The Eastward Dissemination of Western Learning in the Late Qing Dynasty

THE EASTWARD DISSEMINATION OF WESTERN LEARNING IN THE LATE QING DYNASTY

VOLUME 1

XIONG YUEZHI

SILKROAD PRESS

Singapore • Hong Kong • Beijing • Honolulu

Published by

Enrich Professional Publishing (S) Private Limited
16L, Enterprise Road,
Singapore 627660
Website: www.enrichprofessional.com
A Member of Enrich Culture Group Limited

Hong Kong Head Office:
2/F, Rays Industrial Building, 71 Hung To Road, Kwun Tong, Kowloon, Hong Kong, China

China Office:
Rm 1800, Building C, Central Valley, 16 Hai Dian Zhong Jie, Haidian District, Beijing, China

United States Office:
PO Box 30812, Honolulu, HI 96820, USA

Translated by Chen Yanxin, Li Jiao, and Wang Junchao

Edited by Glenn Griffith and Phoebe Wai

ISBN (Hardback) 978-981-4332-24-8
ISBN (ebook) 978-981-4332-79-8 (pdf)
978-981-4332-80-4 (epub)

Printed in Hong Kong with woodfree paper from Japan

Contents

1

Chapter

Introduction

Airplane, space exploration, remote sensing, optical fiber, nuclear power, DNA engineering, and test-tube baby are too commonplace for modern people to astonish at; television, camera, video-recorder, calculator, air-conditioner are too widely-use that almost nobody, except those who work in the patent bureau or intellectual property office, are interested to trace their origins and history. Discussion of these inventions and technology are nothing different from chatting about domestic trivia because modern people are so accustomed to these new products.

We all are members of the global village because of scientific breakthrough and technological progress that narrows peoples' distance. An active international cultural exchange, an instantaneous transmission of information, and a stronger connection among peoples will inevitably lead to a greater unity in the world.

Tracing back to 150 years ago in China — circa the outbreak of the Opium War, most of the people would find the ideas of hydrogen, oxygen, voltage, electricity current, atom and chemical elements confusing or ridiculous. Even scholars with profound knowledge could only remain shocked when they were asked about orbital revolution, geological structure, body cell, and the process of photosynthesis. England, America, Napoleon, and Washington were too well known to even women and children in the West, but these were too alienated to Chinese.

These scientific knowledge became so general to primary and secondary school students as these could be found on every textbooks during the Republican period. So, what kinds of Western learning and how were these knowledge disseminated to China in the decades of post-Opium War? What was the response of the Chinese society towards these new knowledge? Why the arrogant, ethnocentric and xenophobic Chinese scholar-gentries did eventually surrender to Western culture?

Literature Review

This volume aims to look at the relationship between the eastward dissemination of Western learning and the society of the late Qing period. The term "Western learning" has been known to the Chinese since the Ming Dynasty, when the missionaries of the Society of Jesus ("Jesuits") entitled their books "Western learning." These titles included Julius Aleni's *Summary of Western Learning* (*Xixuekao* 西學考) and Alphonsus Vagnoni's *Western Learning Concerning Self-Cultivation* (*Xixue xiushen* 西學修身), *Western Learning and the Establishment of Family* (*Xixue chijia* 西學持家), and *Western Learning, the Governance of Country and the Universal Peace* (*Xixue zhiping* 西學治平).

Liang Qichao suggested in his *Bibliography of Western Knowledge* (*Xixue shumubiao* 西學書目表) that Western learning covered a diverse set of topics including mathematics, mechanics, electrical science, chemistry, acoustics, optics, astronomy, geology, medical science, history, geography, legal studies, mining, military strategy and knowledge, and 14 other fields of study; And Xu Weize added six more subjects of Western learning in his *Bibliography of Japanese-Western Knowledge* (*Dongxixue shulu* 東西學書錄). Since subjects related to Western learning are legion and too comprehensive to study, it is only possible to explore those subjects that had a huge influence on much of Chinese culture and society.

Fig. 1.1 Portrait of Liang Qichao, leader of the 1898 Reform

In addition to the content of these Western subjects, this book seeks to understand the media of disseminating Western learning (Chinese and Western translators, modern schools, journal editors, and translation agencies), the content, targets, ways, and processes of knowledge transmission, and people's response to the new knowledge.

There are various important studies of the dissemination of Western learning in the late Qing period. Notable titles include *An Outline of Translation of Books* (*Yishu shilüe* 譯書事略 , 1880) of John Fryer, *Achievements and Limitations of the Recently Published Books of Western Science* (*Taixi gezhi zhixue yu jinke fanyi zhushu xianglüe deshi* 泰西格致之學與近刻翻譯諸書詳略得失 , 1889) of Sun Wenxin, and *A Research Report on Western Learning* (*Du xixue shufa* 讀西學書法 , 1896) of Liang Qichao. These three titles pioneered the study of the dissemination of Western learning in the last decades of the Qing Dynasty and influenced scholars to conduct more detailed research on this topic. Chen Duxiu, for instance, divided the dissemination of Western learning before the Republican period into four stages in his article "Our Final Realization:" the late Ming Dynasty, the early Qing era, the post-Opium War period, and the post-Sino-Japanese War times. He continued to suggest that the dissemination process matched the modernization level of the late Qing society. The Self-Strengthening Movement, for instance, remained at a superficial level of military and economic reform due to the general ignorance and skepticism towards new knowledge. Around the 1898 Reform and the Late Qing Reform, when the Chinese had better understanding towards Western learning, the Qing court started abolishing old system, such as the absolute monarchy and the civil examination. Chen's short article also reflected people's changing attitude towards Western learning before the May Fourth Movement. Following Chen's research was Liang Qichao's *Intellectual Trends in the Qing Period* (*Qingdai xueshu gailun* 清代學術概論, 1920) and Zhang Xinlang's *The History of European Cultural Dissemination into China* (*Ouhua dongjian shi* 歐化東漸史, 1934), both of which provided a general account of the spread of Western learning in the late Qing period. Quan Hansheng's publication of *Arguments against Westernization in Late Qing* (*Qingmo fandui xihua de yanlun* 清末反對西化的言論) in 1935 presented insightful opinion on the Chinese's rejection to Western culture. Zhou Changshou, who published *A Study of the Translated Science Works* (*Yikan kexue shuji kaolüe* 譯刊科學書籍考略) one year after Quan's completion of his masterpiece, gave an account of the Chinese translated works of Western Science since the late Ming Dynasty to the 1930s. He divided the three centuries into three phases, and he listed in the bibliography of 468 titles of astronomy, mathematics, physics, chemistry, botany, zoology, minerals, biology, and geography, which were translated in the second phase "from mid- to late Qing" according to their publication dates. Zhou's work, however, was nothing more than a book list as he did not elaborate on the books, the translation process, and the social impacts of these translated works.

After 1949, when the People's Republic of China was established, there were only a few new works on the dissemination of Western learning in the modern era. Edited by Du Shiran and others, *Drafted History of Science and Technology in China* (*Zhongguo kexue jishu shigao* 中國科學技術史稿, 1982) discusses the introduction of Western science and technology in China between 1840 and 1919. It also studies the impact of these Western subjects, such as mathematics, physics, astronomy, geology, medical science, railway construction, and metallurgy, on China. This work had a high academic value because of the authors' expertise in science, but it failed to depict the holistic view of the spread of Western learning as well as the society's response as there was almost no mention of the humanities or social science. *A Short History of Translation in China* (*Zhongguo fanyi jianshi* 中國翻譯簡史, 1984) of Ma Zuyi, which aimed at studying the history of translation in the last 80 years, introduced representative translated titles and translators and covered a wide range of Western subjects — from science to literature and art. This work, however, had three main shortcomings: first, it put much emphasis on the translation process, while leaving the social impact of Western learning unmentioned. Second, it employed a considerable amount of political terms that would easily confuse readers. Third, it lacked a concrete analysis of the missionaries and their work in China. Other general research on this topic included Qian Cunxun's "Impacts of Translation to the Modernization of China (1954)," Guo Tingyi's "The Introduction of Western Culture in Modern China (1951)" and "The Introduction of Science and Democracy to Modern China — Translation in Late Qing and Western learning (1952)." Qian and Guo presented their own viewpoints over the stages of the dissemination of Western learning and its social impact in their articles, but their reference work was slightly disappointing. Qian referred to the *Bibliography of Japanese-Western Knowledge* of Xu Weize instead of Gu Xieguang's *Bibliography of Japanese-Western Knowledge (enlarged edition)* (*Zengban dongxi xue shulu* 增版東西學書錄), which contained 300 more entries than the original edition, in collecting his statistical data. Moreover, both Guo and Qian missed analyzing the Japanese-translated Western books — the greatest and largest proportion of the references for Western learning.

Works that focus on the achievements of a particular scholar are multifold. Representative titles include *John Fryer: The Introduction of Western Science and Technology in Nineteenth-Century China* (1967) and *Missionary Journalist in China: Young J. Allen and his Magazines* (1983) by Adrian Bennett; *Young J. Allen in China: His Careers and A Review of the Times* (*Lin Lezhi zaihua shiye yu wanguo gongbao* 林樂知在華事業與萬國公報, 1978) by Leung Yuen-sang; *Yan Fu and His Representative Translated Works* (*Lun Yan Fu yu yanyi mingzhu* 論嚴復與嚴譯名著, 1982) by Wang Shi and others; and *Lin Qinlan* (林琴南, 1935) by Han Guang.

There are also numerous research titles on a particular organization or a group of people. To name a few, these included "What Kind of Organization Was Society for the Diffusion of Christian and General Knowledge among the Chinese? (1963)" by Jiang Wenhan, "China Christian Educational Association and Its Publication (1971)" and "Society for the Diffusion of Christian and General Knowledge among the Chinese in Late Qing Period (1973)" by Wang Shuhuai, "Translation Works of the Chinese Exchange Students in Japan (1960)" by Sanetō Keishū, "Past, Present, and Future of the Sino-Japanese Translation Works (1980)" by Tam Yue-him, "A Discourse on Chinese Learning for the Fundamentals and Western Learning for Practical Use (1982)" by Chen Xulu, *A Debate between Tradition and Westernization in Late Qing* (*Wanqing chuantong yu xihua de zhenglun* 晚清傳統與西化的爭論, 1982) by Sun Guangde, "The Origin of Sinology and Western Learning and the Implicated Cultural and Psychological Trends" and "The Promotion of Chinese Learning for the Fundamentals and Western learning for Practical Use by the Late Qing Intellectuals" by Wang Erh-min, *Foreigners That Contributed to the Modernization in China* (*Yingxiang woguo weixin de jige waiguoren* 影響我國維新的幾個外國人, 1971) by Yao Songling, and *From Morrison to John Leighton Stuart: The Coming of Christian Missionaries* (*Cong Malixun dao Shituleideng: laihua xinjiao zhuan* 從馬禮遜到司徒雷登——來華新教傳, 1985) by Gu Changsheng. Among these profound studies, Yao Songling and Gu Changsheng's books collect biographies of the missionaries, such as Young J. Allen, W. A. P. Martin, Timothy Richard, and Ernst Faber.

Despite the numerous research works on the dissemination of Western learning, most of these works lacked quality in terms of the choice of research topics, the use of historical sources, the explanation of the social impacts of Western learning, and a holistic process of the spread of new knowledge. Scholars mainly relied on Liang Qichao's *Bibliography of Western Knowledge*, Xu Weize's *Bibliography of Japanese-Western Knowledge*, and Gu Xieguang's *Records of Translation* (*Yishu jingyan lu* 譯書經眼錄). These three bibliographies, however, excluded the Western books completed before the reign of Emperor Tongzhi (1862–1875) and after 1904. Books published by the missionaries circa the Opium War (1839–1842) in Malacca, Singapore, Batavia, Guangzhou, and Ningbo were also not documented. And almost no scholar had explored the achievements of the Translation College of the Jiangnan Arsenal — one of the most productive and influential translation organizations in the late Qing era.[1] Another fundamental problem of these previous studies was the absence of introductions to particular translated works. In fact, the understanding of these works was circumscribed to their names; there was little reference to their origins, contents, and the differences between the translated and the original versions. There has been no study to the widely circulated *A New History of Europe* (*Taixi xinshi lanyao* 泰西新史攬要) of Richard Timothy and *Tales of the Sino-Japanese War* (*Zhongdong zhanji benmo* 中東戰紀本末) of Young J. Allen; there has been no research on *Chemistry* (*Gewu tanyuan* 格物探原) of Alexander Williamson and *Civilization and China and Christian* (*Zixi cudong* 自西徂東) of Ernst Faber which had been tribute to the Qing court; and there has been no discussion on *Chambers's Educational Course: Political Economy for Use in Schools and for Private Instruction* (*Zuozhi cuyan* 佐治芻言) of John Frye which has been renowned as the best reference of Western politics.[2]

Fig. 1.2 The Translation College of the Jiangnan Arsenal

Fig. 1.3 Main Gate of the Translation College of the Jiangnan Arsenal

Even the studies of particular series of translated works emphasized much on the works' influence on the upper class and intellectuals. One of the examples was the research on Yan Fu's translated works. Having been regarded as highly influential by scholars, Yan's works were actually too advanced and difficult for commoners, who would rather refer to general textbooks. Western knowledge that was re-imported from Japan was also significant to the Chinese society, but scholars nowadays concentrate too much on the works of Chinese organizations such as the Translation College of the Jiangnan Arsenal and the Society for the Diffusion of Christian and General Knowledge Among the Chinese (*Guangxue hui* 廣學會). The focus on the whole development of Western learning in China, features of each stage of knowledge dissemination, the changing translation style, and the contradictory ideologies between Western science and Christianity were inadequate as well.

Fig. 1.4 The Society for the Diffusion of Christian and General Knowledge Among the Chinese

Four Stages of the Dissemination of Western Learning in the Late Qing Era

The first stage (1811–1842)

Robert Morrison, a missionary of the London Missionary Society, was assigned to China in 1807 on an evangelic mission. He was the first Protestant missionary that pioneered the spread of Western learning in China. The publication of *The Gospel of St. Luke* (Chinese) and *A Summary of the Doctrine of Divine Redemption* (*Shendao lun xu jiushi zongshuo zhenben* 神道論贖救世總說真本, also in Chinese) in Guangzhou in 1811 symbolized the beginning of a new wave of Sino-Western cultural encounters since the banning of Christianity in the last years of the reign of Kangxi. Morrison, however, was soon forced to leave China due to complaints from the Portuguese merchants in Macau. He arrived in the Southeast Asia, where he established schools and presses in some main Chinese settlements such as Malacca, Singapore, and Batavia in order to preach the overseas Chinese through education, books, and journals. During these decades, Morrison and his colleagues published 147 titles and journals in Chinese, 34 titles of which were about world history, geography, politics, and economics. Significant titles included *A Brief History of the United States of America* (*Meilige hesheng guozhi lüe* 美理哥合省國志略, 1838) by Elijah Coleman Bridgman, *A General Account of Trade* (*Maoyi tongzhi* 貿易通志, 1840) by K. F. A. Gutzlaff, *Chinese Monthly Magazine* (*Chashisu meiyue tongji zhuan* 察世俗每月統記傳), and *Eastern Western Monthly Magazine* (*Dongxiyangkao meiyue tongji zhuan* 東西洋考每月統記傳). These new journals opened the way to modern learning for even the most notable open-minded Chinese scholars, such as Lin Zexu, Wei Yuan, Liang Tingnan and Xu Jiyu; and the new schools — Anglo-Chinese College (present-day Ying Wa College) and Morrison Education Society School — nurtured prominent translators of the late Qing society, such as Yuan Dehui.

Morrison's publications and schools, in terms of quantity and quality, were never comparable to those of John Fryer and Young J. Allen. However, he was celebrated for his pioneering role in the introduction of Western learning to China in the mid-Qing period. He opened the first modern press in China, established the first church school that admitted Chinese, and founded the first Chinese journal, as well as published the first Anglo-Chinese dictionary.

This first stage of dissemination of Western learning featured the relatively equal status between the Western preachers and the Chinese learners. Despite the denunciation of Christianity as a heterodox sect as early as 1724 by Emperor

Yongzheng, the Western religion was not an evil to the commoners, who found the free education and medical service appealing and the missionaries not as arrogant as other foreign traders. The cordial relationship between the Oriental Empire and the Occidental states resulted in a peaceful Sino-Western cultural exchange, though the influence of new knowledge was limited to only several coastal ports in South China.

The second stage (1843–1860)

The second stage began with the opening of treaty ports after the Opium War and the signing of a series of unequal treaties — the Anglo-Chinese *Treaty of Nanjing* (1842), the Sino-French *Treaty of Whampoa* (1843), and the Sino-American *Treaty of Wanghia* (1843). The great powers were granted the freedom of movement to both Catholic and Protestant missionaries in China. Hong Kong was declared as the new British colony. Guangzhou (Canton), Fuzhou (Foochow), Xiamen (Amoy), Ningbo (Ningpo), and Shanghai were opened as free treaty ports. These six coastal cities soon replaced Southeast Asia as the bases for evangelization, which was done by not only building churches, but also the establishment of schools and hospitals.

These six ports had their own characteristics because of their different geographical locations. Hong Kong and Guangzhou were the first two contact points of Western culture as their locations in the southern tips of the empire made them the homes of Western merchants before the Opium War. Guangzhou, as the only authorized trading port under the policy of single-port trading (*yikou tongshang* 一口通商), particularly had a considerable Western population and was seemingly the most prepared place for the influx of Western learning. Fuzhou and Amoy, two of the leading cities in Fujian Province, were regarded as the best areas for evangelization because of the absence of a language barrier — the missionaries had mastered Fujianese during their stay in Southeast Asia, where a large overseas Fujianese population was settled. Ningbo and Shanghai, the two rising cities in the Lower Yangtze area, witnessed the fastest spread of Western learning due to the strong economy of the surrounding area and their closer location to the center of the empire. These two Yangtze cities soon surpassed the other four cities in terms of the popularization of Western learning, and they, together with Hong Kong, became the hubs of Western learning during the reign of Emperor Xianfeng (1850–1861). London Missionary Society Mission Press (*Mohai shuguan* 墨海書館) and The Chinese and American Holy Classic Book Establishment (*Huahua shengjing shufang* 華花聖經書房), two of the most representative Western presses, were located in Shanghai and Ningbo, respectively.

During the second stage of the dissemination of Western learning, there were 434 titles of Western knowledge published in these six cities, among which 329 titles were religion propagation and the remaining covered various subjects including astronomy, geography, mathematics, medical science, history, and economics (refer to table 1.1).

Table 1.1 Statistics of Western books published in the six coastal ports

	Religious propagation (title)	Scientific reference (title)	Total (titles)
Amoy	13	—	13
Fuzhou	26	16	42
Guangzhou	29	13	42
Hong Kong	37	23	60
Ningbo	86	20	106
Shanghai	138	33	171

There were four characteristics of the dissemination of Western learning in this stage.

Treaty ports as the bases of dissemination

Southeast Asia, the foothold of the missionaries before their arrival in China, had a large population of overseas Chinese and protection from the colonial governments that allowed the publication of books of Western learning. However, the spread of new knowledge remained only at local levels because Southeast Asia was too distant to influence China. It was not only due to the opening of China that missionaries started to establish their bases in treaty ports along the crescent-like coastal line, build schools and hospitals, and publish books and journals. The establishment of treaty ports, where the Occidental learning first met the Oriental empire, symbolized a new wave of the dissemination of knowledge.

The publication of considerable science titles

A New Discourse on Human Body by Benjamin Hobson and five other titles of him were the first series of Western medical reference works to be published in late Qing society. *A Treatise on Arithmetic* by Edward T. R. Moncriff was the first Chinese-published mathematics textbook compiled in the Western mathematical system. *Questions and Answers of Astronomy* by Andrew Patton Happer and *A Short Discourse on Astronomy* by Hobson were the batches of Western astronomical treatises published in China. *The Sequel of Euclid's Elements* co-translated by Alexander Wylie and Li Shanlan introduced Euclid's theory to China. *Elements of Analytical Geometry and of Differential and Integral Calculus* — also the joint works of Wylie and Li, was the first reference work of advanced mathematics. *Popular Treatise on Mechanics* co-translated by Wylie and Wang Tao was the first textbook of Western mechanics. *An Element of Botany* co-translated by Joseph Edkins, Alexander Williamson and Li Shanlan was the first reference text of Western Botany in China.

An open attitude to Western learning

A group of mid-Qing intellectuals first showed their eagerness in learning Western knowledge. These representative learners — to be specific, the pioneers of the changing academic atmosphere in the Qing society — included Lin Zexu, Liang Tingnan, Wei Yuan, Xu Jiyu, Li Shanlan, and Wang Tao. Their learning focus was many, such as international affairs, world history, geography, science, and technology.

Chinese intellectuals' participation in translation

The first Chinese citizen's participation in Western translation happened in the early nineteenth century, when Leung Fa (also known as Liang A-Fa), a printing worker in a Guangzhou press and later the first Chinese pastor, helped Morrison and William Milne edit and print the Chinese version of *The Bible*. Leung's assistance was undeniably significant for the influx of Western knowledge to China, but his achievements were limited to evangelizing Christianity, which was far from being about the goal of spreading new learning such as science and technology. After 1843, a new group of Chinese translators emerged in Shanghai and Guangzhou. These intellectuals, represented by Li Shanlan, Wang Tao, Guan Sifu, and Zhang Fuxi, were actually active modernists who supported Sino-Western cultural exchange. They worked on a freelance basis but they sometimes cooperated with the missionaries. The translation of *The Sequel of Euclid's Elements*, for instance, was proposed by Li Shanlan to Alexander Wylie. However, they were interested only in science titles and left the books on religion unattended.

The third stage (1861–1900)

China's defeat in the Second Anglo-Chinese War (1856–1860) constituted a turning point in the dissemination of Western learning in China. The Qing court was forced to sign a series of unequal treaties with the Western powers, who received not only a large sum of indemnity but also political rights. Stated in the Treaty of Tianjin (1858) and confirmed in the Convention of Beijing (1860), the Qing court was required to open 11 more treaty ports — Tianjin, Niuzhuang, Dengzhou, Tainan, Chaozhou, Hainan, Zhenjiang, Nanjing, Jiujiang, Hankou, and Danshui, where foreigners enjoyed the right of settlement, purchase of property and construction of churches, hospital, and tombs.[3] The missionaries were also granted the freedom of free passage in most parts of the empire: from Guangzhou to Amoy, Shanghai, Chefoo, Tianjin, and Yingkou; and from Shanghai to Zhenjiang, Nanjing, Jiujiang, and Hankou.[4] Foreign ships would no longer be blocked from sailing in the Yangtze River. These terms also applied to France, Russia, and the United States (due to the most-favored nation clause). The signing of the unequal treaties intensified the Western powers' political aggression and economic exploitation of China yet created a more favorable environment for the spread of Western learning.

Simultaneous to the so-called imperialist invasion of China was the Qing court's initiation of the Self-Strengthening Movement after the death of Emperor Xianfeng and the Coup of 1861. It was the first modernization attempt in China that aimed at mastering Western military technology and science. The Ministry of Foreign Affairs and the Imperial Foreign Language Institute were thus established, which contributed to the spread of Western learning.

There were five characteristics of the dissemination of Western learning in this stage.

Various organizations of the dissemination of Western learning

These organizations included church schools and Chinese-founded modern schools that were located in various parts of the empire, church hospitals that taught Western medical knowledge, and translation and publication houses that issued various books and journals about the new affairs. There were three types of operation: first, the church-sponsored associations. These included the Society for the Diffusion of Christian and General Knowledge among the Chinese, American Presbyterian Mission Press (*Meihua shuguan* 美華書館), School and Textbook Series Committee (*Yizhi shuhui* 益智書會, the former Educational Association of China and China Christian Education Association), Canton Pok Tsai Hospital (*Guangdong bozhai yiju* 廣東博濟醫局), and Shanghai Tou Se We Press (*Tushanwan yinshuguang* 上海土山灣印書館). Second, government-supervised entities. These included the Translation College of the Jiangnan Arsenal, the Imperial Foreign Language Institute, Tianjin Machinery Factory (*Tianjin jiqiju* 天津機器局), and Tianjin Armaments College (*Tianjin wubei xuetang* 天津武備學堂). Third, public organizations. These included The Commercial Press (*Shangwu yinshuguan* 商務印書館), Book Translation Association (*Yishu gonghui* 譯書公會), The Chinese Progress Press (*Shuwu baoguan* 時務報館), and Agriculture Journal Association (*Nongxue baoshe* 農學報社). The Translation College of the Jiangnan Arsenal and the Society for the Diffusion of Christian and General Knowledge among the Chinese were the two most important organizations.

In addition to the above associations, several churches, schools, presses, hospitals, customs departments, and provincial offices also published a proportion of Western books.

Establishment of translation organizations by the government

The study of Western learning prior to the 1860s was limited to only a few enthusiastic scholar-officials such as Lin Zexu, who actually regarded the study of Western learning as a temporary means to help strengthen the country. Neither did these scholars nor the government have long-term plans for promoting Western learning. It was after the beginning of the Self-Strengthening Movement that the Qing court unwillingly took the leading role in encouraging the study of Western learning through the establishment of the Imperial Foreign Language Institute and Translation College of the Jiangnan Arsenal, whose publications outdid the others' in terms of both quantity and quality. This demonstrated the importance of the government's participation in translation as well as the dissemination of Western learning in China.

A considerable amount and various subjects of translated books

Within the four decades, there were 555 Western book titles published in China — five times more than those published in the first half of the nineteenth century.[5] Among the translated works, 123 titles were in social sciences, philosophy, history, legal studies, literature, and education; 162 titles were in mathematics, mechanics, electrical studies, chemistry, optics, and biology; 255 titles were in artisanship, mining, and shipbuilding; and 45 titles were in journals, current affairs and miscellaneous publications. Well-translated titles included *Principle and Applications of Chemistry* (*Huaxue jianyuan* 化學鑒原), *Chemical Analysis* (*Huaxue fenyuan* 化學分原), *Elements of Geology* (*Dixue qianshi* 地學淺釋), *Elements of*

International Law (*Wanguo gongfa* 萬國公法), *Chambers's Educational Course: Political Economy for Use in Schools and for Private Instruction*, *A New History of Europe*, and *The Social Contract* (*Minyue tongyi* 民約通義).

Shanghai as the hub of translation

The emergence of Shanghai as the hub of translation in China was nothing surprising. Prior to 1860, Shanghai, together with Ningbo and Hong Kong, published most of the Western books among the other coastal cities. The rising importance of Shanghai as a modern commercial center in the empire made it the largest hub of the dissemination of Western learning. Most of the translation offices, regardless of clerical, government, or public background, were situated in Shanghai, though a few of the translation houses had their headquarters in Guangzhou or Beijing. Three of the most significant translation organizations — Translation College of the Jiangnan Arsenal, Society for the Diffusion of Christian and General Knowledge Among the Chinese, and School and Textbook Series Committee — were also based in the Lower Yangtze city. In terms of publication quantity and quality, 77 percent of translated works and most of the well-translated titles were published in Shanghai. The formation of a translation hub signified a more concentrated and systematic development of Western learning in China.

The spread of Western learning to the lower classes

The nationwide establishment of modern schools, the issuing of various newspapers and journals, the publication of numerous titles of Western books, and the works of the missionaries helped disseminate Western learning from the elite intellectuals to the lower classes. Judging from the question and answer column in the *Chinese Scientific Magazine* (*Gezhi huibian* 格致匯編) and *Scientific Review* (*Gezhi xinbao* 格致新報), the essay competition organized in *A Review of the Times*, and the abandoned writing of the eight-legged essay initiated by the Shanghai Polytechnic Institute, Western learning influenced all social classes — from intellectuals to commoners, from coastal citizens to inland villagers, and from the general public to the royal family.

The upper class was particularly passionate about Western learning. Zeng Guofan encouraged his son Zeng Jize to study Western science and technology. The son later became a notable diplomat due to his mastery of a foreign language. Zhang Zidong and Li Hongzhang donated to the Society for the Diffusion of Christian and General Knowledge among the Chinese. Tan Jixun, father of the notable modernist

Tan Sitong, employed Western doctors for his concubine and established memorial tablets for the dead missionaries. The rich in Shanghai dispatched their sons to church schools. Even Emperor Guangxu studied Western books. All these were evidence of the general acceptance of Western learning among the Chinese.

The fourth stage (1901–1911)

The reputation of the Qing court sank to its nadir after the Coup of 1898 and its defeat in the Eight-nation Expedition in 1901, making the empire no longer a worthy focus of loyalty to the patriots and intellectuals. A storm of revolution was stirring up in the society. Japan, a previous vassal state of China, had secured its foothold among the great powers after its victory in the Sino-Japanese War in 1895 so as to replace Europe as the most popular destination for overseas study. This decade witnessed a new focus and methods of the dissemination of Western learning.

There were five characteristics of the dissemination of Western learning in this stage.

An unprecedented amount of translation

The decade of the 1900s witnessed a doubling of the translation of Western books compared to the previous three stages. It was estimated that there were at least 1,599 Western titles translated from Japanese, English, and French works — amounting to 69.8 percent — during 1900 to 1911.[6] The first five years of the 1900s alone saw the translation of 899 titles, which was more than the total number of translated works of the previous 90 years.

Table 1.2 Translated Western books from 1902 to 1904

Language of the source text	Number of titles translated	Percentage
French	17	3.2%
German	24	4.5%
English	89	16.7%
Japanese	321	60.2%
Others	82	15.4%
Total	533	100%

A re-importing of new knowledge

The drastic increase for translation was due to the new source of Western books. During the first three stages, Western knowledge was transmitted to China

(Cont'd)

through the translation of English, French, and German books. After 1900, the Chinese turned to Japanese translations of Western subjects as evidenced by the statistics from 1902 to 1904 (refer to table 1.2).

The reasons for the rising importance of Japanese books of Western learning were several: first, the similarity between Chinese and Japanese. These two languages shared numerous Chinese characters (known as *kanji* 漢字 in Japanese) that made it easier for the Chinese to learn. Second, most of these Japanese books were shortcut to Western learning for Chinese. Although Japan initiated its modernization almost simultaneously with China, its translation of Western books was much earlier as most of its political leaders had already noted the significance of mastering Western knowledge. By the time the Chinese scholars got engaged in the large-scale translation of Western books, Japan had already produced piles of well-translated works, which were the essentials of Western learning to Chinese. Third, the proximity between these two Oriental countries encouraged the Chinese to study in Japan. Fourth, Japan's miraculous victory in the Russo-Japanese War in 1905 strengthened Chinese's' confidence towards Japan. A considerable amount of students flocked to Japan, where they believed the key of modernization lied. Even the most notable Chinese historical figures of the twentieth century, such as Sun Yat-sen, Chiang Kai-shek, and Lu Xun, had also studied in Japan for a few years.

A significant impact of Western learning

These students aboard brought not only a great variety of Japanese books of Western learning to China, but also numerous new terms invented by the Japanese for key academic subjects that are still widely used now. To name a few, these terms included *shehui* (社會, society), *zhengdang* (政黨, political party), *minzu* (民族, ethnic group), *jieji* (階級, class), *zhuyi* (主義, ideology), *sixiang* (思想, thoughts), *guannian* (觀念, idea), *zhenli* (真理, truth), *zhishi* (知識, knowledge), *weiwu* (唯物, materialism), *weixin* (唯心, idealistic), *zhuti* (主體, subject), *keti* (客體, object), *zhuguan* (主觀, subjectivity), *keguan* (客觀, objectivity), *juti* (具體, concrete), and *chouxiang* (抽象, abstract). This "big bang" of vocabulary words created a new prosperity in the academic circle and publication industry, paving the way for the promotion of vernacular Chinese (*baihua* 白話) and the New Cultural Movement in late 1910s.

A changing learning focus to Social Science and Humanity

Having suffered from several failed reforms, the Chinese scholars soon abandoned science and technology and turned to culture — the core value of Western learning and the secret of modernization. They started to translate more works of the social sciences and humanities, which soon outnumbered those of science and technology titles. From 1902 to 1904 alone, there were 327 translated titles of literature, history, philosophy, economics, and legal studies — 61 percent of the total translation work. Translated books of natural science and applied science amounted to 112 and 56 titles, respectively.

The emergence of the first generation of Chinese translators

Prior to the fourth stage, the translation of Western books in China was completed based on Sino-Western cooperation because China was facing a shortage of translator who could master a foreign language. Even the early notable intellectuals, such as Li Shanlan, Xu Shou, and Hua Hengfang, had to rely on foreigners because of their limited knowledge of foreign languages.

Fig. 1.5 Portrait of Hua Hengfang and *Elements of Geology*

Fig. 1.6 Portrait of Xu Shou, pioneer of Chinese chemistry

Fig. 1.7 Inscription to the Statue of Xu Shou by Zheng Changyan

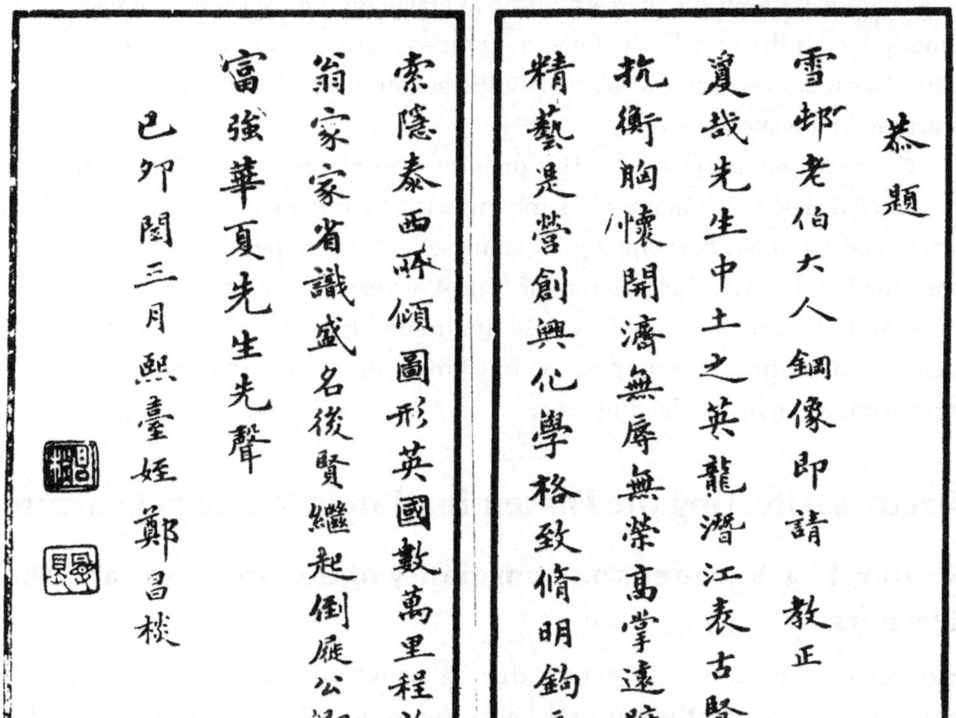

恭題
雪邨老伯大人銅像即請 教正
夐哉先生中土之英龍潛江表古賢
抗衡胸懷開濟無辱無榮高掌遠蹠
精藝是營創興化學格致脩明鉤元
索隱泰西所傾圖形英國數萬里程放
翁家家省識盛名後賢繼起倒屣公卿
富強華夏先生先聲
己卯閏三月熙臺姪鄭昌棪

The opening of modern schools during the Self-Strengthening Movement created a new learning environment, where students were exposed to new knowledge and foreign language. Most of these students continued their studies overseas after graduation, and they returned to China as new kinds of scholars who were eager to introduce what they had learned overseas to the Chinese. These scholars, represented by Yan Fu and Ma Junwu, published articles about Western learning and translated Western masterpieces. The birth of the first generation of Chinese scholars declared the end of the Sino-Western cooperation in translation.

From Morrison's publication of the first Western books in China in 1811 to the end of the Qing Dynasty in 1911, there were at least 2,293 Western titles published and translated in China. Below are the detailed statistics of translation in this century.

Table 1.3 Statistics of translation titles between 1811 to 1911

Period	Total translation (title)	Average annual translation (title)
1811–1842	34	1
1843–1860	105	6
1861–1900	555	14
1901–1911	1,599	145

There were multiple increase of the average annual translation at each stage, among which the fourth stage had a 10 times increase from the third stage. The early twentieth century was obviously the height of the dissemination of Western learning in the late Qing era.

Chinese participation in the promotion of Western learning was also recognized. The first stage was mainly directed by missionaries, the second stage witnessed a limited participation of Chinese with the supervision of Westerners, the third stage was the practice of Sino-Western cooperation in translation, and the fourth stage was eventually dominated by Chinese intellectuals. This demonstrated the changing position of Chinese in the spread of new learning — from a subordinate to a leading role.

Factors Affecting the Dissemination of Western Learning

Cultural backgrounds and cordiality of the preachers and the learners

Similar to a drama performance during which the actors have to suit the audience's appetite, the cultural background and the academic standard of the general Chinese populace had to be considered in the transmission of new knowledge. Despite the enthusiasm of the translators, teachers, and journalists, most of the commoners were neither equipped with a basic knowledge nor interested in new knowledge, so that the dissemination of Western learning had limited success in the early stages.

It was not until the implementation of the modernization reforms in China that Western learning caught the arrogant and ethnocentric Chinese scholar-officials' fancy. Pressured by the frequent defeats in external wars and the outbreak of a series of internal rebellions in the 1850s, the Qing court thus turned to the learning of Western science and technology, which they regarded as an effective means to strengthen the country. The missionaries' works were not an aimless and arbitrary introduction of all the Western knowledge. To suit the officials' appetites, the missionaries had to start writing books of mathematics, chemistry, mechanics, electrical studies, medical studies, and other related subjects — even though the study of philosophy, theology, and legal studies was easier as these humanity subjects required no building of laboratories or equipment purchases. The difficulty in promoting Western science and technology was compounded by the non-scientific background of the missionaries. John Fryer and Richard Timothy, for example, received only basic training on science before their journeys to China. Having noted the high demand for scientific knowledge in China, these missionaries had to take up the study of science by themselves and even to pay the bills for the equipment.

Another decisive factor of the successful dissemination of Western learning was the psychological relationship between the preacher and the learner. It explained the enormous success of Matteo Ricci and his colleagues in their evangelical missions, as well as the early failure of the late Qing missionaries. Because of the relatively equal status between China and the Iberian countries, the humble attitude of Ricci towards the Chinese, their respect of Chinese culture, and the incorporation of Christian teachings into the Confucian value system, the psychological gap between the Occidental preachers and the Oriental learners was narrower. Chinese scholar-officials could convert to Christianity without discarding their traditional beliefs. Missionaries were friends instead of conquerors to the Chinese, even Western science had proved its superiority over Chinese knowledge.

The situation in the late Qing period was, however, completely different. Transportation advancement, communication breakthroughs, and improvements in printing supposedly facilitated the spread of new knowledge, but the missionaries faced even greater obstacles than Ricci. Western learning was influential to only a few treaty ports because of the declining international status of China that created a general disdain towards the Westerners in the Chinese society. Moreover, the Eurocentric missionaries, who were protected by unequal treaties, presented themselves as saviors yet showed no tolerance towards Chinese culture. The resultant resistance in the late Qing society was not surprising.

Technological advancements

Significant advancements in printing methods (from woodblock printing to lead printing), along with developments in transportation (from ships to steamships and trains), and improvements in communication (from in-person delivery to telegraph and telephone) helped accelerate the transmission of information. It explained the greater success of the dissemination of Western learning during the reigns of Tongzhi and Guangxu (1861–1908) than the reigns of Daoguang and Xianfeng (1820–1861). The establishment of more translation organizations and new societies, and the recruitment of more laborers undeniably contributed to the popularization of new knowledge, but technological advancement also played an important role. It was unimaginable for the publication of the 10,000 copies of *A New History of Europe* without the adoption of lead printing. The instant transmission of news from all parts of the world to China was also impossible without the laying of submarine cables and the invention of the telephone.

Mode of translation

The mode of translation directly affected readers' understanding of the new knowledge. The translation was done orally by Westerners who were working with the Chinese who were writing the words down. This method, *xiyi zhongshu* (西譯中述), was the main translation method in the late Qing period. The distortion of the meaning in Western knowledge was because of the distinctive language differences between Chinese and English, compounded by the missionaries' only basic understanding to the Oriental language and the Chinese scholars' unfamiliarity with Occidental culture. This problem was particularly acute in the humanities and social sciences reference works, which required special terms that the Chinese lacked. "American states," for instance, was translated as "provinces (*sheng* 省)". These two local administrative units were actually different in terms of independence from the central government. There was also no term for "President" in Chinese, so the translators correlated "President" with "Emperor" as they explained that the "President" was the head of state. Consequently, articles about "the election of Emperors in the United States" and "the four-year term of service of the Emperor" were common in journals issued during 1860s and 1870s, such as *The Church News* (*Jiaohui xinbao* 教會新報) and *A Review of the Times*. The interpretation towards political affairs was so twisted that it aroused attention from both the missionaries and Chinese scholars. Young J. Allen wrote an article "An Explanation on the Translation of the Terms of Democratic Countries and their Constitutions." Wu Jianren also included these mistranslated phrases in his satirical novel *Eyewitness Account of Bizarre Events over the Past Twenty Years* (*Ershinian mudu zhi guai xianzhuang* 二十年目睹之怪現狀). Such ignorance towards global affairs was the result of China's long-term policy of seclusion and so mistranslation was inevitable. Despite numerous points for criticism in these translated titles, it was better than having none of the new publications that led China out of isolation. Their usefulness should be recognized.

Translation organizations

There were four major types of supervision of the translation activity in the late Qing period: first, individual translations. The choice of translation topics was based on personal academic levels and interest. Second, church-directed translation efforts. Supervised by Westerners, the church-led translations aimed to enlighten the public through the introduction of international affairs. The translated titles covered a wide range of humanities and social science subjects including world history, geography, customs, and current developments. Third, government-supervised translation. The Qing court founded the notable Translation College of the Jiangnan Arsenal and the Imperial Foreign Language Institute, where translated mainly Western titles of applied science helped modernize the state. Fourth, the public agencies. The translated subjects of these public agencies varied according to the political developments. The Translation Society, for instance, focused on the translation of history and geography titles published circa the 1898 Reform, while the Translation Association (*Yishu huibian she* 譯書匯編社) shifted to translate *The Social Contract*, *On Liberty*, and other representative political reference works after 1900, when the ideas of democracy and revolution were gaining more popularity in the society.

Compared to government-supervised translation organizations, the public associations had a greater freedom in choosing the books to translate. The former had to publish titles that had practical use in the Qing court's modernization, so that the translation of the *Encyclopedia Britannica* and philosophy books suggested by John Fryer had to give way to the publication of other titles covering armament production, acoustics, optics, chemistry, and electrical studies.

There was an absence of cooperation among these translation organizations, particularly in the late 1890s, when the Chinese started translating Japanese books. Whenever a new book was published in Japan, these Chinese organizations would start their translations.

Reasons for the Chinese People's Acceptance of Western Learning

Different parties had their own considerations when accepting Western learning. It might have been a plan of the government or an impromptu action of an individual; it might have been controlled by the Westerners or supervised by the Chinese. These parties, however, shared the same aims of modernizing China through the introduction of Western learning.

Understanding the world

As described by Li Hongzhang in his letter to Zhu Jiuxiang the Education Commissioner, China's defeat in the Opium War opened the way for "the transformation unprecedented in three millennia (*sanqianyunian yida bianju* 三千餘年一大變局)" and the Sino-Western encounter in modern times.[7] The Westerners faced an isolated China, while the Chinese faced an alienated Western culture. Having shared the same goal in opening China to Western and global affairs, both the missionaries and the Chinese reformers were devoted in translating a series of Western masterpieces. To name a few, these works included *A Brief History of the United States of America* by Elijah Coleman Bridgman, *A General Gazetteer of the Great Britain* (*Daying guotong zhi* 大英國統志) and *A General Account of Trade* by K. F. A. Gutzlaff, *Gazetteer of Four Continents* (*Sizhou zhi* 四洲志) by Lin Zexu, *Four Essays on Off-shore Countries* (*Haiguo sishuo* 海國四說) by Liang Tingnan, *Illustrated Gazetteer of the Maritime Countries* (*Haiguo tuzhi* 海國圖志) by Wei Yuan, *A General Discourse on the International Law* (*Yinghuan zhilüe* 瀛寰志略) by Xu Jishe, *Elements of International Law* (*Wanguo gongfa* 萬國公法) by W. A. P. Martin, *A General Discourse on the International Law* (*Gongfa zonglun* 公法總論), *Commentaries on International Law* (*Geguo jiaoshe gongfa lun* 各國交涉公法論), and *Commentaries on International Private Law* (*Geguo jiaoshe bianfa lun* 各國交涉便法論) by John Fryer. There were also various gazetteers that introduced the geography, history, political system, economic development, culture, religion, customs, and celebrities of Britain, France, the United States, Russia, Germany, and Japan. Titles that explained international laws were particularly useful for the long-isolated Chinese to understand common diplomatic rules which helped China to enter the international stage.

Strive for a strong and rich country

The humiliating defeat in external wars, particularly in the Second Anglo-Chinese War when the Anglo-French coalitions occupied the Chinese capital and forced the Qing court to sign the unequal treaty, revealed the weaknesses of the Chinese army to counteract Western gunboats. The Self-Strengthening Movement was thus implemented, aiming at learning the advanced Western science and technology. In addition to the purchasing of Western armaments, the Qing court encouraged the translation of science reference works that covered a wide range of subjects, including mathematics, physics, chemistry, astronomy, geography, and biology. These science titles such as *A Guide for Army Marching* (*Xinjun zhiyao* 行軍指要), *Training of Navy* (*Suishi caolian* 水師操練), *Krupp's Discourse on Artillery* (*Kelubo paoshuo* 克虜伯炮說), *The Making of Gunpowder* (*Zhihuo yaofa* 制火藥法), and *A New Treatise on Coastal Defense* (*Fanghai xinyan* 防海新焉), were mainly published by the Translation College of the Jiangnan Arsenal,. Books about economics and other modern industries included *A Practical Treatise on Metallurgy* (*Baozang xingyan* 寶藏興焉), *Essentials of the Records of A Craftsman* (*Gongcheng zhifu* 工程致富), *Digging into Mines and Prospecting Gold* (*Tankuang qujin* 採礦取金), *New Knowledge of Western Technology* (*Xiyi xinzhi* 西藝新知), *An Elementary Manual of Agriculture* (*Nongxue chuji* 農學初級), and *The Complete Works of Agriculture* (*Nongwu quanshu* 農務全書). Both elementary and advance books were available to the Chinese.

Save the country from the edge of extinction

China's disastrous defeat in the Sino-Japanese War proved the failure of science and technology in strengthening the country. Its international status greatly declined, inviting ambitious foreign powers "to cut the Chinese melon." The Chinese intellectuals soon realized the key to modernization was in political reform, as hinted at by Japan's constitutional reform in 1889. Books that introduced various political systems and advocated Social Darwinism and constitutional reform prevailed in China. Popular titles included *A New History of Europe*, whose theme was the Theory of Evolution and modernization; *Tales of the Sino-Japanese War* which revealed government and social malpractice of the era; and *Education in Japan*, which outlined the successful Meiji Modernization in Japan. The publication of these political reference works pushed the demand for a comprehensive reform to the climax.

Rising popularity of democracy and revolution

To the radicals, only the idea of "foreign" could save China from foreign partition. The translated edition of *The Social Contract*, *On Liberty*, *The Origin of Freedom* (*Ziyou yuanlun* 自由原論), *Del' Esprit des Lois* (*Wanfa jingli* 萬法精理), *Declaration of Independence of the United States of America* (*Meiguo duli xuanyan* 美國獨立宣言), therefore, were overwhelmingly popular to the Chinese, especially to the revolutionists who regarded these works as their classics. Western enlightenment philosophers such as Rousseau, Voltaire, Montesquieu, and John Stuart Mill were worshipped more than traditional Chinese sages like Confucius, Mencius, and Master Zhu Xi. Moreover, works that explained the recent independent movements wars, and nation founders were also popular among the intellectuals who believed that the Qing court was too corrupt and incompetent to revive the empire.

Reformists headed by Liang Qichao did not support anti-Qing revolution. Their translated works, however, also broadened people's horizons due to the introduction of democracy or constitutional monarchy. Simultaneous to the publication of these works were the translations of books that advocated socialism or anarchism.

Enlightenment of the public

The literacy rate before the 1900s in China remained low due to the absence of universal education. The achievements of translation organizations, new schools, and journals in enlightening the coastal Chinese should be recognized, but the influence of these media outlets was also confined to the treaty ports. *The Chinese Scientific Magazine* was mainly circulated in Shanghai, the Shanghai Polytechnic Institute admitted mainly students living nearby, and the School and Textbook Series Committee was located in Shanghai. It was not until the abolition of the old civil examination in 1905 that the way was paved for the further dissemination of Western learning. New textbooks were not only available in coastal cities, but also in inland towns. Short and simple nursery rhymes and poems about new knowledge, such as *Astronomy Rhyme* (*Tianwen gelüe* 天文歌略), *Geography Rhyme* (*Dili gelüe* 地理歌略), *Globe Rhyme* (*Diqiu yunyan* 地球韻言), and *Women Studies Rhyme* (*Nuxue gelüe* 女學歌略) were even more popular than the reference works.

The influence of Western learning was increasing throughout the century from 1811 to 1911. Western learning was regarded as nothing different from so-called "barbarous learning" at the beginning of its introduction to China in 1810s, but it soon caught people's fancy because of its practical use in strengthening the country. It remained a prominent school of learning even after the failure of the Self-Strengthening Movement, and its significance reached a climax in the 1900s. As concluded by Zou Rong, an active revolutionist in the Late Qing, Western learning was "a panacea for the current situation (*jiushi zhi lingdan miaoyao* 救時之靈丹妙藥)."

Missionaries: the Conflict between Science and Religion

Missionaries played a leading role in the dissemination of Western learning in the late Qing society. However, the academic circle lacked comprehensive study of the aims and process of the missionaries' work, as well as their attitude towards the contradictory ideologies of science and religion. Previous studies mentioned only about the achievements of Chinese translators in the popularization of new knowledge without recognizing the works of Alexander Wylie and John Fryer. Several research papers asserted that beneath the teaching of science laid only evangelic missions. Missionaries were selfish in bringing the essentials of Western science to the Chinese. Gu Changsheng, for instance, suggested that:

> The so-called science curriculum of the church schools was featured by the metaphysical idealism, religion, and a limited knowledge about manufacturing and export trade. There was almost no teaching of science …The selfishness of the missionaries was revealed from the publication of the Society for the Diffusion of Christian and General Knowledge Among the Chinese…they urged the Chinese to surrender to colonial rule without encouraging the study of Western learning.[8]

Ma Zuyi shared the same view with Gu, who criticized that:

> The Chinese reformists, who upheld their core value of "Chinese learning for the fundamentals and Western learning for practical use (*zhongti xiyong* 中體西用)," did not encourage the study of Western political theories and philosophy. Missionaries, who represented the interest of the colonial powers,

did not want to confront a strong and rich China. Consequently, they left the Western humanity subjects unmentioned.[9]

The achievements of both the Chinese translators and the missionaries should be recognized. Without the contribution of either one party, the mode of "translation by Westerners and narration by Chinese" could never be practiced. The main issue towards the missionaries' work was their ambiguous attitude towards science.

The relationship between science and religion was more complicated than people might expect. The Catholic church's persecution of Renaissance scientists, such as the excommunication of Galileo, the burning of Bruno, and the denunciation of the theory of evolution were all part of the church's heterodox ideology and these had left a deep impression of the hostility between the Church and the scientists on the people. Nevertheless, during the prolonged conflict of science and religion there was the conversion of scientists, such as the notable Kepler, Boyle, Newton, and some Nobel prize laureates, the vindication of the solar-center theory, and other cordial responses of the Church towards the emergence of science. The Western world, the originator of modern science, had the largest Christian population as well.

In fact, their relationship varied throughout the ages. Science, particularly the ancient Greek mathematics, always appeared in the theology curriculum in the Middle Ages. The ancient Greeks had two schools of mathematics, represented by the rationalism of Pythagoras and mechanism of Ptolemy. The former school believed that the universe was formed for ruled by mathematical principle, while the latter ideology derived the operation of the universe from classical mechanics. Both of these two groups of philosophy were useful to interpret the natural harmony and the greatness of the God. Although the persecution of scientists during the sixteenth century had resulted in a temporary decline of science, the new subjects gained an upper hand after the Reformation and the rise of the Protestant church, whose ethics stimulated the development of science. The new church advocated that: first, the appreciation of God and his greatness was the duty of all the people. Second, "the study of natural phenomena is an effective means for promoting the glory of God," whose wisdom completely laid in the natural order created by himself.[10] Third, the quest of welfare and the creation of wealth lied in science and technology.[11] Fourth and last, working hard was a means to praise the Creator and one should endure a pristine life to thank God.

These are all reasonable explanations for the non-exclusive nature of science and religion. Their confrontation broke out only when the conclusion of scientific research contradicted religious creeds. For instance, the solar-center theory of

Copernicus that went against the earth-center theory of the Church, and Darwin's postulation of the common ancestry of humans and apes seemed to contradict the story of God's creation of man. On the contrary, when scientific theories proved themselves more accurate in explaining the universe through meticulous logic ai derivation and the scientific method, some portions of the Christian world would adjust accordingly. In fact, Protestant Christianity was never an unreceptive religion.

Judging from the missionaries' evangelic activities in China, it could be concluded that: first, they were pleased to introduce general science knowledge about mathematics, physics, chemistry, geography, geology, biology, and medical science. Second, they followed their church's attitudes towards science. The Jesuits in the seventeenth century avoided mentioning the theory that the earth revolved around the sun. While the missionaries in late Qing era were generous to explain the theory, they held a cautious attitude towards evolution which postulated the common ancestry of humans and apes, an idea which was only seen in the *Chinese Scientific Magazine*. Third, the teaching of inferior scientific knowledge was a groundless accusation. Several missionaries might not be proficient in science, but they did encourage the learning of new subjects as science and religion were compatible:

> Without religion, science would lead to human selfishness and moral degradation; without science, religion would result in a narrow mind and superstition. Real science and a real religion are not mutually exclusive. They are similar to a twin brother — two angels that represent brightness, vividness, and happiness, coming from heaven to bless the people. Our society [Society for the Diffusion of Christian and General Knowledge Among the Chinese] is the representative of religion and science. We declare to the Chinese the non-exclusive nature of religion and science through our publications.[12]

To conclude, there were various attitudes towards science among the religious schools and churches. In general, Protestant missionaries devoted more time to propagating Western science than the Catholic missionaries did. Among the Protestant missionaries, those who were inclined to Liberal Christianity, such as Young J. Allen and Richard Timothy, were more active in preaching than the fundamentalists represented by J. H. Taylor. Works done in the twentieth century also outnumbered those done in the nineteenth century. A complete exclusion of science was never witnessed no matter in which sect and which period.

Bibliography of the Western Books

Biographies of the Jesuits in Chinese Diocese (*Yuan Zhongguo chuanjiaoqu de Yesuhuishi zhuanji* 原中國傳教區的耶穌會士傳記) edited by Louis Pfister (1833–1899) and translated by Feng Chengjun was published in 1932. It was the first comprehensive account of the Jesuits' evangelic missions in China, and it later became the reference for Joseph Dehergne, a French missionary, in compiling the *Collected Biographies of the Jesuits in China* (*Ruhua Yesuhuishi liezhuan* 入華耶穌會士列傳) with reference to other historical documents in Europe. Dehergne's book was translated by Geng Sheng and was published in 1995 by the Zhonghua Book Company. The book featured a list of works of the Jesuits during their stay in China from 1552 to 1880, and classified statistics of their works.

Edited by Xu Zongze, *A Summary of the Translated Works of the Jesuit Missionaries in between the Ming and Qing Dynasties* (*Mingqing jian Yesuhuishi yizhu tiyao* 明清間耶穌會士譯著提要) is an important book for understanding the works of the Jesuit missionaries completed during the last years of the Ming Dynasty. The 10 volumes extensively covered the process of the dissemination of Western learning during the late Ming period, the translated works of the Jesuit missionaries, a short biography of each translator, and a catalog of the book collections of the libraries in Xujiahui (the present Xuhui District in Shanghai), Paris, and the Vatican. A list of the translated titles was also attached in the book. Volumes two to eight of the collectanea included an introduction to the *Holy Bible*, a defense of Christianity against other religions, and an explanation on theology, the history of Christianity, calendric calculation, science, and information on The Gospels. A summary of the book, names of the authors and the translators, publication date, and preface and postscript were documented as well. The author Xu Zongze was a descendant of Xu Paul Guangqi, a Chinese friend of Ricci and the first Chinese convert to Christianity in the Ming Dynasty. In 1907, Xu Zongze joined the Jesuit Novitiate, where he prepared for his study for the doctoral degree in the United States. He was promoted as a sacredos after he returned to China, and was later employed as the curator of the Library of the St. Ignatius Cathedral in Xujiahui, Shanghai. Xu, an expert in the history of Catholics, also compiled *A Summary of the History of Catholics in China* (*Zhongguo Tianzhujiao chuanjiao shigai* 中國天主教傳教史概).

Compiled by John Fryer, *An Outline of Translation of Books* was serialized in the 5th to 8th issues of the *Chinese Scientific Magazine*.[13] The English edition was published in the January issue of the *North-China Herald* (*Beihua jiebao* 北華捷報)

in 1880. This book aimed to introduce the characteristics of the translation projects of the Jiangnan Arsenal, and was attached with a book list that recorded 98 published titles (up to 1879), such as *Practical Geometry* (*Yungui yuezhi* 運規約指) and *Algebra* (*Daishushu* 代數術). Among the 98 titles, 45 had finished translation but not been published, 13 were still being translated, and the process of the remaining titles was unknown. There was also the information of the author, the translator, the publishing date, the number of volumes, and the price. The English edition included "The Book Catalog of the Planned Titles" and "The Book Catalog Translated by Westerners Living in China." The former catalog documented 42 titles, part of which had already been published, such as *Written Calculation of Mathematics* (*Bisuan shuxue* 筆算數學) by Calvin Wilson Matteer and *A General Gazetteer of the Great Britain* by William Muirhead. The latter catalog recorded 62 titles, including *A New Discourse on the Human Body*. These two catalogs, together with *An Outline of Translation of Books*, covered almost all the translated Western books published from 1842 to 1879, such as *A New Discourse on the Human Body* by Hobson, *A Brief Survey of the United States of America* (*Lianbang zhilüe* 聯邦志略) by Bridgman, and *Introduction to Science* (*Gewu rumen* 格物入門) by W. A. P. Martin. These Western authors mainly settled in the treaty ports, such as Shanghai, Guangzhou, Tianjin, Hankou, Dengzhou, Chefoo, and Fuzhou, where their rights were well protected by the unequal treaties. Some of them lived in Beijing and Suzhou.

Achievements and Limitations of the Recently Published Books of Western Science by Sun Weixin was the author's examination paper completed in spring 1889, when Gong Zhaoai, Surveillance Commissioner of Zhejiang Province, issued a question to the students of the Shanghai Polytechnic Institute to comment on the translated Western works. Sun, who had written about 10,000 words explaining the merits and shortcomings of 140 titles, came out first in the examination. He first classified the subjects of Western learning into "mathematics, mechanics, astronomy, geology, geography, mining, chemistry, electrical studies, optics, heat, hydrology, climate, medical studies, cartography, botany, and zoology. He then commented on representative titles of mathematics treatise:

> Translated mathematics treatises included *Euclid's Elements* by Ricci and Alexander Wylie, *Compedium of Arithmetic* (*Shuxue qimeng* 數學啟蒙), *Elements of Algebra* (*Daishuxue* 代數學), *Elements of Analytical Geometry and of Differential and Integral Calculus* by Alexander Wylie, *Written Calculation of Mathematics*, *Guide of Geometry* (*Xingxue beizhi* 形學備旨) by Calvin Wilson Matteer, *Explanation to Mathematics* (*Shuxue li*

> 數學理), *Collected Mathematical Questions* (*Suanshi jiyao* 算式集要), *Algebra*, *Difficult Questions on Algebra* (*Daishu nanti* 代數難題), *Explanation to Trigonometry* (*Sanjiao shuli* 三角數理), and *The Origin of Calculus* (*Weiji suyuan* 微積溯源) by John Fryer, and *On Conic Section* (*Huanzhui quxian shuo* 圜錐曲線說) by Joseph Edkins. These works were concise and suitable for advanced level students. *Enlightenment on Western Mathematics* (*Xisuan qimeng* 西算啟蒙), *Enlightenment on Mental Calculation* (*Xinsuan qimeng* 心算啟蒙) by Harriet Newell Noyes, and *An Elementary Manual of Mental Calculation* (*Xinsuan chuxue* 心算初學) were too simple.[14]

He also compared the translated *Guide of Geometry* with *Euclid's Elements*, saying that:

> There are considerable sample problems in each volume of *Euclid's Elements*. The translator arranged the sample problems according to their difficulty and included a clear explanation. This book should be the best mathematics reference work. The *Guide of Geometry* was similar to *Euclid's Elements*. However, it replaced the difficult questions by other mathematical tips, which were useful to the study of trigonometry[15], statistics, and maritime expedition. The *Euclid's Elements* was no longer needed with the publication of this book.[16]

Gong Zhaoai, the chief examiner of Sun and a diplomat in the late Qing period, found Sun's paper highly impressive. Sun's work was an introductory paper, but the author managed to "make appropriate comparison and clear explanation, demonstrate his profound knowledge through extensive reading, and be attentive to current affairs and new books of Western learning."[17] Wang Tao, the College Head of the Shanghai Polytechnic Institute, compiled and published all these excellent examination papers, Sun's work included. These works were referred to by other intellectuals in their studies of Western learning, such as Liang Qichao's compilation of the *Bibliography of Western Knowledge*.

Edited by Liang Qichao and published by *The Chinese Progress Press* (*Shiwu baoguan* 時務報館) in 1896, the four-volume *Bibliography of Western Knowledge* introduced 352 titles of Western books translated in the post-Opium War period and attached a list of 293 titles of Western books completed before 1842. There was also a guide for the study of new knowledge. Liang explained the compilation background, the classification, and the importance of Western learning in the preface. He classified all the works of Western learning, religious titles excluded, into three branches and 28 sub-branches (refer to table 1.4)

Table 1.4 Branches and sub-branches of Western books in the Bibliography of Western Knowledge

Branches	Sub-branches	
Western subjects	Mathematics	Mechanics
	Electrical Studies	Chemistry
	Acoustics	Optics
	Thermodynamics	Astronomy
	Geology	Biology
	Zoology and Botany	Medical Studies
	Cartography	
Western affairs	History	Political Institution
	Education System	Law
	Agriculture	Mining
	Industry	Commerce
	Military	Maritime Affairs
Miscellany	Travelogue	Newspaper
	General Science	General Commentary
	Unclassified	

Compiled by Kang Youwei and published in spring 1898, *Catalog of Japanese Translated Books* (*Riben shumu zhi* 日本書目志) classified the books of Western learning completed by Japanese scholars into 15 categories: biology, science, religion, books and historical accounts, politics, law, agriculture, industry, commerce, education, literature, linguistics, fine art, hearsay, and military affairs. Under each category, there were also sub-branches for each subject, such as physics, chemistry, astronomy, anthropology, and psychology. The title, volume number, author, and price of each book, as well as Kang's comments on each book and the academic development in Japan were included but the Chinese translation of most of these recorded titles was unavailable. According to Kang, the Japanese language was much more acceptable here to the Western language than to the Chinese. He believed that adopting the Japanese translation would be much more efficient as the study of Western knowledge was already well developed in Japanese academia, so he compiled this catalog.

A Summary of the Bibliography of Japanese-Western Knowledge (*Dongxixue shulu tiyao zongxu* 東西學書錄提要總敘) by Shen Tongsheng was published in 1897. Shen, whose date of birth and death was unknown, was born in Kuaiji (present-day Shaoqing) in Zhejiang Province. He had received the degree of recommended man (*juren* 舉人) in the civil examination, but he continued his study in a modern school, Shanghai Nanyang College. During his study in Shanghai, he compiled *Bibliography of Japanese-Western Knowledge*, the namesake of Xu Weize's bibliography but with different content. This bibliography covered the books of various subjects, including astronomy, geology, gazetteer, education system, military matters, agriculture, industry, commerce, legal studies, diplomacy, history, mathematics, cartography, mining, chemistry, electrical studies, optics, acoustics, mechanics, thermodynamics, medical studies, biology, zoology, and botany. The bibliography had never been published, but Shen compiled all the prefaces of each subject into a concise edition, *A Summary of the Bibliography of Japanese-Western Knowledge*. The author traced the origin of each Western subject and explained the relationship between Western and Chinese learning, helping the public to have a better understanding of the new learning.

Common Titles of Chinese and Western Books (*Zhongxi putong shumu biao* 中西普通書目表) by Huang Qingcheng (1863–1904) was published by the Shanghai Journal of Mathematics Office. Huang, named as Bingda before he was renamed to Qingcheng, was also called Yuanchu, Yuchu (虞初), or Yuchu (愚初). Born in the Muxian Village in the Pingyang Country (present Chendong Village of the Cangnan County) of the Zhejiang Province, Huang was fortunate to study under the guidance of Sun Yirang, a notable scholar of the Lower Yangtze. In 1889, he was employed as a teacher in the Shanghai Medhurst College, where he first encountered Western learning. With the sponsorship of a philanthropist Shen Dunhe and Wang Fengzao, the Chinese ambassador in Japan, Huang traveled to Japan for two months, visiting important cities like Tokyo, Kyoto, Nara, Nagasaki, Kobe, Osaka, and Yokohama, and meeting about 80 Japanese celebrities.

After returning to China, he published the *Diary of the Journey to Japan* (*Dongyou riji* 東遊日記) to advocate the application of the Japanese mode of modernization in China. He received the degree of recommended man in 1894, but he was devoted in the dissemination of new knowledge instead of serving the absolute monarch. The publication of the *Common Titles of Chinese and Western Books* was one of his achievements to recommend useful reference works for beginners in Western learning (refer to table 1.5).

Huang also attached a short comment to these books. *A Short History of Europe* (*Ouzhou shilüe* 歐洲史略), for instance, was praised that "[one can] examine the ancient development of that territory (Europe) after reading the book." *On the Prolongation of Life* (*Yannian yishou lun* 延年益壽論) was merited as being "very concise."

Table 1.5 Categories and reference in the *Common Titles of Chinese and Western Books*

Category	Reference
Elementary Manual for Sinology and Western learning	*Books for Beginners of Chinese and Western Learning*
	On Education
	Chambers's Educational Course: Political Economy for Use in Schools and for Private Instruction
Reference of Sinology	*Questions and Answers to Book Catalogs*
Reference of Western learning	*Bibliography of Western Knowledge*
	A Research on Western Learning
Chinese Classics	*The Analects*
Chinese Masterpiece of Collectanea	*Commentaries and Sub-Commentaries on the Thirteen Classics*
Western Classics	*Euclid's Element*
	Guide of Geometry
Western Masterpiece of Collectanea	*Chinese Scientific Magazine*
	A Comprehensive Study of Western Learning
Specific Subject	*Discourse on Astronomy*
	Discovery of Astronomy
	Elements of Geology
	A Comprehensive Study of the Human Body

Fig. 1.8 *A Comprehensive Study of Western Learning*

In addition to the publication of the *Common Titles of Chinese and Western Books*, Huang established the *Journal of Mathematics* (*Suanxue bao* 算學報) in 1897 and *Journal of Historical Studies* (*Shixue bao* 史學報) in 1898, the first specialized mathematics magazine and the first journal of modern history, respectively. The history journal was renamed to *Journal of European Studies* (*Ouxue bao* 甌學報), adding articles of geography, philosophy, and politics.

Bibliography of Japanese-Western Knowledge was edited by Xu Weize and was published in 1899. Xu was born in a distinguished family in Shaoxing County in Zhejiang Province, and his father Xu Youlan and Uncle Xu Shulan were both famous book collectors. Xu, who found John Fryer's *An Outline of the Translation of Books* and Liang Qichao's *Bibliography of Western Knowledge* too simple, decided to compile a new book catalog, with newly-published Japanese references included. Xu compiled this book based on the 170,000 books stored in the Guyue Library and Zhuxue Study, two familial libraries established by his father and Uncle, respectively.[18] It also included a preface written by Cai Yuanpei. Cai, one of the most influential intellectuals in the Republican period and a fellow villager of Xu, was working for Xu's family as a private tutor and helping Xu Shulan to edit his books.[19]

Xu continued to collect books even after the publication of the bibliography. Gu Xieguang, a friend of Xu, donated all his collections to Xu, who thus published the enlarged edition of the book, with the name of Gu included in the authorship. Cai also wrote the preface for the new edition. There were 31 branches and several sub-branches of books in the enlarged edition. The History branch, for instance, was divided into general history, annals, ancient history, specific history, political institutions, war tales, and biographies of the emperors, ministers, and other commoners. The Agriculture branch, for example, collected books on cultivation, silkworm raising, plantation work, pasturage, and farming customs. The number of the volumes, editions, and the names of the author and translator of each book were documented. A summary of the contents of each book, which noted the content, the reason for compilation, and the authors' comments, was also included. In the end of the book, there were the "List of Old Translated Books by Chinese and Western Scholars" and the "List of Collection of Books Edited by Chinese."

Questions and Answers of Western Reference Works (*Xixue shumu dawen* 西學書目答問) was edited by Zhao Weixi and was published in 1901. Zhao Weixi, also named as Zhao Zhishan, was born in Nanfeng County of Jiangxi Province. He joined the government as a junior compiler in the Hanlin Academy after his graduation as the advance scholar (*jinshi* 進士) in the 16th year of the reign of Guangxu (1890). He worked as the Education Commissioner of Shaanxi and

Guizhou Provinces, Superintendent of Training, and Provincial Surveillance Commissioner of Gansu Province before the collapse of the Qing Dynasty, and he continued to govern Gansu Province as the Commissioner-in-chief until his death in 1917. During his term of service in Guizhou, he submitted a memorial to request the establishment of a translation bureau in the province in response to the educational reform, which examined students' understanding to current and global affairs and other new knowledge. He stressed the difficulty of implementing the new examination curriculum and founding of the modern school in the remote and inland Guizhou province in the memorial, and he suggested the establishment of a translation bureau helped introduce new knowledge to the people.

He followed the compilation style of Zhang Zhidong's *Questions and Answers to Book Catalogs* in editing the *Questions and Answers of Western Reference Works*, which classified all the Western books into three branches — general affairs, religion, and science, but he excluded religious titles. There were 221 titles of general affairs, covering a wide range of subjects including history, politics, education, law, logic, economics, agriculture, mining, industry, commerce, military matters, maritime affairs, diplomacy, travelogue, and other miscellaneous subjects. The remaining 151 titles were about mathematics, cartography, applied science, chemistry, thermodynamics, acoustics, optics, mechanics, electrical studies, astronomy, geology, biology, zoology, botany, and medical studies. There was a summary for each subject to introduce the features of the subject, and comments for several titles. *On Education* (*Yiye yaolan* 肄業要覽), for instance, was praised for its inclusion of new ideas though the book was a children's textbook. *Confrontation between Human and Microorganism* (*Ren yu weishengwu zhengzhan lun* 人與微生物爭戰論) was described as having "original arguments that serve as a key to hygiene problems." Volume numbers, names of the author and translator, and the publishers of the books were recorded as well. Moreover, the author made several changes to the translated names of new subjects. Economics, for example, was changed from *jixue* (計學 , literally meaning "the study of calculation and statistics) to *jingji* (經濟 , romanized as *keizai* in Japanese)[20] — a Japanese imported term.

Summary of Western Reference Works (*Xinxue shumu tiyao* 新學書目提要) in four volumes was published by Shanghai Tongya Press during 1903 to 1904. According to its preface, this book was co-edited by the staff in the Tongya Press, who was believed to be a group of Chinese exchange students in Japan.[21] This book introduced 218 titles published after 1900. And each volume collected reference works of different subjects — volume one had 93 titles of legal studies, volume two had 72 titles of history, volume three had 30 titles of geography, and volume four had

23 titles of literature. Most of the introductory articles, amounted to from between 500 to 1,000 words, and were longer than others' catalogs which had been collected. In addition to the documentation of the basic information of the books, this work was recommended for its comparison of the new books with other existing titles. Published in 1904, *The Newest Reference Works for Economics* (*Zuixin jingji xue* 最新經濟學)[22] was better than Adam Smith's *The Wealth of Nations* translated by Yan Fu, because the authors found Smith's work "only a demonstration of the economic theory of one school" and "failure to trace the holistic study of economics." *The Newest Reference Works for Economics*, on the contrary, was an insightful and appropriate guide for elementary students as it summarized the thoughts of various economics schools.[23] *The Newest Reference Works for Economics* was so popular that it was reprinted thrice within two years.

Records of Translation was edited by Gu Xieguang and published by Hangzhou Jinjia Stone House in 1934. Gu Xieguang, also known as Gu Dingmei, was born in Shaoxing County of Zhejiang Province. During his early years, he moved with his father to Pingxiang County in Jiangxi, where he studied in the Aozhou College and graduated as a Tribute Student (*gongsheng* 貢生). Being a keen student in the calligraphy of Clerical Script, he had copied more than 700 stone inscriptions, which were collected in the *Catalog of Cauldron Inscriptions in Northern Yellow River* (*Heshuo jinshi mu* 河朔金石目). Prior to his compilation of the *Records of Translation*, he also completed a literary collection — *Literary Collections of the Feiru Feixia Study* (*Feiru feixia zhai shiwen ji* 非儒非俠齋詩文集). This record introduced 533 translated books and 644 locally published books completed during 1902 to 1904, and these books were categorized into 26 branches and various sub-branches (refer to table 1.6).

Table 1.6 Categories in the *Records of Translation*

Volume	Branch	Sub-branch
1	History	
2	Legal Studies	
3	Education	Educational System
		Education Curriculum
		Teacher
		Reference Textbook
		Elementary Learning
	Diplomacy	
	Military	Barracks
		Naval Vessels
		Navy
		Guns and Cannons
		Gunpowder
		Armaments
		Military Strategy
4	Agriculture	
	Mining	
	Handicraft Industry	
	Commerce	
	Maritime Affairs	
	Physics and Chemistry	
	Astronomy and Climate	
5	Geography	
	Biology	
6	Museology	
	Hygiene	
	Cartography	
	Philosophy	
	Religion	
	Physical Education	
	Travelogue	
	Newspapers	
7	Current Affairs	
	Miscellany	
	Fiction	Political
		Scientific
		Detective
		Romantic
		Adventurous
		Myths
8	Locally Edited Titles	

Edited by the Educational Association of China in 1903, the *Catalog of the Education Association of China* (*Zhongguo xueshuhui shumu* 中國學塾會書目) collected 172 titles that were later categorized into seven branches. There were 18 titles of mathematical treatises, 57 titles of scientific references, eight titles of history, 14 titles of geography, five titles of religion and philosophy, six textbooks, and 64 unclassified titles. Established in 1878 in Shanghai, The School and Textbook Series Committee was the precursor of the Education Association of China, which was re-organized and renamed in 1890.[24] As a result, this catalog was almost the same as the *Catalog of the School and Textbook Series Committee* (*Yizhi shuhui shumu* 益智書會書目) edited by John Fryer and published in 1894 by The American Presbyterian Mission Press. *The Catalog of the School and Textbook Series Committee* was recommended for its record of the original author, publication house and date, which helped trace the sources of the books collected in the *Catalog of the Education Association of China*.

In addition to the above catalogs, there were several important bibliographies of Western learning, such as the catalog of the Society for the Diffusion of Christian and General Knowledge Among the Chinese, *Summary of Mathematical Works* (*Suanxue shumu tiyao* 算學書目提要, 1889) by Ting Fubao, *Summary of Historical Works of Various Countries* (*Lieguo shixue shumu tiyao* 列國史學書目提要) by Zou Shouqi, *The First Summary of Science Works* (*Kexue shumu tiyao chubian* 科學書目提要初編, 1903) by Wang Jingyi, and *Summary of the Translated Works of the Jiangnan Arsenal* (*Jiangnan zhizaoju yishu tiyao* 江南制造局譯書提要, 1909) by Chen Zhu. There are only two recommended bibliographies for Western books published during 1905 to 1911: *Catalog of Translated Japanese Books in China* (*Zhongguo yi Riben shu zonghe mulu* 中國譯日本書綜合目錄) edited by Tan Ruqian and published by the Chinese University of Hong Kong Press in 1980, and *Catalog of the Books Published in Late Qing Period* (*Wanqing yingye shumu* 晚清營業書目) edited by Zhou Zhenhe and published by Shanghai Bookstore in 2005.

2

Chapter

A Homage to Matteo Ricci

The Ming-to-Qing dynastic transitional period witnessed a large-scale introduction of Western learning to China. These decades of cultural exchange have been extensively studied by scholars who looked at the collection of historical sources, translation of important documents, and the exploration of the ancient scholars and their works.[1] Among these research works, "History of Sino-Western Cultural Exchange in the Ming-to-Qing Dynastic Transition," chapter four of Fang Hao's *The History of Chinese-Western Communication*, clearly presents the background, process, and content of the dissemination in the late Ming period, as well as the missionaries' activities. Another representative work was *Jesuit Missionaries and Science in China* by Fan Hongye, who analyzed the impact of the new knowledge and the development of science in China in a systematical way.

To repeat the content of these authoritative works seems to be unnecessary. However, having considered the legacy of this period of history as the origin of the revival of Western learning in the late Qing period, it would be clear to trace the first encounters between Oriental culture and Occidental religion. It is also helpful to highlight the differences of the dissemination method and society's response towards the new knowledge between these two periods. Therefore, this chapter focuses on the missionaries' activities in China up to the late eighteenth century, the knowledge introduced, response from the Chinese scholars, and the impact of Western learning to the traditional academic development.

The Two Centuries of Vicissitudes

The world had never seen such unprecedented changes in communication and such enthusiasm about discovering the world before the fifteenth and sixteenth century. Triggered by the discovery of America by Columbus and furthered by the sailing across the Cape of Good Hope by Vasco da Gama, and the circumnavigation of Magellan, the "Age of Discovery" constituted a new page in human history. The Europeans, propelled by the pursuit of gold, and in search of glory were anxious to plow their way through the waves, head to the unknown world, and turn the Asian territories into their conquered territories.

Cooperation among these European powers, including Portugal, Spain, the Netherlands, Britain, France, and Prussia, was rarely seen in the struggle for colonies. Several of the countries involved themselves in conflict, generating a hostile relationship that resulted in the eventual outbreak of wars. China was too strong for the European states to conquer by that time, so that they shifted their attention to subduing the weaker neighbors of China, such as the Indian, the Southeast Asian, and the Taiwanese (known as Formosan by the time) areas. In general, the fifteenth to sixteenth century was "the Age of Portugal and Spain." The Dutch became dominant after the second half of the sixteenth century but their rise was terminated in the early seventeenth century, by the British, who dominated the world until the twentieth century.

The term "century" was employed only by the Westerners to describe a period. The Chinese, on the contrary, counted time by "era periods (*nianhao* 年號)," which represented a specific period of the reign of emperors. They addressed 1587 as the 15th year of the reign of Emperor Wanli, and they called 1662 as the 1st year of the reign of Kangxi. China was misunderstood as an empire of gold by the Westerners before the age of exploration. The mutual recognition between the Oriental empire and the Occidental countries had long been established, but it remained only a superficial understanding before the arrival of the Westerners, who brought along not only war but also a new culture which helped to bridge their cultural gap even if by force, understanding China through the colonization of overseas Chinese communities in Southeast Asia. All these elements constituted the background of the eastward dissemination of Western learning that began with the coming of Jesuit missionaries in the sixteenth century, until the banning of Christianity by the Qing court and the dissolution of the Jesuits in the eighteenth century.

Established in Paris in 1534 and operated under the patronage of the Pope in 1540, the Society of Jesus aimed to uphold the authoritativeness of the Pope and to oppose the Reformation initiated by the Protestant Church. The society and its founder Ignatius Loyola, a Spanish noblemen, were criticized by Enlightenment philosophers such as Voltaire because of its conservative nature, but the features of the society should be recognized. First, all the missionaries paid absolute obedience to their seniors. Second, the wearing of a uniform was not required in order to make it more convenient to preach to people of various classes as countries, showing a flexible evangelic method. Third, the emphasis of education and the establishment of schools helped to nurture knowledge of considerable well-known scholars, including Molière, Montesquieu, and Galileo. Fourth, the bravery and perseverance of the missionaries, added by their passion in conquering the world in the name of Christianity, propelled them to move to hot Africa, mysterious Asia, and desolate South America. All these factors contributed to the enormous success of the Jesuits in disseminating both Christianity and Western learning in the late Ming society.

In 1552, 30 years prior to Matteo Ricci's arrival in China, Francis Xavier from Spain was dispatched by the Jesuits to the Oriental empire. Xavier, the first Jesuit missionary in China, landed on Shangchuan Island[2], 150 kilometers southwest of Guangzhou, and made the island a base for his mission. It is difficult to imagine the limited achievement of Xavier then judging from the establishment of more than 100 schools that are named after Xavier nowadays. Actually, during his four-month stay in China, he did nothing more than to seek help from the Portuguese Ambassador to request a residency permit in China, which ended in failure. He soon died a feverish death, leaving a few legacies to later generations. Eight more Jesuits missionaries visited China following Xavier's journey, and they settled in Macau, which had been made the sphere of influence for Portugal. These eight missionaries had almost no achievement in preaching because of their incompetence in speaking Chinese. Having considered their unfamiliarity with the Oriental language and culture as a great obstacle to evangelical work, the Jesuits decided to dispatch Alexandro Valignano, Michele Ruggieri, Franciscus Pasio, and Matteo Ricci, four Italians who had mastered Chinese and were well acquainted with Chinese culture, to continue the work of the preceding members.

Fig. 2.1 Portrait of Matteo Ricci, an Italian missionary of the Jesuits

Valignano, the Superior in India of the Order, had the highest superiority among the four missionaries. Graduated as a Doctor in Canon and Civil law (Doctor in *Utroque Iure*) from the University of Naples, he joined the Jesuits and afterwards he was sent to China. He first arrived at Macau, and he left the Portuguese colony for Japan one year later. He was responsible for planning and directing the Jesuits' evangelical activities in the Far East. Ruggieri was called upon by Valignano to assist his mission in China. He was the first Jesuit missionary to visit the inner parts of China (Shaoqing, Shaoxing, and Guilin) and he was also the first who completed Catholic reference works, *Compendium Creed of Divinity* (*Shengjiao shilu* 聖教實錄) in Chinese. He returned to Rome in 1588 at the age of 44, and he never visited China again in his lifetime. Pasio, who had arrived at China two years after Ruggieri did, only accompanied Ruggieri to visit Shaoqing. He soon started his mission in Japan. These three missionaries, though qualified to be the pioneers of preaching in China, were far from paving the foundation for the dissemination of Western learning to China when compared to Ricci.

Ricci was born in 1552 in Macerata, a small town in Central Italy and part of the Papal States. During his study in a Jesuit school in Rome, he was particularly interested in mathematics and theology. He joined the Jesuits after his graduation in 1571. Prior to his journey to China, he joined a missionary expedition to India. Summoned by the Jesuits, Ricci departed Goa and headed to Macau, where he started his unprecedented mission until his death in 1610. He made enormous contributions to the introduction of Western learning and culture to China in his 28 years of settlement in China as is explained in the following passage.

First, Ricci started the Sinification of Western learning. In order to ensure the Chinese people's acceptance of the alien Christianity and Western culture Ricci adopted a Chinese form of preaching. He pretended to be a Buddhist monk initially, comparing himself with the Indian monks, to which the Chinese were familiar. The church that he built in Shaoqing was called Xianhua Temple[3], with a tablet inscribing the phrase "the Pure Land from the West (*Xilai jingtu* 西來淨土)." It was not until he had realized the inferior social status of Buddhist monks that he discarded the wearing of Buddhist attire and dressed as a Confucian scholar. In addition to the change of clothing, Ricci learned to read and write in classical Chinese, and he adopted a Chinese name Li Madou with the pseudonym of Xitai (literally, a Western monk), which was similar to the practice of the Chinese scholars. He followed the Chinese custom to bow instead of shaking people's hands in greeting. He even performed *koutou* (叩頭 , a respectful act done by kneeling and bowing and had the head touching the ground) to high officials. His main key to entering the Chinese scholarly world was the incorporation of Christianity into the Confucian belief system. "Shangdi," the high emporor mentioned in the Confucian classic *The Book of History* (*Shangshu* 尚書), was correlated to God because the terms carried the meaning of "the heavenly king." He tolerated the Chinese people's ancestor worship, which he regarded as a common practice that involved no idolatry. In sketching the world map, he also strove to avoid challenging the concept of "the middle kingdom" of the Chinese scholars, who used the term to describe China as the center of the world surrounded by barbarous tribes.[4] He skillfully adjusted the position of the Meridian on the map, placing China in the center instead of the easternmost part. Ricci's amendment successfully pacified the Sino-centric scholars, who were willing to study the map and were thus indoctrinated with the knowledge of the five continents. Presenting the Western learning with appropriate adjustment was effective to avoid direct conflict with the Confucians, while assuring the dissemination of new knowledge. This method, invented by Ricci, was widely adopted by latter missionaries in dealing with the conservative and arrogant Chinese.

Second, Ricci expanded the influence of Catholics to the rest of China. Since the coming of Xavier to China in 1552, the development of Christianity in China had limited success. Most of the missionaries had never travelled to other parts of China except Macau and Guangzhou, which were however too distant to influence the majority of scholar-officials in the North. Ricci, who was invited to cure a son of an official, had the opportunity to visit Nanjing, but he was not permitted to stay in the Southern capital permanently. He then went to Nanchang, another prosperous city in the middle Yangtze River, to gather students who wished to know more of the West. People in Nanchang, who had never seen any Westerner, were astonished by Ricci's knowledge of the Four Confucian Books. His popularity continued to rise with his accurate prediction of the solar eclipse. Having received the order from A. Valignano, Ricci attempted to visit Beijing, but his efforts were hindered by the outbreak of the Japanese Expedition to Korea (1592–1598) during which the Ming court was responsible to send army to protect Korea, its vassal state. He thus stayed in Nanjing, where he befriended several high officials — Ye Xianggao, Li Zhi, and most importantly, Xu Guangqi. Before his arrival in Beijing in 1601, Ricci had successfully converted 40 people, with the majority of followers who were scholars and officials. The 1600s saw a multiple increase in Chinese converts which amounted to 2,500 people. The growth of Christianity in China did not cease even after Ricci's death in 1610. Up to the 9th year of the reign of Kangxi (1670), the number of Chinese Christian converts reached 270,000, and about 40 churches were established in most parts of China. Such a flourishing could not have been achieved without the pioneering work of Ricci.

Third, Ricci secured the patronage of court officials, paving the way for latter missionaries to enter the bureaucratic circle. The Jesuits regarded the catching of officials' fancy the quickest means to spread Western culture. Ricci first befriended Qu Taisu in Shaozhou. This was the first significant step for Ricci to establish the relationship with the Chinese officials because Qu, as a son of the Minister of Rites, had an excellent personal network. Most of the high officials were introduced by Qu to Ricci during his stay in Nanjing, though Ricci's charisma and profound knowledge also played a role in earning the cordiality with the Chinese officials. Feeling proud of making friends with Ricci, these scholars frequently visited Ricci's house in Nanjing to discuss astronomy, calendars, geography, and other Western subjects with the "Confucians in the Far West (*Taixi zhi ru* 泰西之儒)," what Ricci used to refer to the Chinese.[5] In addition to Xu Guangqi, Li Zhizao, and Yang Tingjun, the three main supporters of Ricci, there were many other friends of Ricci that might not be familiar to us. According to the tomb inscription of Ricci written by Wang Yinglin and other historical documents, friends of Ricci included Guo Yingping the Vice Minister of the Ministry of Military, Wang Pan the Prefect of Shaoqing County, Liu Jiwen the Governor-general of Guangdong, Wang Yingling the Prefect of Nanxiong and Shuntian, Wang Zhongming the Minister of Rites, Zhang the Minister of Revenue, Zhao the Minister of Justice, Ye the Minister of Rites, and Li Zhuowu, a celebrated Confucian. The scholar-gentry was one of the dominant classes in ancient China as it represented the essentials of Chinese culture and moral standards because of their profound knowledge, gentle and graceful personalities, and their role in maintaining the social order and providing education. To catch the fancy of the scholar-gentry class was the key for Western learning to enter the Chinese cultural circle, and this mission was completed by Ricci.

Fourth, Ricci assured the support from the emperor. Ricci and his colleagues well understood the importance of the emperor's permission for their evangelic work. This strategy of "working from the top down" was regarded as the quickest way to make hundreds of people Christian converts. To secure protection from the emperor, Ricci brought along with him a memorial, written in a humble manner, to state his experience in learning Chinese, and his respect to Chinese culture, and his desire to work for the Celestial Empire. Ricci also presented plies of gifts, including Western clocks, musical and astronomical instruments, bells, Western paintings, and other items, as tributes. Three days after Ricci's presentation of the Western inventions, he and his colleagues were allowed to visit the Forbidden City. He had never seen Emperor Wanli, who had hidden himself from morning meetings with officials for more than 30 years. What he only did was to pay homage to the throne.

The emperor, though he did not receive Ricci, was interested in the presented musical clock and the Western music. He thus invited Ricci to teach the eunuchs the making of the clock as well as Western musical theory. He also permitted Ricci to settle in Beijing with an imperial stipend. Ricci's influence to the royal members was never limited to the emperor. More than 50 royal family members, such as the Empress Dowager, princesses, and princes of the later Emperor Yongli were converted to Christianity, so as to create a "Catholic Chinese court."

Fifth, Ricci demonstrated the essentials of Western science and technology. The concept of "middle kingdom" established since ancient times and the implementation of the tributary system added to the difficulty for the "barbarous" Western learning to enter the Chinese academic circle. Instead of mentioning about God initially, Ricci adopted the method of "preaching through teaching," an indirect evangelic way aimed at arousing the curiosity of the learners to their belief, or to incorporate several Christian ideas during the teaching. Both Ricci and Ruggieri demonstrated various Western products, such as the mirror, musical clock, world map, Venetian prism, textile products, a portrait of the Madonna, clavichord, a globe, various astronomical instruments, and their scientific knowledge to both officials and the public.

Sixth and lastly, Ricci pioneered the Sino-Western translation. Translation was proven to be the most important means to popularize foreign culture in China, as evidenced by the translation of Buddhist classics from Sanskrit to Chinese during the Six Dynasties to the Tang Dynasty that made Buddhism one of the most influential religions in China. The translation of Buddhist classics was done by Indian or Chinese monks, who usually worked independently. The notable monk Xuanzhuang, for instance, was proficient in both Sanskrit and Chinese and thus managed to translate by himself. Ricci, on the contrary, invited Chinese scholars to participate in the translation project. The translation of *Euclid's Element* was done together by Ricci and Xu Guangqi, and the *Rules of Arithmetic Common to Cultures* (*Tongwen suanzhi* 同文算指) was jointly translated by Ricci and Li Zhizao. It was not because of Ricci's impotence in Chinese that he sought help from the Chinese scholars. It was actually a valuable opportunity for Ricci to explain the essentials of Western knowledge in detail and eventually, to enlighten the Chinese scholars about the greatness of the creator. Ricci cooperated with the Chinese to translate 19 treatises of Western science and technology. Ricci's unprecedented achievements in pioneering the dissemination of Western learning were concluded in prose in Yao Dong's *Collections of Foreign Folk Songs* (*Waiguo zhuzhici* 外國竹枝詞):

The opening of the Catholic Church unifies the sounds of nature.
Musical pitch flows from high to low following the ringing of bells and the sound of a piano.
Roses bloom outside the Fucheng Gate.
Pour wine on the ground to pay homage to Ricci the Western Confucian.[6]

Ricci died in May 1610 at the age of 57. He was the first missionary that enjoyed the privilege of having a grand funeral and a tomb in Erligou, 2 *li* (里)[7] away from the Fucheng Gate in Beijing, while most of his counterparts had to be buried in Macau.

Ricci's position as the Superior of the Chinese Diocese was succeeded by Nicolaus Longobardi, also an Italian missionary. His goal in China was similar to Ricci and other missionaries: to establish a preaching base in the Southern China before heading to Beijing. However, he was vindictive toward Ricci's strategy of accommodating Confucianism. His banning of the worship of other Chinese deities, ancestors, and the Confucian masters aroused discontent among the Chinese scholars, most of whom were friends of Ricci. These officials, headed by Shen Que the Nanjing Minister of Rites, submitted a joint petition to the court in 1616, requesting the banning of Christianity because of its propagation of worshiping and being loyal only to God and not just to the family. Defending arguments by Xu and other Chinese converts were not accepted and, eventually, the Ming court ordered the missionaries to leave the capital. Diego de Pantoja, Sabatino de Ursis, and other missionaries were dispatched to either Guangzhou or Macau for temporary settlement. They changed their names to live in remote areas to avoid having their identities unveiled.

A few years after the Nanjing Religious Incident in 1616, the Catholic Church regained its influence in China. The reasons were mainly related to the political circumstance of the time: first, the Western mathematics and astronomical knowledge was useful in formulating the calendar. Western mathematics proved that it was more accurate to predict the eclipses and it was thus adopted to amend the outdated Chinese calendar in the reign of Tianqi (1620–1627). Xu Guangqi was responsible for the formulation of the new calendar, and he suggested inviting Longobardi and Johannes Terrenz, who were living privately in Beijing, to assist in the project. Second, Western weapons were adopted by the Ming court to confront the Manchus. Western cannons were first used by general Yuan Chonghuan in the Battle of Sarhu against the Manchu. And the weapon demonstrated its strength in creating hundreds of deaths and injuries, the Manchu leader Nurhaci included. With the help of the Western weapons, the fierce Manchu could no longer gain any upper hand in war. The Ming court continued to employ Western merchants to Beijing to assist in the making of Western guns, providing a change for the introduction of Western science. The superiority of Western learning was consolidated. Third, the opposition party against the introduction of Western learning, headed by eunuch Wei Zhongxian and Minister Shen Que, lost their control in court affairs after the enthronement of Emperor Chongzhen. The new emperor was more sympathetic to the missionaries because of their assistance in the frontier battles. Consequently, J. Aleni and Franciscus Sambiasi were granted the freedom of passage in the empire, the right of building churches and preaching. By the 7th year of the reign of Tianqi (1627), there were approximately 13,000 Chinese Catholic converts. Moreover, Adam Schall and other missionaries were permitted to enter the Forbidden City without permission because there were court women, princes, and eunuch converts. Several unofficial historical accounts even suggested that Emperor Chongzhen was a Christian.

In 1644, when Beijing was conquered by the Manchu troops, the royal members escaped to the south, running across the River Yangtze, and reached Shaoqing in Guangdong, where they established the new Nanming regime (literally, the southern Ming Dynasty). This exiled government was dominated by Catholic ministers (Qu Shisi), eunuchs (Pang Tianshou), the Queen, Emperor Dowager, and princes. Facing the devastating raid of the Manchu troops, the Empress Dowager even sent letters to Pope Alexander VII to request military assistance.

These Jesuits missionaries served the Qing court after the collapse of the Southern regimes. They attempted to earn credence from the Manchu rulers by presenting interesting Western inventions, such as the new calendar, the celestial globe, sundial, horoscope, and world map. The Manchu rulers, in response, welcomed the missionaries even though they had been helping the Ming court to confront them. Adam Schall, who was respected as "*mafa*" (literally, teacher or master) by the young Emperor Shunzhi, was appointed as the director of the Imperial Board of Astronomy in 1644. No missionaries in China had received such favorable treatment like Adam Schall, who was granted the freedom to submit memorials to the emperor directly, and to be exempted from *koutou*. The emperor frequently summoned Adam Schall to the palace, and visited his residence to discuss astronomy or political affairs. Adam Schall was even promoted thrice within a year — from the fifth ranked Grand Master for Thorough Counsel to the third ranked Chamberlain for Ceremonials. He was bestowed with the title "Master Heavenly Secret (*Tongxuan jiaoshi* 通玄教師)" and the post of Grand Master for Splendid Happiness, a first-ranked prestige title for civil officials. Adam Schall's profound knowledge, to a certain extent, secured his foothold in the Manchu court as a foreigner, but his respect to local practice, such as shaving hairs and keeping a hair tail, also played a role.

Following the death of Emperor Shunzhi in 1661, the influence of Adam Schall and the Church on the court affairs drastically declined. The throne was taken by Emperor Kangxi, aged 6, who was too young to govern. Four regents were appointed to assist Kangxi, and Oboi, the most overbearing regent, was a traditional Manchu aristocrat who showed no appeal to any policies undermining the Manchu customs, the employment of Jesuits missionaries included. Despite his disdain towards the Westerners, Oboi dared not take any action against them for his fear of triggering a diplomatic dispute. The opportunity to remove the missionaries came in 1664, when Yang Guangxian, a conservative Han scholar, impeached Adam Schall and other missionaries for planning a rebellion, confusing the public with evil ideas, and formulating a ridiculous calendar. The fatal accusation of Adam Schall was his referral to a calendar published in the Ming Dynasty in arranging for the funeral of a prince, leading to the death of two emperors' concubines, another prince and eventually, Emperor Shunzhi. The court officials were so frightened that they ordered the arrest of Adam Schall, F. Verbiest, G. de Magalhães, and Lodovico Buglio. Adam Schall was given the death penalty, while the remaining were expelled from China. On April 16, 1665, when the memorial of Schall's death penalty was submitted to the emperor, an earthquake suddenly broke out in Beijing, resulting in the collapse of houses and the falling of the cross of the church on the ground. Most of the court officials believed this natural disaster a signal of misjudgment of the missionaries. And Oboi, even recognized as the "first warrior in Manchu tribes," dared not to offend the deities. With the pressure from the Empress Dowager, Oboi decided to release Adam Schall, and allowed the missionaries to settle in Guangzhou. Schall, aged 70 by the time, was frustrated and died of sickness soon.

The emperor's attitude was decisive for any formulation of policies under an absolute monarchy, China included. In 1668, when the 14-year-old Emperor Kangxi took up the rule by himself, he ordered a remand of Adam Schall's case. Yang Guangxian, who had replaced Adam Schall to direct the Imperial Board of Astronomy, was invited by the emperor to have a contest with F. Verbiest. Yang and Verbiest had to predict the position of the sun at noon by referring to their own method. During the competition, Verbiest could make an accurate prediction while Yang failed to do so. The emperor thus dismissed Yang, whose job would be taken up by Verbiest.

Fig. 2.2 Portrait of Ferdinand Verbiest

The result of the competition had two immediate effects: the vindication of Adam Schall and the encouragement of the emperor to study Western learning. The emperor was too astonished at the accuracy of Western learning and the ignorance of his ministers. He was determined to master this advanced learning. He had lessons with Verbiest about Western astronomy with reference to 120 treatises compiled by the Jesuits missionaries. He learned algebra, logarithm, and the usage of scientific instruments.[8] He also directed Franciscus Gerbillon Joan and Joachin Bouvet to translate the first six books of Ignace-Gaston Pardies' *Elements of Geometry* (*Jihe yuanben* 幾何原本) and *Applied and Theoretical Geometry* (*Yingyong he lilun jihexue* 應用和理論幾何學) into Manchu. His study stopped temporarily with the outbreak of the Revolt of the Three Feudatories, but the rebellion also gave further rise to the Jesuits in China, as the Western cannons, produced by F. Verbiest, demonstrated their strength in overcoming the traditional Chinese army again. In addition to science and technology, the Jesuit missionaries introduced various Western subjects, including geography, zoology, music, anatomy, and philosophy, to Emperor Kangxi. It was not until the emperor's deterioration in health that his study terminated.[9]

The short-lived cordiality between the Qing court and the Church was because of the Church's banning of ancestral worship and the failed negotiation between the two parties. The emperor explained to the Church that the worship of ancestors and the ancient sages was a mere expression of respect, and no idolatry was involved. The emperor also stated that Westerners who failed to respect the Chinese tradition like Ricci would not be permitted to stay in China. Their relationship eventually broke up in 1717, when all evangelic activities were officially forbidden in China, and missionaries were expatriated. The decline of the Catholic influence in China was compounded by the dismissal of the Jesuits in 1773 due to conflict among the Christian associations. The 200-year history of Jesuits in China came to its epilogue, and the dissemination of Western learning came to a halt until the coming of the Protestant missionaries in the early nineteenth century.

Knowledge from the West

The introduction of the most advanced Western knowledge to the Oriental country was not expected because of the inherent conservativeness and anti-reformation characteristics of the Jesuits whose ultimate goal was preaching not teaching. The Chinese, however, still found the Western knowledge new and interesting because they had long isolated themselves from the outside continents since the end of Zheng Ho's seventh maritime expedition in the early-Ming period. The Chinese's ignorance of European culture, knowledge, and customs thus created the favorable conditions for the Jesuits' missions.

Since the coming of Ricci to the dismissal of the Jesuits, the missionaries translated 437 Western titles, 251 among which were religious books that mentioned *The Bible*, theology, and rituals; 55 were humanity titles that explained geography, maps, languages, philosophy, and education; 131mentioned about natural science such as mathematics, astronomy, biology, and medical studies.[10]

Astronomical treatise

Ricci's presentation of a self-made celestial sphere and mechanical clock to the local governor of Shaoqing symbolized the beginning of the introduction of Western astronomy to China. The translation of Western astronomical treatises began after Ricci's settlement in Beijing in order to aid in the amendment of the Chinese calendar. Xu Guangqi and Li Zhizao were assigned to assist in the work, but Ricci found it necessary to equip his friends with astronomical knowledge. He then translated considerable Western astronomic and calendric treatises.

Ricci's counterparts, such as D. de Pantoja, S. de Ursis, and N. Longobardi, who were proficient in astronomy and calendric formulation, also helped translate astronomical treatises.

Treatise on Isoperimetric Figures

Treatise on Isoperimetric Figures (*Huanrong jiaoyi* 圜容較義) was orally translated by Ricci and was recorded by Li Zhizao. It was published in Beijing in 1614 in one volume. It introduced the shapes of celestial spheres, the celestial movement, and the concept of a spherical earth.

Explication of the Structure of Heaven and Earth

Explication of the Structure of Heaven and Earth (*Qiankun tiyi* 乾坤體義) was edited by Ricci during the reign of Wanli. The first volume introduced the armillary sphere, the concept of a spherical earth, and Ptolemy's nine-leveled heaven. The second volume argued for the larger volume of the Sun to the earth, and the large volume of the earth to the moon. The third volume explained the calculation of area and volume.

The concept of the nine-level heaven originated from Ptolemy's *Almagest*, the most representative Western astronomical treatise in Medieval Europe. Ptolemy suggested that the unmoving Earth was the center of the universe. The seven stars — the moon, Mercury, Venus, the Sun, Mars, Jupiter, and Saturn — orbited around the Earth at different levels, while other stellar bodies were fixed on the eighth heaven. Ptolemy's model suited the ancient Chinese concept of a nine-leveled heaven.[11]

Questions about Heaven

Questions about Heaven (*Tianwen lüe* 天問略) was compiled by Emmanuel Diaz, reviewed by Zhou Xiling, Kong Zhenshi, and Wang Yingxiong, and published in 1615. It was written in the question-and-answer style, interpreting the structure of the nine heavens, the five planets, the sun, the moon, the seasonal climate, duration of day and night, and the eclipses.

Calendric Treatises of the Chongzhen Reign

Calendric Treatises of the Chongzhen Reign (*Chongzhen lishu* 崇禎曆書), also entitled *New Treatise on the Western Calendric Formulation* (*Xiyang lifa xinshu*

西洋曆法新書), was compiled by the officials of the Imperial Board of Astronomy, N. Longobardi, Joannes Terrenz, Jacobus Rbo, Adam Schall, Xu Guangqi, and Li Tianjing during their formulation of the new calendar.

This book contained 11 sections. The first section "the origin of the principle" introduced elementary knowledge of Western astronomy, such as the five planets, the sun, the moon, the celestial movement, and spherical astronomy. The second section "the principle of mathematics" explained the observation of the celestial movements and related calculation. The third section "the principle of calculation" included formulae of trigonometry and geometry. The fourth section "the principle of instruments" explained the production and the use of astronomical instruments. And the fifth section provided "comprehensive" lists of the conversion table of the Sino-Western units of measurement. This book was the largest compendium of Western astronomy at the time.

In addition to the translation of books, these missionaries also produced or brought along with them various astronomical instruments, such as the quadrant of the seven stars, celestial globe of various stars, celestial template, a telescope to observe the waxing and waning of the stars, a celestial sphere, a sundial, a zodiac globe, and an equator globe.

The most important contribution of these astronomical treatises was the introduction of the geocentricism of Ptolemy and heliocentricism of Copernicus. These two Western universe structures differed from the traditional Chinese concept of the universe in terms of the distance among the stars and the celestial movement. The Chinese theory of a hemispherical heaven (*gaitian shuo* 蓋天說) suggested that the universe was a dome, with the earth as the ground while the arc was the heaven and the home to various stars. Another two Chinese universe models that emerged since the Han Dynasty were the theory of the spherical heaven (*huntian shuo* 渾天說) and the "theory of visibility and invisibility" (*xuanye shuo* 宣夜說). The former asserts that the earth was similar to an egg, with the earth as the yolk and the eggshell as heaven; the latter suggested all the stars, which are "floating" in the shapeless universe, had to rely on "*qi*" (氣 , ether) to move. Although the theory of the spherical heaven seemed to share the same universal view of Ptolemy's geocentricism, it was not popular among the scholars, who found the traditional theory of a hemispherical heaven more reliable. Ptolemy's geocentricism, though it had been regarded as outdated in the West, was still new to the Chinese.

Despite the Church's hostility towards the concept of heliocentricism, these Jesuits missionaries did not avoid introducing Copernicus' theory.[12] His notable title *On the Revolutions of the Celestial Spheres* was frequently quoted in the *Calendric Treatises of the Chongzhen Reign*. J.Rbo, though he disagreed with Copernicus, included the theory in the book, suggesting that the Earth's rotation made the stars appear to revolve around the Earth.[13] Jesuits missionaries that arrived at China in the eighteenth century held a more cordial attitude to Copernicus' theory. Michael Benoist (1715–1774), a French Jesuit missionary who assisted in the amendment of the Chinese calendar during the reign of Qianlong, showed his affirmation of heliocentricism as he found Copernicus' theory accurate in predicting the celestial movement. He stated that:

> The Sun was placed at the center of the universe by Copernicus. The nearest star to the Sun was Mercury, followed by Venus, the Earth, Mars, Jupiter, and Saturn. The Moon revolves around the Earth. There are five little stars (the satellites) revolving Saturn, and there are four small stars revolving Jupiter. Each of the small stars has their own orbit. The farthest level is the home to various stellar objects. Heaven is always in constant stability...Copernicus, in discussing [the nature of] the seven stars, stated the immovable Sun and the movable Earth. People who first heard this theory were so surprised that they regarded [this theory] as heterodox as they saw the Sun spinning around the earth everyday.[14]

Galileo, equally famous with Copernicus, also had his theory introduced. The Italian scientist supported and developed Copernicus' theory after he had observed the innumerable stars in the galaxy — evidence that refuted that the Earth was the center of the universe. His discovery of the satellites spinning around Jupiter and Saturn was also introduced to the Chinese through the Jesuit missionaries. Adam Schall, for instance, openly denied the Ptolemaic model and supported Galileo:

> With the death of Tycho came the popularization of the telescope. All the delicacies of the universe are observed by it. For example, Galileo who drew a new graph 30 years ago, gave an epochal explanation to cosmology. Since then, various scientists emerged and completed more reference works, so that [the public] realized the presence of four little stars (satellites) beside Jupiter known to the people. These four stars revolve in quite a high speed. There are two little stars beside Saturn. There are different phases of Venus. All these concepts were unheard of before.

Regarding the formation of the galaxy, Adam Schall introduced the idea that:

> The ancient people did not regard the celestial river (the galaxy) as stars. Having found the light of the galaxy dimmer than the Sun and the Moon, they believed that the galaxy was a group of pure ether, so that they placed the galaxy in the ninth heaven. With the invention of the telescope, [people can] observe the galaxy and realize the presence of various stars in the galaxy.[15]

The Chinese people were so proud of their brilliant culture that they seldom referred to foreign tradition. In the aspect of astronomy, China was one of the earliest civilizations that interpreted political affairs with reference to celestial operation. The emperor, regarded as the son of heaven under Chinese cosmology, was responsible for worshipping the deities on an auspicious day selected by the astronomical officials. It was necessary to ensure the accuracy of the calendar as any miscalculation might result in unfortunate events. The Datong calendar, compiled based on the excellent Shouli Calendar of Guo Shoujing, was too outdated to predict the eclipses of 1450, 1479, 1610, and 1629. Emperor Chongzhen was so furious that he decided to adopt the Western calendar.[16] Xu and Li, who had learned the Western method, requested the revision of the calendar. From 1630 to 1632, Xu had successfully predicted five lunar eclipses and one solar eclipse. They gathered their valuable experience and the research method in the *Calendric Treatises of the Chongzhen Reign*, which they believed beneficial to the latter generations. Such an act violated the dignity of the conservative Chinese, who thus initiated a petition to express their discontent. Wei Wenkui, a commoner geomancer, submitted a memorial to challenge the Western calendar in predicting the encroachment of the five stars.[17] The court, therefore, invited Wei to compete with the other three boards — one referred to the Datong calendar; one used the Muslim calendar; and one adopted the Western calendar (Shixian calendar). The Western bureau, headed by Adam Schall, was edged out by the other two boards, which cooperated with Wei to move a bit the instrument which resulted in Adam Schall's failure in predicting the celestial movement. Adam Schall reported the incident to the emperor, who promised to organize another competition in the coming year. In the second competition, only the Western bureau could predict the solar eclipse in 1643. However, the Ming Dynasty was too short-lived to implement the new calendar as it collapsed a year after the second competition.

The succeeding Qing court planned to adopt the Western calendar after its establishment, but it faced fierce opposition from the conservative officials though the Western calendar had demonstrated superiority to both the Chinese and Muslim calendars. The outbreak of the Nanjing Religious Incident that created great political turmoil further delayed the court from implementing calendric reform. The Datong and the Muslim calendars were readopted without amendment. In 1668, when Emperor Kangxi grasped real power, he invited Yang and F. Verbiest to have a competition on astronomical knowledge. The young emperor headed to the imperial observatory with curiosity and excitement and was delighted with Verbiest's correct prediction of the position of the shadow at noon, and other climatic phenomena, while Yang failed to predict this. Yang was soon replaced by Verbiest as the director of the Imperial Board of Astronomy.

The obstacles of the Jesuits missionaries in promoting Western astronomy in China were clearly narrated. It was a painstaking process to overcome the stubborn and conservative Chinese, who still refused to surrender to the Western methods even though they had been proven better than any other calendars through experiments.

Geographical treatises

In addition to the knowledge of the universe, the Jesuits missionaries were also enthusiastic in indoctrinating the Chinese with a broader worldview. When Ricci arrived at Shaoqing and Beijing, he presented a world map (written in English) to the Chinese to arouse the officials' curiosity. Ricci's work set a precedent for other missionaries, such as J. Aleni, L. Buglio, and F. Verbiest to the create maps.

A Map of the Myriad Countries of the World

Wang Pan, the Assistant Provincial Surveillance Commissioner of Lingxi and a friend of Ricci, appreciated his introduction and requested Ricci to translate the map into Chinese. The translated map was entitled *A Map of Mountains and Seas* (*Shanhai yuditu* 山海輿地圖) and was published by Wang in 1584. The publication of this map not only symbolized the Chinese people's first encounter with Western geography, but also triggered scholars' study of world maps and cartography. There were piles of world maps drawn based on Ricci's map, such as *A Map of Mountains and Seas* (1598, Suzhou) by Zhao Kehuai, *A Complete Map of Mountains and Seas* (1600, Nanjing), *A Complete Map* (1601, Beijing) by Feng Yinging, and *A Map of the Myriad Countries of the World* (1602, Beijing) by Li Zhizao.[18] Li's work, the most informative map at that time, projected the world on an oval and placed China at the center of the map with a detailed explanation. The map also introduced the five zones — the tropical area, the two temperate areas, and the two poles, and the five continents (Asia, Europa [Europe], Libya [Africa], the Americas, and Magallanica [Antarctica]). Most of the translated terms, such as *Yazhou* (Asia), *Ouzhou* (Europe), *Daxiyang* (Atlantic Ocean), *Luoma (Rome), Jia'nada* (Canada), *Nanbeiji* (the North and the South poles), *Nanbeijiquan* (the Antarctic and Arctic circle), and *chidu* (the equator) are still in use at presence.

Illustrated Record of the World Maps

Illustrated Record of the World Maps (*Wanguo tuji* 萬國圖記) was an atlas edited by Ricci during his stay in Nanchang in 1595 and was presented as a tribute to Emperor Wanli in 1600. This atlas was well printed on excellent Japanese papers imported from Macau, and was bound in Western style. Ricci referred to the *Theatrum Orbis Terrarum* (Theatre of the world), a collection of maps by Flemish cartographer Abraham Ortelius, in completing his atlas. *The Illustrated Record of the World Maps* was not a mere duplicate of the 53 maps in Ortelius' book as he supplemented the map with explanations of the places, a diagram of the nine-leveled heaven, and an article about the four oceans.[19]

Geography of Foreign Countries to China

Translated by J. Aleni in oral form, recorded by Yang Jingyun, and published in 1623, *Geography of Foreign Countries to China* (*Zhifang waiji* 職方外紀) was completed based on the study notes of D. de Pantoja and S. de Ursis. "*Zhifang*," the book title, also referred to an ancient Chinese clan responsible for map-drawing and handling tributary affairs suggested by the *Rituals of Zhou* (*Zhouli* 周禮). There were five volumes in this geographical account. The first volume introduced Asia, followed by the introduction of Europe, Africa, the Americas and Antartica. The last volume was a summary of the four oceans, listing the names of the seas and bays, islands, islanders, marine products, and the situation of the oceans. This book focused on describing the geography, people, climate, and landmarks of the five continents, particularly on "those countries which are extremely distant [to China] and had never established communication with China."[20] Columbus' discovery of the new continent, a well-known story in the West yet almost unheard of to the Chinese, was introduced in detail.[21] The European education system was also explained in detail in the preface of volume two of the book.[22] This book, written in Chinese and with diagrams included, was one of the most systematic and influential geography accounts in the late Ming period.

Illustrated Discussion of the Geography of the World

Published in 1674, this book was edited by F. Verbiest to explain his *A Map of the Whole World* (*Kunyu quantu* 坤輿全圖). The first volume described the natural geography of the continents, the spherical nature of the Earth, the poles, famous mountains and rivers, and various natural phenomena such as earthquakes, ocean currents and tides, and storms. The second volume covered the customs of the various countries. Most of the content of this book was similar to Ricci's description, but it added 24 diagrams of fantastic creatures, such as the Italian beaver, African sugar glider, and South American ostrich. There were also seven diagrams of the ancient Seven Wonders — the Hanging Garden in Babylon, the Colossus of Rhodes, the Giza Pyramid at Memphis, the Mausoleum at Halicarnassus, the Temple of Artemis at Ephesus, the Statue of Zeus at Olympia, and the Lighthouse of Alexandria.[23]

Questions and Answers Regarding the West

Questions and Answers Regarding the West (*Xifang dawen* 西方答問) was composed by J. Aleni, edited by E. Diaz, João Fróis, and J. Rbo, and published in 1637, during Aleni's evangelic mission in Fujian. The first volume accounted for a wide range of topics, including the European countries, transportation, seas, local products, kings, officials, clothes, customs, laws, trade, catering, medicine, palaces, cities, military, marriage, and funeral. The second volume mentioned the maps, calendars, Western scholars, and divination. This book, the most comprehensive reference work of European culture completed in the Ming-to-Qing transitional period, was recommended to Emperor Kangxi as a manual of Western learning by the missionaries. It was summarized as the *Imperially Authorized Occidentalium* (*Yulan xifang yaoji* 御覽西方要紀) at the request of Emperor Kangxi in 1668.

The introduction of Western geography had an epochal impact on the field of Chinese geography. The new cartography technique and the invention of instruments, broadened the Chinese people's understanding of the world, challenged the traditional belief of a hemispherical universe that was Sino-centric, and fostered the development of Chinese geography. The breakthrough in cartography was well demonstrated in the drawing of the *Map of the Imperial Territory (Huangyu quanlan tu* 皇輿全覽圖 *).* In the 47th year of the reign of Kangxi (1708), the emperor organized a group of Jesuits missionaries including J. Bouvet, Joan-Bapt Regis, Petrus Jartoux, Guillaume Fabre Bonjour, and J. F. M. A. de Moyriac de Mailla, to complete the map. The Qing territory, stretching from the northern border at Heilongjiang and Mongol to the southern periphery at Yunnan, with the easternmost edge touching Taiwan and the Western boundary reaching Tibet, was surveyed by the Western method and instruments and clearly depicted. However, this unprecedented map was stored in the Imperial Household Department after its completion and had never been disclosed to the public until the reign of Xianfeng, when Hu Linyi, the Provincial Governor of Hubei, referred to the Map of the Imperial Territory in drawing his *Map of the United Qing (Qing yitong yutu* 清一統輿圖). The missionaries, on the contrary, brought along their research data to Europe and made further studies of it.

Mathematical treatises

Mathematics, the key to understanding astronomy, calendar formulation, geography, and other natural science subjects, was widely introduced to the Chinese scholars through the translation of mathematical treatises. Representative titles included *Euclid's Elements* and *Rules of Arithmetic Common to Cultures*.

Euclid's Elements

Translated by Ricci in oral form and recorded by Xu Guangqi in the 35th year of the reign of Wanli (1635), this book was the first Western mathematical treatise introduced to the Chinese during the Ming-to-Qing transitional period.[24] Ricci referred to the revised edition of *Euclid's Elements* by Christoph Clavius and translated only the first six books. Volume one covered the triangle, volume two discussed lines, volume three explored the circle, volume four discussed the inscribed circle, volumes five and six studied ratio. Each volume included a definition of the terms, formulae, and sample questions.

The translation of *Euclid's Elements* was a significant milestone in establishing geometry as a branch in Chinese mathematics, and confirming the Chinese translation of geometric terms, such as point, line, plane, parallel lines, right angle, obtuse angle, acute angle, triangle, and quadrilateral. This book was so influential that it was published thrice within a century since its translation. The remaining nine books were translated by Alexander Wylie and Li Shanlan in the late Qing period.

Rules of Arithmetic Common to Cultures

This book was translated by Ricci in oral form, documented by Li Zhizao, and published in the 42nd year of the reign of Wanli (1614). The original manuscript was the *Clavius Epitome Arithmeticae Practicae* by Christoph Clauvius, Ricci's

Italian mathematics teacher. The first two volumes introduced the integer and fractional arithmetic, and the remaining eight volumes discussed ratio and proportion, false position method, sequences and series, elimination, and extraction of roots. Exercises were also attached. Li stated the motive of translation in the preface:

> There are no differences between Chinese and Western addition, subtraction, multiplication, and division. However, the parts that discuss fractions and *regula societatum* (rule of society) were mysterious so that even the ancient sages had never explored them. Trigonometry, extraction of roots, and theory of the circle were difficult to study by the ancient (Chinese) method, but the newly translated works helped overcome the diffulculties.[25]

Li found the similarities and differences of Chinese and Western mathematics, as well as the strengths of Western mathematics through comparison.

Calendric Treatises of the Chongzhen Reign

There are a few chapters discussing Western mathematics in this astronomical treatise. The book *Great Measurement* (*Daice* 大測) discusses Ptolemy's spherical trigonometry; the book *Eight Segments of the Circle* (*Geyuan baxian biao* 割圓八線表) explores the application of the circle segment in trigonometry; and the book *Complete Treatise on Measurement* (*Celiang quanyi* 測量全義) explains trigonometry and spherical trigonometry, and Archimedes' theories on areas and volumes. There is a full-translated text of Archimedes' *Measurement of the Circle*.

A Comprehensive Study of Heaven

A Comprehensive Study of the Heaven (*Tianxue huitong* 天學會通) was compiled in 1664 by Xue Fengzuo, who had studied astronomy, mathematics, medical science, and physics from the missionary Nicolas Smogolenski. The mathematics section of this book has three chapters: "Logarithmic Scale" that lists frequently seen ratio (correct to 6 decimal places), "Four Logarithmic Functions" that explains the ratio of the segments of sine, cosine, tangent, and cotangent, and "Trigonometry" which interprets trigonometry and spherical trigonometry. These three chapters are more precise and informative than those articles in the *Calendric Treatises of the Chongzhen Reign*. The publication of this book symbolized that logarithms, one of the important topics in modern mathematics, were introduced to China systematically.

Essentials of Mathematics

Essentials of Mathematics (*Shuli jingyun* 數理精蘊) was compiled by Mei Juecheng at the request of Emperor Kangxi, who had a keen interest in studying mathematics.[26] The first volume had five chapters that introduced fundamental mathematical theories, with quotations from the translated *Euclid's Elements* and Bouvet's *Elements of Mathematics* (*Suanfa yuanben* 算法原本). The second volume had 40 chapters that explained various topics, including the units of measurement, numeral systems, arithmetic calculation, fraction, ratio, simultaneous equation, extraction of roots and cubic roots, trigonometry ratio, inscribed circle, inscribed square, pi, areas and volumes of prisms, logarithm, and algebra. The remaining eight chapters were mathematical tables.

Mei spent 31 years — from 1690 to 1721 — to complete this compendium. It was published in the first year of the reign of Yongzheng (1723), and it became an authoritative reference for latter Chinese mathematicians, such as Dai Xu and Xiang Mingda.

Biological treatises

Memorial of the Real Christianity

Published in 1593, *Memorial of the Real Christianity* (*Wuji tianzhu zhengjiao zhenchuan shilu* 無極天主正教真傳實錄) had five chapters that explained woods and herbs around the world, the distribution and habits of animals — though its title seemed irrelevant to animals and zoology. The original manuscript of the book is collected in the National Library of Spain at the present time.[27]

Miscellaneous Works

On Lion (*Shizi shuo* 獅子說) was compiled by L. Buglio after the presentation of an African lion by the Portuguese Ambassador in 1678. Buglio, who was frequently asked about the lion, decided to publish this book to introduce this alien animal to the Chinese. This book introduced the appearance, characteristics, and fierceness of the lion.

Buglio, at the request of Emperor Kangxi, compiled another biological treatise *On the Eagle* (*Jingcheng ying shuo* 進呈鷹說), which introduced the appearances and characters of eagles, and the methods of catching and raising eagles. Buglio had referred to the authoritative work *On Animals* by Ulisse Aldrovandi (1522–1607) in compiling the eagle treatise. *The Geography of Foreign Countries to China* by J. Aleni also introduced various fantastic creatures.

Medical and pharmaceutical treatises

The establishment of hospitals in Macau might have introduced Western medicine to the Chinese commoners. The upper class, who were affluent enough to employ private Chinese doctors, did not need to visit Western hospitals. Medical and pharmaceutical treatises thus became the gateway for the scholar-officials to understand Western medical science. *De Providentia Numinis* (*Zhenzhu lingxing lizheng* 真主靈性理證) by Martinus Martini, *A Brief Outline of the Study on Human Nature* by J. Aleni, and *On Divine Providence* (*Zhizhi qunzheng* 主制群徵) by Adam Schall discussed the respiratory, circulatory, and sensory systems.

The most representative work on Western anatomy was the *Western Views on the Human Body* (*Taixi renshen shuogai* 泰西人身說概). It was translated by J. Terrenz in oral form and documented by an anonymous imperial scribe, and was later edited by Bi Gongchen, an advance scholar in the reign of Wanli who found the translated text too vulgar to read. He also attached the *Western Graphs of the Human Body* to the book.

This book was divided into two parts: the first part explained the bones, tendons, skin, fat, pulse, nerves, and veins; the second part mentioned the motor, muscular, circulatory, nervous, and sensory systems. The description of the brain was the most interesting yet confusing to Bi, who commented that:

> [The book] continues to argue that the brain is where people store all the memories. Having heard this concept all of a sudden, [I] find this concept astonishing. However, when people are thinking, they close their eyes and contract the brows. It seems that they are "seeking" something from the upper organ (the brain). Moreover, as suggested by an idiom, "a man who cannot remember is brainless." It can also prove that the concept of the book was trustworthy.[28]

Another missionary, Franciscus Furtabo, also argued that the brain controls human learning, memory, mind, and sentiment in his *In Universam Dialecticam*. All these concepts were new to the Chinese, who used to believe that the heart, on the contrary, governed the mind instead. Because of the absence of empirical study to the heart, while the function of the brain had been well explained by the missionaries, the Chinese started to accept the Western medical knowledge. Even Li Shizhen, Jin Sheng, and Wang Qingren, three notable medical researchers, were also persuaded. It was the greatest achievement of the introduction of Western medical knowledge to China.

Western medicine, a completely different system to Chinese medical herbs, was also introduced to China through pharmaceutical treatises. *On Medicine* (*Yaolu shuo* 藥露說), completed by S. de Ursis in the 46th year of the reign of Wanli (1618), was the first Western pharmaceutical reference work published in China. This book, together with the *Occidentalium* compiled by L. Buglio and F. Verbiest, also mentions the herbal distillate, the making of medicine stove and medicine. *Supplementary to Herbs* (*Bencao bu* 本草補), compiled by missionary Pedro de la Piñuela in the 15th year of the reign of Kangxi (1676), was the first treatise on Western *materia medica* in China.

Macau, the home of the first Western hospital in China, also witnessed the wide use of Western medicine. Even the upper class started employing missionaries as doctors. Emperor Kangxi, for instance, had his malaria, palpitations, and a tumor on the mouth cured by Western medicine. Cao Yan, a trusted minister of Kangxi, was given cinchona (quinine) for his malaria. The application of Western medicine was also narrated in the *Dream of the Red Chamber* (*Honglou meng* 紅樓夢), a mid-Qing novel tracing the rise and decadence of an imaginary eminent aristocratic family. Chapter 52 described that:

> Were you (Ch'ing Wen) to treat yourself exclusively with Western medicines, I'm sure you'd be all right," Pao-yü added smiling. "Go," he accordingly implored She Yüeh, "to our lady Secunda, and ask her for some. Tell her that I spoke to you about them. My cousin (Hs Feng) over there often uses some Western plaster, which she applies to her temples when she's got a headache. It's called 'I-fo-na (Ephedra).' So try and get some of it![29]

All these examples were evidence of the common use of Western medicine among the upper class Chinese in the early Qing period.

Musical instruments and treatises

M. Ruggieri, Lazarus Cattaneo, and Ricci brought along Western musical instruments on their mission to China. Ricci also presented a clavichord to Emperor Wanli, who found the instrument appealing and he appointed four music officials to learn playing the clavichord from Diego de Pantoja. With the construction of churches in China came Western religious music. Bassoons and other musical instruments were played at Ricci's funeral.

Western music continued to catch the upper class' fancy in the Qing Dynasty. Emperor Kangxi invited an orchestra, led by missionaries Thomas Pereyra and

Ludovicus Pernon, to the Forbidden City. Musical theory was also studied. Pereyra and Theodorico Pedrini were employed, at the request of Emperor Kangxi, to teach the princes musical theory and to compile a Chinese theory reference work, entitled as the *Correct Meaning of the Principle of Music (Lülü zhengyi 律呂正義)* after its publication in the 52nd year of the reign of Kangxi (1713). This book explained the reading of a musical score, the composition of songs, and the denotation of pitch names as *wu (* 烏 , do*), le (* 勒 , re*), ming (* 鳴 , mi*), fa (* 乏 , fa*), shuo (* 朔 , so*), la (* 拉 , la*), and qi (* 其 , ti*).*

Painting

In addition to musical instruments, Ricci and Adam Schall brought along religious paintings such as the portraits of the Madonna to China. L. Buglio and F. Verbiest were proficient in painting, but Emperor Kangxi did not consult them on Western painting, as it had no practical use to him. Emperor Qianlong, on the other hand, was interested in Western painting. He found painting a useful means to demonstrate his achievements, and he was much delighted by the drawings of Giuseppe Castiglione, who had mastered both Chinese and Western painting and attempted to incorporate the two methods in his masterpieces. Castiglione and other missionaries were invited to present 16 drawings on the emperor's conquest of the Junggar and Muslim tribes.

Western painting had a mixed influence in China. As suggested by Ricci, "Chinese painting, which does not emphasis the drawing of shadows, makes people dull and flat...Our painters understand this technique (the drawing of both light and shadow), and they adopted it, making their paintings more lifelike."[30] The introduction of Western painting techniques propelled the development of Chinese painting as several painters, such as Zeng Jing, Jiao Bingzhen, Men Yingzhao, and Xu Yaopu, referred to Western painting methods, particularly on the way of depicting people. Several painters, on the contrary, found the religious aspects and "improperly dressed women" in drawings unacceptable, and the Sino-Western incorporated painting strange.

Architecture

While the study of science was limited to a particular group of people, Western architecture was well demonstrated to the public through the construction of churches. The historical and grandiose St. Lazarus Church, St. Lawrence Church, St. Antony Church, the Ruins of St. Paul's, St. Augustine Church, and St. Dominic

Church in Macau were opened to the Chinese. Among these churches, the Ruins of St. Paul's, built in a baroque style, has since become the symbol of Macau though it suffered from a devastating fire that left only the façade undestroyed.

The first Western church in a non-colonial area was built during the reign of Wanli in Nanjing, widely known as *Wuliangdian* (無梁殿 , meaning a palace without room beams). Other prominent cities, such as Beijing, Hangzhou, Shanghai, and Guangzhou, were home to Catholic churches as well. The Cathedral of the Immaculate Conception in Beijing, also known as the Xuanwumen Chapel or Southern Chapter by the local people, featured a dome, an arch, pavilions, and fountains. The Cathedral of the Immaculate Conception in Hangzhou was well decorated with golden ornaments and exquisite paintings, making the cathedral the most splendid around the country. Western residences were also situated in the coastal cities such as Macau, Guangzhou, Yangzhou, and Anqing.

The largest compound of Western buildings was the Summer Palace in Beijing. It was first built during the reign of Emperor Kangxi as a present to his fourth prince, later the Emperor Yongzheng. It was redesigned by Castiglione with assistance from Jean-Denis Attiret and M. Benoist at the request of Emperor Qianglong. The royal garden saw a mixture of Chinese, baroque, and rococo styles, represented by the fountain, pillars, and roof decorated with Chinese tiles.

Miscellaneous Inventions

Simultaneous to the dissemination of Western culture, a considerable amount of Western inventions were introduced to China (refer to table 2.1).

Table 2.1 List of Western inventions introduced to China in the Ming-to-Qing transitional period

Franco cannon	watermill	telescope
microscope	musical clock	chain watch
celestial sphere	globe	theodolite
sundial	star-dial	eclipse telescope
compass	Archimedes' screw	lighthouse[31]
thermometer	hygrometer	fan
organ	flute	guitar

The public's response to these new inventions was interesting. Chapter 6 of the *Dream of the Red Chamber* described the first glimpse of a musical clock of Goody Liu, an old widow from the village:

> ...old Goody Liu could hear nothing but a "lo tang, lo tang" noise, resembling very much the sound of a bolting frame winnowing flour, and she could not resist looking now to the East, and now to the West. Suddenly in the great Hall, she espied, suspended on a pillar, a box at the bottom of which hung something like the weight of a balance, which incessantly wagged to and fro. "What can this thing be?" thought Goody Liu in her heart, "What can be its use?" While she was aghast, she unexpectedly heard a sound of "tang" like the sound of a golden bell or copper cymbal, which gave her quite a start. In a twinkle of the eyes followed eight or nine consecutive strokes; and she was bent upon inquiring what it was, when she caught sight of several waiting-maids enter in a confused crowd.[32]

Factors affecting the dissemination of Western culture in the Ming-to-Qing transitional period

Political attitude of the rulers

The gunboat policy of the European countries might have been successful in conquering the weaker Indian and Southeast Asian peoples. In turning China into the European sphere of influence, the military seemed ineffective due to the relative strength of China. Ricci, having granted the permission from the Jesuits, formulated the policy of "acculturating, supplementing, and surpassing Confucianism" to secure the missionaries' foothold in China. The introduction of knowledge that suited the appetite of the Chinese, particularly of the rulers, was not a mere flattering, but a shortcut of preaching. In a highly centralized state like China, the emperor's appreciation of Western learning implied the freedom of dissemination of new knowledge. It would be also easier for the missionaries to gain acceptance of the court. Adam Schall was trusted because Emperor Shunzhi favored Western learning; he was imprisoned after the conservative minister Oboi came into power. Western learning regained its upper hand after Oboi's death. The compilation of the *Essentials of Mathematics* was due to Emperor Kangxi's fondness for Western mathematics. And the Western mansions in the Summer Palace would not be constructed without Emperor Qianlong's appreciation of Western architecture.

It also explained how the introduction of Western science was more successful than humanity subjects as the ruler found the knowledge more practical. Astronomical and mathematical knowledge was the key to a precise calendar that helped maintain an agricultural economy, as well as the legitimacy of the regime. The ruling class found geography knowledge useful because of its relevancy to the territory. The study of geography was triggered by the signing of the Treaty of Nerchinsk, during which Emperor Kangxi found China was not well depicted on the Western maps.

Attitude of the Church and the missionaries

Most of the Jesuit missionaries were well educated and equipped with profound knowledge. They were also pious Christians who did not fear spending two to three years sailing to the Far East for preaching. The missionaries attempted to introduce Western learning to the Chinese, but because of the Church's hostility to the new knowledge, the missionaries dared not to openly oppose their society. Neither did they leave the new theories unmentioned or vaguely explained. The teaching of Copernicus' heliocentricism well demonstrated the struggle of the missionaries. They, on the one hand, did not introduce Copernicus' theory to the Chinese because it contradicted the concept of geocentricism suggested by the Church; at the time on the other hand, they relied on Copernicus' *On the Revolutions of the Celestial Spheres* in compiling the *Calendric Treatises of the Chongzhen Reign*. It was not until the nineteenth century that the Church released the ban of Copernicus' theory in response to the theory's general acceptance in Europe. It was also when the Jesuits made a systematic introduction of heliocentricism to the Chinese.

The method of dissemination

The method of "preaching through teaching" generated a complicated effect to the Chinese scholars. Only a small proportion of scholars, such as Xu Guangqi and Li Zhizao, accepted both the Western knowledge and religion. The majority of the Chinese found Western learning useful yet they were unwilling to convert to Christianity due to the Western religious creeds which were contradicted by traditional Chinese belief. Representatives included Emperor Kangxi, Wang Xichan, and Mei Wending. The abstract of *Questions about Heaven* in *The Catalog of the Complete Library of the Four Branches of Literature* (*Sikuquanshu* 四庫全書) well demonstrated this lopsidedness:

> The sections of the positions of the stars, the Sun, the climate, the land, the lunar cycle, and the eclipses are comprehensive and clear. However, this book extensively praises the achievements of the heavenly lord and

> the location of the heavens...[the missionaries, in fact,] attempted to use the accurate experimental result to prove the presence of heaven. [Their] intention was doubtful and shrewd. However, they made better predictions on astronomical phenomena than the ancient methods. [The editor decided] to discard their absurd teachings but to study the precise and justified methods.[33]

The last group of Chinese included the conservatives, represented by Wei Wenkui and Yang Guangxian. Yang's quotation of "I would rather have an incorrect calendar in China than allow Westerners to settle in China"[34] clearly depicted their opposition towards everything Occidental.

The opposition to Christianity in the early-Qing period was not a blind outburst of anti-foreignism. The conservatives used to criticize the Church's intolerance to Chinese customs and parts of the Christian belief that contradicted Confucian teaching. Ricci's policy of "accommodation," actually, proved that the gap between the Occidental religion and the Oriental tradition could be overcome. The Church might have its consideration in banning ancestral worship, but beneath the surface of the conflict of ritual laid the struggle for legitimacy of the Chinese emperor, who saw the superiority of God a potential threat to his mandate of heaven. Without the permission of the emperor, it was difficult for Christianity to enter the Chinese academic circle. Scholars' conversion to Christianity was common during Ricci's time, but only the illiterate joined the Christian family in the mid-Qing period. Christian converts were excommunicated in several distinguished clans.

Scholars' Response: Acceptance, Rejection, and Acculturation

The introduction of the alien Western learning to China aroused a complicated response that varied from periods and the targeted learners. Generally, there were three kinds of responses to the Chinese: to accept Western learning, to reject anything Occidental, and to acculturate the two distinct cultures.

To accept Western learning and to develop Chinese learning

Scholars who belonged to this group included Xu Guangqi, Li Zhizao, Yang Tingyun, Wang Zheng, Wang Xichan, and Mei Wending.

Xu Guangqi

Xu Guangqi was the pioneer at introducing Western learning to China in the late Ming Dynasty. Born in Shanghai, where plenty of scholars were nurtured, Xu was also devoted in the study of traditional Chinese learning. He first heard about Western culture from missionary L. Cattaneo in 1595. After meeting with Ricci in 1600 and being taught about Western astronomy and geography, Xu was so impressed that he decided to befriend Ricci. He was baptized in 1603, a year prior to his examination. The employment of Xu as a Hanlin Academic did not stop him from studying Western subjects. He frequently visited Ricci's house in Beijing, discussed with him, and translated a series of scientific treatises such as *Euclid's Elements*, *Principles of Right Triangles* (*Gouguyi* 勾股義), *Hydraulic Machinery of the West* (*Taixi shuifa* 泰西水法), *Method and Meaning of Measurement*, *Similarities and Differences in Measurement*, *Description of the Simple Altazimuth Quadrant* (*Jianpingyi shuo* 簡平儀說), and *De Anima*. Xu's contributions to open the way for Western learning into China were recognized in the *Biographies of the Astronomers* (*Chouren zhuan* 疇人傳):

> Since the arrival of Ricci to the Oriental land, the one who had the deepest comprehension of his teaching on astronomy and mathematics was Guangqi. Moreover, the formulation of the new calendar exhausted Guangqi's energy. [Xu] examined the celestial phenomena and translated thousands of words into Chinese. He conducted research frequently to make his works reasonable and understandable to the public. Those who kept the new knowledge in secret were incomparable to Xu. Even when comparing those who managed to master Western learning nowadays (the mid-Qing period), [the achievements of] Guangqi should be recognized.[35]

Li Zhizao

If Xu had been the most influential scholar in introducing Western learning in China, Li Zhizao would have been the second fiddle. He was born in Renhe County (present-day Hangzhou) and he received the degree of advanced scholar in 1598. After a prolonged chat with Ricci, he was so impressed with both Ricci and his knowledge that he decided to spend his lifetime in Western learning. He translated a series of Western scientific treatises with the missionaries, such as the *Rules of Arithmetic Common to Cultures*, *Treatise on Isoperimetric Figures*, *In Universam Dialecticam*, *Explanation on the Celestial Spheres* (*Huanyouquan* 寰有詮), and other titles, making great contribution to the promotion of mathematics, geography, and logic in China. He was not made a convert until his divorce with his concubine in 1610.

Yang Tingjun

Yang, a fellow villager of Li and an advanced scholar, graduated in 1592. He was also friends with Ricci after a discussion on logic. Prior to his conversion to Christianity, Yang became a Buddhist and had a concubine. His conversion was harshly criticized by his Buddhist friends, who even composed an article "Censure on Yang." He translated less than Xu and Li did, but his work *Geography of Foreign Countries to China* (co-translated with J. Aleni) was the most informative geographic accounts in the Ming-to-Qing transitional period.

The baptisms of Xu, Li, and Yang had an epochal meaning in opening the way for Western learning into China. The trio relied on their knowledge, influence as degree holders, and personal networks as high officials to promote Western learning. After the outbreak of the Nanjing Religious Incident, they spared no effort to defend and protect the missionaries. Their generosity brought them laudatory title of "the three pillars of Chinese Christianity."

Wang Zheng

Wang Zheng, also called Wang Liangpu (pseudonym Kuixin), was born in Jingyang County of Shaanxi Province. He graduated with the degree of "recommended man" at the age of 24, but he did not pass the examination for the advanced degreed until 52. He was baptized in 1624 as he found Western learning appealing. With the assistance of Nicolaus Trigault and Han Yun, he translated *An Aid to Western Scholars* (*Xiru ermuzi* 西儒耳目資), a systematic linguistic reference work that introduced Chinese grammar and phonetics to Westerners. *Illustrations and Explanations of Various Machines* (*Xinzhi zhuqi tushuo* 新制諸器圖說), another work translated by Wang and J. Terrenz, was the first mechanical engineering treatise in China. The first volume mentioned basic knowledge on mechanical engineering, a bibliography and a list of instruments. The second volume explained elementary theories of mechanical engineering, including the principle of levers, the use of balances, pulleys, and screws. The third volume included 54 diagrams of cranes, river intakes, grindstones, and other devices invented by him.[36] Wang was praised as "the reborn Zhuge Liang." It might be an exaggerated comment, but his application of the new devices in daily use was recognized:

> I (a fellow villager of Wang) heard from the elder villagers that, before Wang's employment as an official, a scarecrow was utilized in sowing in spring and summer. Also, [the villagers would] grind, winnow, take water from the well and exhaust the air by manual methods. The new machines operated vividly. During harvest, [the villagers] used an automatic machine to bundle up the grain, spending half the effort but yielding twice the result.[37]

During a conversation with his guest, Wang showed his respect of Western science, which the Confucians regarded as an inferior system and one with superficial learning:

> A friendly guest told me that, "Your compilation of *An Aid to Western Scholars* was still considered an effort to the scholars. What you have just documented was nothing more than a manual of craftsmanship and technique, on which a gentleman should not place emphasis. Why were you devoted in doing this? Moreover, Western Confucians (the missionaries) who resided in our China were our close friends, so that [we] understand their intelligence. However, they were nothing more than the products of a vulgar scholarship in their countries. Why have you been so partial and biased like this?
> I responded, "To learn, [one] should not concern oneself with the excellence and demerits of the knowledge. [One] should strive for what has practical use. [One] should not be concerned for the Chinese or Occidental origin of the knowledge. [One] should study the knowledge that does not violate the principles of heaven. What I have just documented was related to craftsmanship, but this knowledge is beneficial to daily life, and the strengthening of the country.[38]

Wang's attitude towards Western learning was seldom shared by other conservative scholars, who used to dig into the study of classics, to engage in hollow discussion, or to indulge themselves in extravagant articles. Wang was outstanding according to his counterparts for not only his translation works but also his production of Western machines.

Wang Xichan and Mei Wending

Wang Xichan, also named Wang Yanxu (pseudonym Xiaoan), was born in Wujiang County of Jiangsu Province. He had been a supporter of Neo-Confucianism in his early age, but he turned to the study of calendar formulation and Western astronomy after the introduction of the Western calendar system in China. Wang, unlike the general scholars who were astonished by the accuracy of the Western calendar, held a skeptical view of the new method. When there was extreme climatic phenomena, Wang climbed up to the roof and studied the stellar movements. He carefully documented his observation results of the eclipses, and analyzed with both Chinese and Western methods. His conscientiousness and non-superficiality enabled him to surpass the achievements of the previous scholars. He applied the circle bearing in predicting the eclipses and the last contact with the umbra, invented a new method in calculating the transit of Venus and Mercury, and predicted the duration of the encroachment of the five planets.

Mei Wending, also named Mei Dingjiu (pseudonym Wu'an), was born in Xuancheng County of Anhui Province. He spent his lifetime in the study of astronomy and mathematics, compiling more than 80 titles. As an astronomer, he compiled about 40 titles that studied the ancient Chinese calendar, the newly introduced Western calendar, recently composed astronomical treatises, and the new astronomical instruments. As a mathematician, he compiled about 40 titles that explained general mathematical branches, arithmetic, algebra, geometry, trigonometry, and spherical trigonometry. By applying the Chinese *gougu* method (勾股, trigonometry), he proved plenty of questions in *Euclid's Elements*, solving the Western questions in a simple way. He was so eminent that even Emperor Kangxi invited him to have a discussion.

Both Wang and Mei had no prejudice towards Western learning. When the conservative scholar-officials were arguing about the introduction of Western learning, Wang was working hard to incorporate the two distinctive knowledge systems. He neither rigidly adhered to the Chinese method nor blindly believed the Western method. He was praised in the *Biographies of the Astronomers* that:

> [Wang] conducted research on the mistakes of the ancient method while preserving its correctness; to learn the strengths of Western ideas while discarding its shortcomings. In conducting the research, he did not follow the court's guide, so his works were not consulted. However, he received unanimous recognition from the scholars at the time.[39]

Mei also declared his acceptance of Western learning:

> Those who govern would rule according to the doctrine. Those who

> study mathematics would follow the absolute principle. Mathematics and principles are indifferent in both China and the West...[The conservatives] discard all the learning of the West. To follow the excellent path, [one] should not be so narrow-minded.[40]
>
> The calendar is adopted to tell the time. Why be concerned about its Chinese or Western origin? I adopt [the method] that suits the heavenly principle and follow it only.[41]

From Xu Guangqi to Mei Wending, these scholars faced various circumstances and held different attitudes towards the new knowledge. Xu, Li, Yang, and Wang Zheng found both Western learning and religion appealing, while Wang Xichan and Mei Wending respected Western learning but they were not converted. These scholars, however, shared similarities in their studies: first, they tolerated foreign culture. Having been trained with traditional Chinese learning and possessing honorable degrees, they studied instead of discriminating against the foreign culture. Second, they adopted the strengths of Western culture, as evidenced by the invention of various devices by Wang Zheng and the drawing of maps by Emperor Kangxi. Third, they did not hesitate to abandon any outdated Chinese method. They criticized the traditional concept of the hemispherical universe, and they discarded the belief of the heart controlling the mind. Fourth, they avoided being superstitious to any schools. Unquestioning support of the new knowledge was never seen among these scholars though Western learning had been proven superior to several Chinese concepts. To translate Western reference works and to understand the new knowledge were keys for the Chinese to surpass the Occidental culture, as suggested by Xu Guangqi.[42] To study the new knowledge without careful identification was regarded as dangerous by Wang Xichan as well.

To reject Western learning without conducting research

The core reason for the irrational rejection of Western learning lied in the Sino-centricism of the conservative scholar-officials. They followed strictly the traditional belief though it had proven less accurate to Western knowledge and they concluded before conducting scientific research. Calendar formulation, geography, and medical science were fiercely attacked by these conservatives. And their opposing criticisms were interesting to study.

Wei Wenkui, a conservative minister of the Imperial Board of Astronomy, opposed the implementation of the Western calendar because it failed to predict the encroachment of the five planets and the eclipses. Such failure was, in fact, the result of his cheating in the contest with Adam Schall, during which the ministers moved the Western instruments for a bit.

The argument of Yang Guangxian after his defeat by F. Verbiest in the competition was too incredible to understand:

> When asked by Emperor Kangxi about his inaccurate prediction, Yang replied, "We do not know how to calculate [it]."
> The emperor asked, "I have asked you before, and you said that you are confident in predicting the shadow of the sun. How come you have no idea now?"
> Yang answered, "The calendar that your minister referred to was the calendar imparted from Emperor Yao and Shun (the two ancient sages). The throne that your majesty inherited was imparted from Yao and Shun. The legitimacy that your majesty held was imparted from Yao and Shun. Therefore, The calendar that your majesty implemented should be the calendar of Yao and Shun. Your majesty follows everything of Yao and Shun, and [you] should make no exception in the choice of calendar. F. Verbiest is a Catholic. The sacred emperor should follow only the principle of Yao and Shun instead of the Catholic creeds. F. Verbiest attempted to destroy the instruments imparted from Yao and Shun, and replaced them with Western devices. The destruction of the machines of Yao and Shun implies the annihilation of literature, history, rituals, music, and the institutions of Yao and Shun.[43]

The Sino-centric and stubborn attitude was well demonstrated through Yang's defense. To Yang, the Chinese method was an orthodox belief, while the Western knowledge suited only the barbarians. The application of Western instruments in explaining Chinese culture would result in the extinction of the Chinese tradition. Therefore, the emperor should consult Yang instead of F. Verbiest, and the inaccurate traditional method rather than the Western calendar.

The geographical concept of a spherical earth, the five continents, and the non-centered China was too new and unbelievable for the Chinese to accept. It aroused harsh criticism from the conservatives, who believed the knowledge was fabricated by Ricci. Wei Jun, for instance, argued that:

> [Ricci's map] described the places which are invisible and unreachable to us. His unjustified argument is nothing different from the drawing of a

> ghost. For example, China is placed a bit northwest. When we observe the sky at night, the Polaris is located at the zenith, so that China should be the center of the world. It is ridiculous for the map to place China in the west.[44]

Wei's argument revealed his ignorance of the concept of the celestial pole and the coordinate system that the missionaries had explained in their translated works. However, Wei was not alone in doubting the Western learning. The majority of Chinese, who had long been indoctrinated in the concept of "nine continents," found Ricci's map unreliable. The so-called "nine continents" was an imaginary concept suggested by Zou Yan, a naturalist in the pre-Qin period. To Zou, the world was divided into nine continents, which were further divided into nine sub-continents. China was situated at the center of the Red Continent, which had eight other sub-continents. There were seas separating the continents that prevented the communication of people and animals. And there was a large ocean surrounding the continents serving as the periphery of the world.[45] Several scholars believed Ricci's world view originated from the Chinese concept of "nine continents." Li Weizhen, for instance, mentioned that:

> The humble man (Li) is used to studing the *Records of the Grand Historian* (*Shiji* 史記), in which Zou Yan's mysterious idea is documented. Chinese mountains, rivers, valleys, animals, crops, and other wonderful creatures are introduced. Zou's suggestion that the Chinese territory occupied one eighty-first of the world was similar to the description of the foreigner Li Xitai (Ricci) in his map.[46]

There were opinions suggesting that Ricci's map was completed based on the *Classic on Divine Marvels* (*Shenyijing* 神異經), a mysterious Chinese novel that narrated foreign myths.[47]

The idea of geocentricism received more criticism than the concept of five continents because the moving speed of the Earth was too slow to be felt by humans. The "arch-conservative" Yang Guangxian continued to express his astonishing view:

> If the world were a sphere, those who settle in the lower part of the sphere would have fallen down, and those who reside in the two sides of the sphere would have lied horizontally. How can it be possible? The ancient sages taught us to "butt the sky and to stand still on the ground (*dingtian lidi* 頂天立地, meaning to develop an indomitable spirit).[48]

The opposing opinion to the Western medical knowledge would have been the most ridiculous to understand. In response to the compilation of *Western Graphs of Human Body* and *Western Views on Human Body*, Yu Zhengxie suggested a different human body structure between the Chinese and the Westerners:

> Because of the difference in organs, [the Westerner] holds a distinct religious belief. The Westerner is enthusiastic in preaching, hoping to convert the Chinese. However, they do not understand that the Chinese have developed special organs and nerves. Those Chinese who can be baptized must be physically handicapped.[49]

To acculturate the Sino-Western culture

Nomadic tribes outside the Great Wall had demonstrated their military strength to the Chinese through endless battles. To the Chinese, humiliation in war was insignificant, as they had developed a sense of cultural superiority that they adopted to subjugate the "uncivilized" nomadic tribes. The general acceptance of Buddhism, which was initially regarded as a barbarous religion by the Chinese scholars, well demonstrated the ability of Chinese culture to incorporate any foreign customs and philosophy.

The distance between the East and the West, as well as the political instability in the Muslim area hindered the development of large-scale Sino-European cultural exchange, which relied on only a few passionate travelers or monks prior to the Age of Discovery. Advancement in maritime technology enabled the dispatch of more missionaries to Asia. Western inventions could be brought along as well, helping the missionaries to bridge the cultural gap between China and Europe. In response to the introduction of Western learning, the Chinese scholars followed the habit to incorporate the two distinctive cultural systems. Mei Wending, for instance, listed five similarities between Chinese and Western astronomy about the azimuth and the orbits of the five planets, axial precession, and the motion of the Sun, showing to the public the compatibility of Chinese and Western astronomy.[50]

Most of the scholars, however, tended to believe Western knowledge originated from Chinese learning. Huang Zongxi, for instance, suggested the *gougu* method was the legacy of the Duke of Zhou and was learnt by the Westerners.[51] Fang Yizhi also suggested the "official scholarship" had been missed yet disseminated to the West after the collapse of the Zhou Dynasty. *Mathematical Treatise of Zhou Gnomon* (*Zhoubi suanjing* 周髀算經), the first Chinese mathematical treatise, was believed to be the origin of the Western mathematics and astronomy. *The History of the Ming Dynasty* (*Mingshi* 明史) suggested that:

> Westerners who visited the Chinese territory called themselves European. Their calendar originated from but was an improvement on the Muslim calendar...After the collapse of the Zhou Dynasty, astronomers and their students escaped to various areas. The west Asian and the Arabian states neighbor the west periphery of China. There are neither oceans nor an extremely cold environment that separates the West and China. It is convenient for the astronomers to travel to the West. Europe is located in the West of the Muslim world, and Europe shared similar customs with the Muslim world...After the death of the ancient astronomers, the Chinese left only the *Mathematical Treatise of Zhou Gnomon*. Therefore, the Western astronomical instruments, the concept of five zones and geocentricism should be originated from the *Mathematical Treatise of Zhou Gnomon*.[52]

Essentials of Mathematics also shared the same view with the *History of the Ming Dynasty*:

> The Chinese rituals and knowledge had been lost during the wartime in the late Zhou and the Qin Dynasties. On the contrary, those Chinese astronomers who escaped to the West preserved the essentials of the ancient knowledge, which was developed into the Western learning nowadays.[53]

Prior to the establishment of the term "*daisu* (algebra)" as the corresponding translation for "algebra," the term "*donglaifa* (東來法, method from the East)" was employed by the missionaries to introduce algebra to the Chinese. To the missionaries, the "method from the East" meant the Arabian origin of algebra, but it was mistaken as the method from China to the Chinese.[54]

China, as an ancient civilization, had introduced various inventions and techniques, such as papermaking, printing, compass use, and gunpowder, to the West. The Chinese were so familiar with this history that they believed everything in the West originated from their country. By advocating the Chinese origin of Western learning, scholars in the Ming-to-Qing transitional period attempted to make Western learning less a "barbarous" learning for the conservatives to accept.

The Impact of Western Learning on the Ming-to-Qing Society

Theoretical framework

The level of dissemination is defined as connectivity between the source of dissemination and the audiences. The more distant the receiver to the source of dissemination (in terms of time), the higher the inaccuracy of the knowledge transmitted. Most of the Chinese, who were taught about Western knowledge through the demonstration of inventions or the translated works, might not be familiar with the Western origin of the new knowledge. This problem became more acute in the mid-Qing dynasty, when all the missionaries were expelled from China yet several of the Western reference works were left.

Corrected Practice in Medicine (*Yilin gaicuo* 醫林改錯) by Wang Qingren (1768–1831), medical research in the mid-Qing period, well reflected the misunderstanding of the origin of Western learning. The author believed that Jin Zhengxi was the first to suggest that the brains controlled the human mind. Jin, an advanced degree holder and a general of the late Ming period yet without any training in medical science, should have had no idea of the function of brain. The real story lied in the Christian background of Jin, who had learned the human structure from the missionaries. Jin might have failed to record where he had learned the knowledge from so that Wang made such a mistake, but the absence of a direct connection between Wang and Jin also explained the misunderstanding. Actually, both the oral transmission of knowledge and the anti-foreignism after the banning of Christianity also added to the difficulty in tracing the origin of Western learning.

Western learning and the School of Empirical Studies

A trend of the "practical use of knowledge" emerged in the academic circle of the late Ming Dynasty. The composition of *Comprehensive Treatise on Agricultural Administration* (*Nongzheng quanshu* 農政全書) Xu Guangqi, *Compendium of Materia Medica* (*Bencao gangmu* 本草綱目) by Li Shizhen, *Illustrations and Explanations of Wonderful Machines* (*Qiqi tushuo* 奇器圖說) by Wang Zhengyu, and *The Ingenious Creation of Things by Nature* (*Tiangong kaiwu* 天工開物) by Song Yingsheng all evidenced scholars' reactions to the School of Mind that advocated discussion of metaphysical matters. Such a change in academic trend and the latter rise of the School of Empirical Studies in the early Qing Dynasty were multiple factors. In terms of external factors, the stable political environment and the prosperous economy allowed scholars to devote more time to academic research. And in terms of the intellectual trend, the introduction of Western science challenged the orthodox status of Confucianism, the dominant philosophy in Chinese society since the Han Dynasty. Under the influence of Western science, which emphasized empirical study and logical reason, scholars started to conduct textual inquiry into the Confucian classics, which their ancient counterparts regarded as sacred books that should not be amended. These scholars, represented by Yan Ruoqu, Quan Zuwang, Hui Dong, Wang Mingsheng, Qian Daxin, and Dai Zhen, spent their lifetimes in editing, clarifying, and explaining the ancient books. Another group of scholars, including Wang Xichan, Mei Wending, Xue Fengzuo, and Juan Yuan, studied "practical subjects" such as mathematics and astronomy that were too vulgar and technical for general Confucians to learn. Scholars who excelled in both classical studies and science were also seen. To name a few, they were Jiang Yong, Dai Zhen, Qian Daxin, Jiao Xun, Ruan Yuan, and Yan Ruoqu. It is impossible to distinguish the impact of Western learning on particular scholars, but their works hinted at the application of Western science into the study of Chinese classics. Yan Ruoqu, for instance, indicated the unauthentic information of the eclipses recorded in the *The Book of History in the Ancient Text* (*Guwen shangshu* 古文尚書) with the use of Western astronomical knowledge, thus proving that *The Book of History in the Ancient Text* was a forged work.

The influence of Western learning on the Ming and Qing societies was summarized in five aspects: first, Western learning influenced only the scholars. Uneducated Christian converts, such as Hu Er and An San, had no idea of Western knowledge. Second, Western knowledge was accepted by scholars who had basic scientific knowledge. Those who were interested only in Confucianism and the writing of the eight-legged essay did not find Western learning appealing. Third, Western learning had a larger impact in the Lower Yangtze area, the chief areas of evangelic activities. Zhejiang, Jiangsu, and Anhui Provinces had the largest population of missionaries as well as Chinese Christian converts, followed by Jiangxi and Fujian Provinces. According to the *Biographies of the Astronomers* and the *Collections of Xu Guangqi*, there were 173 scholars influenced by Western learning. Among these scholars, only 120 had their place of birth known (refer to table 2.2). The Lower Yangtze provinces were home to Xu Guangqi, Li Zhizao, Yang Tingjun, Wang Xichan, and Mei Wending as well.

Table 2.2 Scholars in the Ming to early Qing Dynasty who were influenced by Western Learning

Place of birth (province)	Number of scholar
Zhejiang	31
Jiangsu	29
Anhui	22
Jiangxi	7
Fujian	6
Hebei	5

(Cont'd)

Place of birth (province)	Number of scholar
Shandong	4
Henan	4
Shanxi	3
Hubei	3
Guangdong	2
Sichuan	2
Mongol	2

Fourth, the influence of Western learning declined soon after the banning of Christianity. Because of the limited circulation of the translated works and maps, Western knowledge was known to only a minority of scholars. Having found the world maps as "military secrets," Emperor Kangxi ordered the storage of the maps in the palace after their completion. Most of these works were untouched after the expulsion of missionaries from China, so that the Chinese lagged behind the Westerners in the learning of geography. Ignorance of global geography was not limited to the public, but also the upper class. Emperor Daoguang, who had received the ambassadors of the East Indian Company in the early nineteenth century, had no idea the location of Britain. Fifth and last, Western learning influenced mainly mathematics and calendar formulation. Western mathematics became the key to Western astronomy and thus the formulation of an accurate calendar.

Western learning might have influenced particular scholars, but it had more contributions to the revival of the "practical use of knowledge." As concluded by Zhang Weihua:

> Scholars in the reign of Emperor Qianong and Jiaqing were proficient in Western learning. Dai Dongyuan was not the only one [who mastered Western learning]. Western learning mostly demonstrated its influence in China in the rise of the School of Empirical Studies. There are comments suggesting the spirit of science featured Sinology in the early Qing Dynasty. Actually, this "spirit of science" originated from the Western learning. Such an argument might be a bold assertion, but the development of Sinology was propelled by Western learning.[55]

3 Chapter

Western Learning from the Southern Ocean

The development of Western learning in China was suspended because of the banning of Christianity by the Qing court. The development was also delayed due to the dismissal of the Jesuits in the eighteenth century. Western imperialism triggered the second wave of the dissemination of Western learning with the Protestants as the pioneers this time, not the Catholic missionaries.

Robert Morrison: the Prologue

Robert Morrison was born on January 5, 1782 in Morpeth, a small town in Northumberland. His father, James Morrison, moved from Scotland to northern England, where he married Morrison's mother, Hannah Nicholson. Morrison, the youngest child of eight in the poverty-stricken family, had to help his father make shoes to earn a living.

Fig. 3.1 Portrait of Robert Morrison

The whole family relocated to Newcastle, 40 kilometers south of Morpeth, in 1785. Morrison studied with his uncle James Nicholson, a respected primary school teacher. Morrison was influenced by his father, who worked as an Elder in the Presbyterian Church in Newcastle, as well as the religious environment of the city, to participate in the church's activities. He started his study of Latin, Greek, and Hebrew under the guidance of a Presbyterian priest in 1801. He left

Newcastle to continue his studies in a church school in Hoxton, London, in 1803. Graduating with excellent results, he joined the London Missionary Society two years after and he was dispatched to pursue further education in Gosport Missionary Academy where he majored in theology and was equipped with basic medical and astronomical knowledge. During his three years of study at the Gosport Missionary Academy, he met Yong Sam-tak[1] and learned Chinese.

Morrison's church, the London Missionary Society, was established in 1795 through a combination with the Church of England, the Presbyterian Church, and the Congregational Church. It aimed to launch evangelic missions in Asian countries, particularly India and China, the two most populated countries. Morrison and several missionaries were chosen to participate in the church's first mission to China, but Morrison's colleagues were too frightened to go on the journey to the East. In January 1807, Morrison, at the age of 25, left Britain. He sailed across the Atlantic Ocean to the United States instead of following the Africa-India-China route having rejected by the East Indian Company, which saw evangelic missions as negatively affecting their business. On April 20, he arrived in New York, where he was warmly welcomed by the local Protestants, and was received by Secretary of State James Madison. Madison even wrote him a recommendation letter, requesting help from the American merchants in Guangzhou for Morrison. Morrison departed on May 26 and arrived in Macau on September 4.

The policy of single-port trading was still in effect when Morrison arrived in China and this policy forbid Westerners from starting evangelic missions even in the only open port of Guangzhou. With the recommendation letter, Morrison was welcomed to settle in the American Consul. He continued to learn Cantonese and Mandarin from his Chinese servants, but he was forced to pay a high tutorial fee. He attempted to dress in Chinese clothes as Ricci did, but he was viewed with suspicion by the locals. Morrison's difficult early arrival period, as evidenced by the tight budget and unfavorable policy of the Qing court, ended after his marriage to Mary Morton, the daughter of a manager of the East Indian Company. He was paid 5,000 British pounds (increased to 10,000 pounds after two years) as a translator in the company.

Due to the limited success in China, the London Missionary Society dispatched W. Milne to assist Morrison.[2] After Milne's arrival in China in 1813, he suggested establishing a new association that focused on evangelic missions in Southeast Asia, where there were less restrictions on religious activities. They established a new association, the Ultra Ganges Mission, to coordinate their activities. Based in Malacca and Batavia, the edges of the sphere of influence of the Western powers, the association soon became a gathering point for missionaries from Europe and the United States, such as W. H. Medhurst[3], William Young[4], William Dean[5], and David Abeel[6]. The works of Morrison and Milne secured the foothold of the Protestant church in Southeast Asia. Moreover, they established the four guiding principles of their work: preaching, publication, education, and medical service.

Fig. 3.2 Portrait of William Milne

The most well-known work of Morrison was the translation of *The Holy Bible*. Jean Basset was the first to translate the *New Testament,* but he finished only a few sections. Under the advice of the London Missionary Church, Morrison undertook the translation of the *New Testament* from 1808 to 1813, and continued to translate the *Old Testament* from 1814 to 1819 with the help of Milne. The book was typeset into 21 volumes and printed in Malacca in 1823, entitled *The Holy Book of the Divine Heaven* (*Shentian shengshu* 神天聖書). After the publication of the translated *Holy Bible,* a translation committee was organized to edit Morrison's work. *The Testaments* was edited by K. F. A. Gutzlaff[7] and W. H. Medhurst[8], and it was reprinted in 1840. The new edition was studied by Hong Xiuchuan, who was thus inspired to initiate the Taiping Uprising, an anti-Qing and Christian movement plaguing the Lower Yangtze and southern China. In addition to the publication of *The Holy Bible*, the Ultra Ganges Mission translated *A Summary of the Doctrine of Divine Redemption* and other religious materials for the Chinese public. Most of these leaflets were reprinted and referred to by the later missionaries.

The first group of Chinese converts included the printing workers, whose presses were responsible for printing Morrison's books. Cai Gao, the first Chinese convert, was a woodblock-printing worker in the East Indian Company Press in Macau. He was baptized by Morrison in July 16, 1814. His brothers Cai Xing and Cai San followed Gao and converted. Another influential figure was Leung Fa (1789–1855). Leung was born in Gaoming (present-day Gaohe), a small town in Guangdong. Seeking a job in the town, he left his hometown at the age of 15 to go to Guangzhou, where he learned woodblock printing and befriended Morrison and Milne. He worked for Morrison after 1810 to print the translated *Holy Bible*, and, influenced by Morrison, he converted to Christianity in Malacca in 1816. He returned to Guangzhou and continued to work for Morrison. In 1823, he was ordained by Morrison as the first Chinese Protestant missionary. Apart from printing the *Holy Bible*, Leung also published considerable religious leaflets. One of the publications, the *Lasting Stories to Awaken the World* (*Quanshi liangyan* 勸世良言), was said to have enlightened Hong Xiuquan's belief.

Morrison and his colleagues also attempted to introduce China to the West through the publication of reference works (refer to table 3.1). The most important treatise was *The Chinese Dictionary* (*Zidian* 字典), which included numerous vocabularies, idioms, sample sentences, and a translation of *A Reference Work of Arts and Literature* (*Yiwen Beilan* 藝文備覽), a Chinese dictionary published in the 12th year of the reign of Jiaqing (1807).

Table 3.1 Chinese reference works published before 1842

Subject	Title	Author	Publishing date
Chinese classics	*The Analects*	Joshua Marshman[9]	1812
	The Great Learning		
	Translated Commentaries of the Four Books	David Collie[10]	1828
	Three Character Classic	E. C. Bridgman	—
	Thousand Character Text		
	Book of Filial Piety		

(Cont'd)

Subject	Title	Author	Publishing date
Chinese history and current affairs	*La Chine à Tire-d'aile*	R. Morrison	1817
	Notices Concerning China and the Port of Canton		1823
	China: Dialogues Between A Father and His Two Children Concerning the History and Present State of That Country		1824
	The Sacred Edicts: Emperor Kangxi and Yongzheng	W. Milne	1817
	A Sketch of Chinese History	K. F. A. Gutzlaff	1834
	China Opened		1838
	A View of China: for Philological Purposes	W. H. Medhurst	1838
	A Sketch of China	Samuel Kidd[11]	1841
Chinese language	*Elements of Chinese Grammar*	J. Marshman	1814
	Grammar of the Chinese Language	R. Morrison	1815
	Dialogues and Detached Sentences in the Chinese Language		1816
	The Chinese Dictionary		1823
	Vocabulary of the Canton Dialect		1828
	A Dictionary of the Hok-Keën Dialect of the Chinese Language	W. H. Medhurst	1832
	Translation of a Comparative Vocabulary of the Chinese, Corean and Japanese Languages		1835
	Chinese-English Dictionary		1842
	Three Thousand Common Words in Chinese	Samuel Dyer[12]	1834
	Vocabulary of the Fukien Dialect		1838
	Phonetic Notation of the Canton Dialect	E. C. Bridgman	1841

Malacca, Singapore, and Batavia: the Southern Bases

Failing to secure a foothold in China in early nineteenth century, Morrison and Milne retreated to Southeast Asia to resume their evangelic missions. Malacca, Singapore, and Batavia were chosen as their bases because of their positions as European colonies, and the presence of a large overseas Chinese population. Working in these cities, they might have been too distant to influence China, but their activities — publication, education, and medical service — had epochal meaning to both the development of Christianity and the dissemination of Western learning in China.

Publishing in the Southeast Asian ports

According to the *Memorials of Protestant Missionaries to the Chinese* by A. Wylie, there were seven major publishing hubs for Chinese Christian books: Guangzhou, Macau, Malacca, Singapore, Penang, Batavia, and Bangkok. Among these cities, Malacca, Singapore, and Batavia had most publications(refer to table 3.2). Malacca and Batavia had the highest number of publications from 1811 to 1833. Followed by Morrison's death in 1834, the center of publication shifted to Singapore.

Table 3.2 Statistics of Chinese books published by missionaries (1811–1842)

Location	1811–1833	1834–1842	Total
Malacca	45	2	47
Singapore	—	50	50
Batavia	20	10	50
Guangzhou	11	—	11
Macau	—	7	7
Penang	—	1	1
Bangkok	—	1	1

Source: Alexander Wylie, *Records of the Protestant Missionaries in China* (Taipei: Cheng Wen Publishing Co., Ltd., 1967). Su Jing 蘇精, *Malixun yu Zhongwen yinshua chuban* 馬禮遜與中文印刷出版 (Morrison and Chinese Publications) (Taipei: Student Book Co., Ltd, 2000).

The idea of opening his own publishing house in Southeast Asia came to Morrison after the unauthorized publication of *A Summary of the Doctrine of Divine Redemption* and *An Annotated Catechism on the Teachings of Jesus* (*Wenda qianzhu Yesu jiaofa* 問答淺注耶穌教法) in Guangzhou. After the establishment of the Ultra Ganges Mission, Morrison submitted a letter to the London Missionary Society to suggest the opening of an independent press.[13] He also dispatched Milne to develop evangelic missions in Malacca in 1814. Among the Southeast Asian cities, Malacca had the highest priority to Morrison as the city was under the dominance of Britain. It was more prosperous than Penang and Singapore, the other two British colonies in the Malay Peninsula, and there was a larger overseas Chinese population. All of these were favorable conditions which helped the missionaries in their preaching efforts and made it easier for them to learn Chinese.

Milne headed to Malacca along with his wife, Leung Fa, and several printing workers. After two years of preparation, Milne found a site in the harbor in front of the city to serve as the office and dormitory. The Malacca Press, the first press in Southeast Asia organized by the Protestant missionary, was formally opened in 1817. It published 43 titles up until 1842.

Four years after the establishment of the Malacca Press, the Batavia Press was opened by W. H. Medhurst, who had assisted Milne in Malacca from 1816 to 1820. The Batavia Press soon replaced the Malacca Press as the mainstay publisher of the London Missionary Society after Milne's death in 1822. From 1823 to 1842, the Batavia Press published 30 titles, 28 of which were Medhurst's works, and the remaining two titles were compiled by W. Young.

The Singapore Press, formally named as *Jianxia shuyuan* after its opening on November 29, 1834, was established at the suggestion of The Society for the Diffusion of Useful Knowledge.[14] Presided over by a British merchant James Matheson, with E. C. Bridgman, K. F. A. Gutzlaff, and John Robert Morrison as the committee members, this society aimed to enhance Sino-Western communication by coordinating with the British, American, Dutch, and others, as well as publishing "books that enlighten and introduce Western techniques and science to the Chinese."[15] Ira Tracy, a missionary from the American Board of Commissioners for Foreign Missions, was dispatched to Singapore to purchase printing machines to prepare for the opening of the Singapore Press.[16] The first publication of the Singapore Press was *Cessation of Opium Smoking* (*Yapian sugai wen* 鴉片速改文), also completed by Tracy. It published 50 titles, including works by Gutzlaff and Bridgman, up to 1842.

Among the 147 Chinese books published during 1811 to 1842, 113 titles were religious works, such as the *Holy Bible*, a collection of hymns, theoretical treatises, biographies of the religious figures, and the history of religion (refer to the appendix for the whole book list). The rest of the titles were about world history, geography, politics, and economy. In addition to books, the missionaries published several important journals in Southeast Asia: *Chinese Monthly Magazine* (*Chashisu meiyue tongji zhuan* 察世俗每月統紀傳), *A Monthly Record of Important Selections* (*Texuan zuoyao meiyue jizhuan* 特選撮要每月紀傳), *Eastern Western Monthly Magazine* (*Dongxiyang kao meiyue tongji zhuan* 東西洋考每月紀記傳), and *Universal Gazette* (*Tianxia xinwen* 天下新聞).

Chinese Monthly Magazine

Chinese Monthly Magazine began its publication on August 5, 1815 in Malacca. "A philanthropist"(W. Milne) was the chief editor and Leung Fa was the printer. It was freely distributed to the overseas Chinese, several of whom brought the journal to China to the local scholars. Morrison, who wanted to develop the readers' critical thinking through observation, established this journal and entitled it *chashisu*, meaning to observe the world.[17]

Fig. 3.3 *Chinese Monthly Magazine*

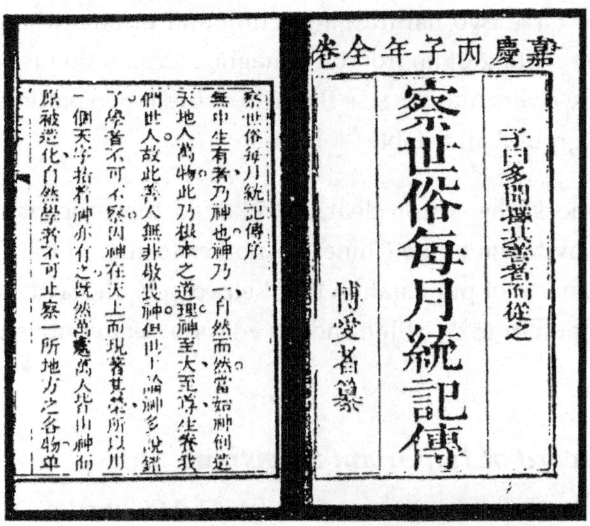
嘉慶丙子年全卷
察世俗每月統記傳
子曰多聞擇其善者而從之
博愛者纂

察世俗每月統記傳序
無中生有者乃神也神乃一自然而然當始神創造
天地人萬物此乃根本之道理神至大至尊生養我
們世人故此善人無非敬畏神但世上論神多說錯
了學者不可不察因神在天上而現著其榮所以用
一個天字指着神亦有之既然萬處萬人皆由神而
原被造化自然學者不可止察一所地方之各物单

More than 80 percent of the articles in the *Chinese Monthly Magazine* explained the teachings of Christianity. The remaining short essays introduced world history and geography, which were new to the Chinese. Representative articles included "Ship with Hot Air" which described the steamship and its wide application in Britain and the United States; "On Astronomy and Geography," which explained elementary astronomy and geographic knowledge in detail; "Brief Introduction of World Geography," which included basic information on hundreds of modern countries;[18] and five translated stories from *Aesop's Fables*.[19]

Having realized that Western knowledge might be too difficult for the Chinese, Milne attempted to write in plain language and to include diagrams. For example, diagrams about the spinning of the earth and the eclipses were added in the astronomical essays. He also explained the concept of heliocentrism in a question-and-answer style. The editor first raised questions about the contradiction between the spinning of the earth and the rising stars in the article "On the Revolution of the Earth around the Sun." Milne answered by using a metaphor:

> Humans are too small to sense the moving of the earth...The movable earth is similar to the experience on a ship. Mountains, trees, and shores seem to be passing away during sailing, but it is in fact the moving of the ship. The earth is equivalent to the ship and the stars are the surrounding scenery.[20]

The editor raised another question about why humans did not fall down when standing on a movable earth. Milne continued to answer with metaphors:

> All creatures have two natures: attraction and orientation. Attraction is similar to the pulling of an iron by a magnet. Orientation is similar to the flowing of the rivers into the sea. Because of these two natures, human are stuck on the ground and stable.[21]

With metaphors, the editor clearly explained the concept of heliocentrism and universal gravitation to the Chinese. Another feature of the *Chinese Monthly Magazine* was the use of punctuation that helped split the sentences. Up to when it ceased publication in 1821, Milne and his editorial team published more than 80 issues.

A Monthly Record of Important Selections

Established in Batavia by "a virtuous man (W. H. Medhurst)," *A Monthly Record of Important Selections* began its publication in July 1823 and was suspended in 1826. As stated in the preface of the first issue, the publication of this journal was a continuation of the *Chinese Monthly Magazine*:

> There was a journal explaining various concepts seven years ago in Malacca. Unfortunately, the author, an old philanthropist, had passed away, so that journal was no longer published. This journal was the *Chinese Monthly Magazine*...The junior (Medhurst) wanted to continue the work of the senior (Milne). The composition of articles and the publication of

journals benefit later generations, ignite readers' benevolence, and deliver people from unnecessary desire. The journal title is changed, but the spirit of the *Chinese Monthly Magazine* is preserved.[22]

The editorial team planned to issue 1,000 copies for each volume initially, but they soon increased the printing amount due to better-than-expected sales. This journal was particularly popular among the overseas Chinese in Indonesia because of Medhurst's article "A Complete Discourse on Kelapa" (present-day Jakarta) that introduced the history, geography, and customs of the Java archipelagos. This article was published as an "offprint" and reprinted four times.

Eastern Western Monthly Magazine

Organized by "a Sinophile (K. F. A. Gutzlaff)," *Eastern Western Monthly Magazine* was first published in Guangzhou in August 1, 1833, and it stopped its publication in September in 1838.[23] It included articles that covered a wide range of topics, such as current affairs, history, geography, religion, philosophy, news commentary, science, astronomy, arts, commerce, and literature. Gutzlaff founded this journal to present the advanced and civilized Western culture to the Chinese, who still regarded the foreigners as barbarians.

Fig. 3.4 ***Eastern Western Monthly Magazine***

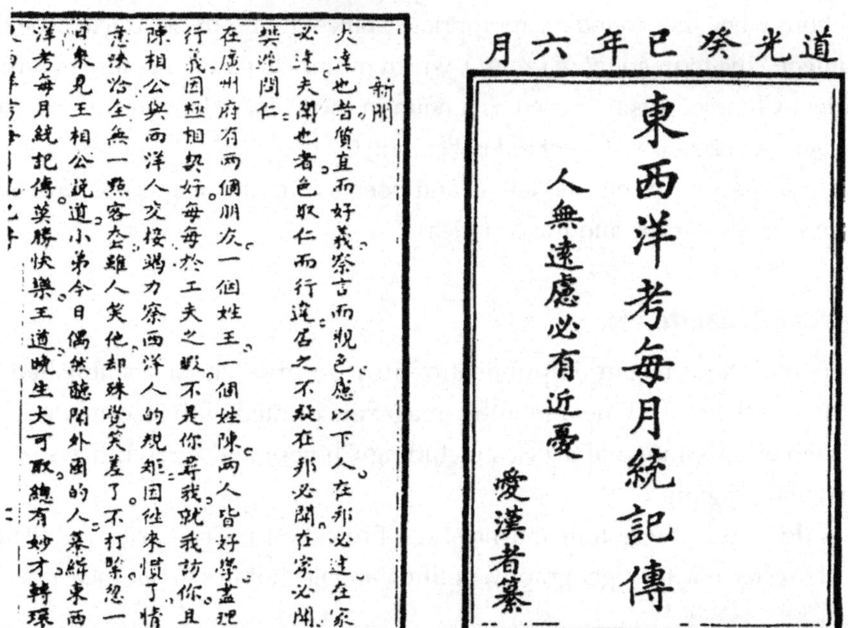

新聞
大達也者。質直而好義。察言而觀色。慮以下人。在邦必達。在家
必達。夫聞也者。色取仁而行違。居之不疑。在邦必聞。在家必聞。
樊遲問仁。
在廣州府有兩個朋友。一個姓王。一個姓陳。兩人皆好學。盡理
行義。因極相契好。每每於工夫之暇。不是你尋我。就我訪你。且
陳相公與西洋人交接。竭力察西洋人的規矩。因往來慣了。情
意浹洽。全無一點客套。雖人笑他。卻殊覺笑差了。不打緊。忽一
日來見王相公說道。小弟今日偶然聽聞外國的人。纂輯東西
洋考每月統記傳。英勝快樂。王道。晚生大可取。總有妙才轉環

道光癸巳年六月
東西洋考每月統記傳
人無遠慮必有近憂
愛漢者纂

One of the features of the *Eastern Western Monthly Magazine* was the news written in novel form. In the first issue, the news of the publication of the *Eastern Western Monthly Magazine* was reported as:

> Wang and Chen are friends living in Guangzhou. Both of them are studious and do justice. They visited each other during free time...One day, Mr. Chen visited Mr. Wang and said, 'I heard from the foreigners about the compilation of the *Eastern Western Monthly Magazine*. I am extremely delighted!'[24]

It is suggested that the novel style of news was influenced by the popular fictions of the Ming and Qing Dynasties. Another feature of the *Eastern Western Monthly Magazine* was the use of Chinese terms and phrases to correlate with Western affairs. For instance, "*shiqiang duwu* (恃強黷武)," a commonly used phrase to criticize rulers who frequently trigger wars, was used to comment on Napoleon's raging of wars. "*Zili weiwang* (自立為王)," meaning self-enthronement, correlated to the crowning of Napoleon as an emperor by himself.[25] "*Shichong shanquan* (恃寵擅權)," meaning to arrogate power to oneself with the rulers' affection secured, described pompous parliament members. "*Niexian* (臬憲)," a respectful title to address the provincial surveillance commissioner, corresponded to the local judges in the British judicial system.[26] Moreover, the editors invented new terms to explain Western institutions when they found no appropriate Chinese terms. In the article "The British Parliament," the term *gonghui* (公會), which meant "to gather because of business" in ancient Chinese, was first used as a noun in the Chinese language to refer to the parliament, an organization that did not exist in China.[27]

The journal also published letters and poems from the overseas Chinese about their journey in Europe and the Americas.[28]

Universal Gazette

Universal Gazette began its publication in 1828 in Malacca. Established by S. Kidd, it was the first Chinese monthly magazine printed with lead-made types. It published a wide range of articles including Chinese and foreign news, science, history, and religion.

In addition to these four journals, the Protestant missionaries published 34 titles of Western history, geography, politics, and economics in Southeast Asia.

Brief Introduction of Geography

Edited by W. H. Medhurst and published in 1819, the *Brief Introduction of Geography* (*Dili biantong lüezhuan* 地理便童略傳) was a short (21 pages) and elementary textbook for primary school students. This book was divided into eight chapters: introduction to the four continents, on China, on India and Persian states, on Arabian and Judaea states, on United Kingdom, on European states, on Africa, and on America. It also included four maps about the world, China, Asia, and Europe. This book explained the basic information of the countries, such as the boundaries, areas, local products, population, and religion, in a question-and-answer form. For instance, question 44 introduced the government of the United Kingdom as:

> Question 44: What is the court of the United Kingdom?
> Answer: The court is presided over by an emperor, who cooperates with the heads of the bureau to govern the country. The emperor decides the matters of war, signs treaties, considers urban construction, military expenses, minting of coins, employment of officials, and the use of the death penalty. However, the emperor has no power on legislation and tax collection. There are two large associations in the United Kingdom: the Aristocratic Hereditary Association (the Upper House) and the Gentry Association (the Lower House). These two associations, after discussing the new laws, amendment of laws, collection of tax, and other urgent matters, report to the emperor for a final decision. The tripartite power prevents the emperor from exploiting the people, the aristocrats from dominating the power, and the commoners from revolting.[29]

Question 69 explained the government of the United States as:

> Question 69: What is the court of the United States?
> The court of the United States is similar to the English court in terms of the presence of two large associations (the Upper and the Lower House) that are responsible for legislation and tax collection. There is no emperor in the United States, but a man called the President to govern the country. After the president ends his term of service, which lasts for four years, another man would inherit his position.[30]

A Brief Account of Things Seen and Heard during the Journey to the Western Hemisphere

Edited by R. Morrison and published in 1819, *A Brief Account of Things Seen and Heard during the Journey to the Western Hemisphere* (*Xiyou diqiu wenjian lüezhuan* 西遊地球聞見略傳) was a fiction of an anonymous villager from Sichuan Province, who crossed Tibet and India, arrived in France, travelled to the Americas, and returned to China.

Comparative Chronology of East and West

Compiled by W. H. Medhurst and published in Batavia in 1829, the *Comparative Chronology of East and West* (*Dongxi shiji hehe* 東西史記和合) was the first reference work of Sino-Western comparative history.[31] Through the listing of the important events in China and Europe in two columns, this book introduced to the Chinese the idea that Europe also had a long tradition. Part of the content was serialized in the *Eastern Western Monthly Magazine* and reprinted in 1833.

Narrative Record of the Countries of the World: Past and Present

Published by the *Jianxia shuyuan* in Singapore in 1838, the *Narrative Record of the Countries of the World: Past and Present* documented the history of the Church and various countries.[32] Books one to six included the events before the Flood, the history of Israel, ancient Greece, Athens, and the Roman Empire. Books seven to eleven mentioned the birth of Jesus, the evangelic mission of St. John, the history of the Byzantium Empire, the Muslim tribes, and British, Italian, and Spanish history. Books 12 to 20 described the discovery of America, the history of the French, Portuguese, Swedish, Russian, and other nations.

The editor, K. F. A. Gutzlaff, focused more on pre-Renaissance European history, particularly ancient Greece and Rome. China had only known the history of the pre-historical times. Nevertheless, this book was a relatively comprehensive reference work of world history published before the Opium War. This book was reprinted twice in Japan, entitled as *Bankoku kōkanroku wakai* (萬國綱鑑錄和解) and *Kokon bankoku kōkanroku* (古今萬國綱鑑錄), respectively.[33]

A Brief Account of the English Character

Originally written in English by Charles Majoribanks, a *taipan* in the British East Indian Company, the Chinese version of *A Brief Account of the English Character*, translated by R. Morrison, was published in 1832. This book, with less than

2,000 words, was introductory material of the British and their aims to trade in the Orient. The author stressed the difficulties for foreigners when establishing trading relationships with the Chinese and it described exhortations from Chinese officials and other maltreatments. British sailors, though seemingly stronger than the Chinese, were kind and benevolent. The Chinese should bear the responsibility for the outbreak of the conflict between themselves and the British. The book ended with a reminder to the Chinese to treat the British kindly in order to demonstrate favor to the foreigners.

The author brought along 500 copies of the book during his commercial trip to China, and distributed the copies in coastal ports such as Amoy, Fuzhou, and Ningbo for free. Brigade vice Commander of Fuzhou, Chen Xiansheng, read the book and found it informative. This book was reprinted and widely distributed in Singapore.[34]

A General Gazetteer of Great Britain

Compiled by K. F. A. Gutzlaff and published in 1834, *A General Gazetteer of the Great Britain* had five books that covered a general description of the United Kingdom, representative scholars and warriors, customs, cities, and British colonies. It was also attached with a portrait of King George III, a painting of St. Paul's Cathedral in London, and a world map.

Unlike a general encyclopedia that lists everything in bullet points or short paragraphs, this book was written in a dialect style. Such a literature style was commonly adopted by the missionaries as it avoided top-to-down indoctrination that might result in readers' aversion to Western affairs. Ye Duhua and Lin Dehao, the leading characters of the story, were two villagers from Guangzhou. Ye continued to study in London after participating in the civil examination, while Lin, a friend of Ye, started his business in the British capital. The duo returned to Guangzhou after two decades, and they introduced Britain to their fellow villagers. To make the book more understandable to the Chinese, the editor correlated the English institutes with its Chinese variants. Each section began with quotations of the ancient Chinese sages to make the narration more familiar to the Chinese readers.

In addition to the basic information on the United Kingdom, this book introduced various Western concepts that did not exist in Chinese tradition. For instance, the high social status of the commoners, the parliamentary system that prevented the tyrannical rule of the Prime Ministers, a monotheist religion that worshipped only the Creator, the banning of idolatry, sexual equality, and the freedom of marriage but the banning of keeping concubines.

A Brief History of the United States of America

Edited by E. C. Bridgman, *A Brief History of the United States* was published by *Jianxia shuyuan* in 1838 with the help of Liang Zhi, a villager from the Duanxi County of Guangdong Province and a student of Bridgman. In addition to the basic information about the territory, population, local products, and economic development, the author attempted to introduce historical events and concepts that were new to the Chinese.[35] The independence movement and the concept of a "United States," for instance, were explained as:

> The English king repeatedly exploited our country. We tolerated this for months and years, but the English king continued to do it. We had no choice but to elect a leader. We could never obey England. We named our country the United States as we had combined the states into a country.[36]

This book was the only Chinese encyclopedia of the United States published before the Opium War, as the United States, a newly established country, was seldom mentioned in the works of early Protestant missionaries, let alone the works of the Jesuits. This book was reprinted in Hong Kong and Shanghai in 1844 and 1861, respectively.

Brief Essentials of Governance

Compiled by K. F. A. Gutzlaff and published in Singapore, the *Brief Essentials of Governance* (*Zhi guoyong zhi dalüe* 制國用之大略) was a 24-page manual of political science and economics that argued for the principle of governance in a multitude of ways: monetary system, tax, national expenditure, military, education system, and source of income. *Memorials of Protestant Missionaries to the Chinese* of A. Wylie suggested that 1839 was the publication date of this book.

A General Account of Trade

Compiled by K. F. A. Gutzlaff and published in Singapore, this manual of Western commerce and trade covered a wide range of topics. Volume one began with an introduction and basic concepts about commerce, merchants, companies, and free trade. Volume two described the situation of modern commerce and international trade. Volume three explained the land and maritime transportation processes and facilities. Volume four accounted for the monetary system, bank and bank notes, currency conversion, and insurance agents. The last volume documented the commercial regulations of the newly established countries.

The Chinese commerce system had developed since the pre-Qin period and reached its height at the Song and Ming Dynasties. Various financial organizations and financial products, such as paper money and banks, had emerged in China, but the Celestial Empire, unlike the modern European states, relied more on agricultural production. Commerce flourished merely in the capital area or the coastal cities. Moreover, the disdain on commerce by the Confucians added to the rulers' general ignorance of the economy and international trade. This manual opposed the Chinese emphasis on agriculture yet it favored restrained commercial activity, as these two economic sectors had equal importance to people's livelihoods. It commented that:

> Merchants devote themselves in a different way to the farmers. Their hard works benefited not only themselves, but also the public...Although merchants produced nothing from the land, they helped to create national wealth through the transportation of products by providing sufficient food and clothes to the people. During the outbreak of famine, when bodies are lying along the roads, merchants soon delivered food to the people. Their generous act is similar to pouring water into a dried pool for the fish, or the rain after a prolonged drought. When people become affluent, merchants help store their wealth, enabling them to use the money in all parts of the nation. Without merchants, having a large amount of wealth would be useless.[37]

The author also compared the commercial systems of the East and the West. Both China and Europe had banks, but the Chinese banks were established by private merchants, while the European banks were operated by the merchants under the supervision of the rulers. Chinese paper money emphasized the credibility of the bank, while the credibility of European notes depended on the ruler. To protect the goods during the long journey, the Chinese merchants employed security guards from *biaoju* (鏢局), an organization established by men proficient in martial arts. The Europeans, on the contrary, invented the insurance system that compensated for any disasters during transactions, such as fire, flood, and the death of the traders.

Trade on Justice

Published by W. Milne in Malacca in 1818, this 10-page brochure mentioned the basic regulations of trade, methods to check unfair trade in China, Chinese units of measurement, unauthentic products and money, and the termination of contracts. This brief yet informative manual was reprinted in Malacca and Ningbo in 1832 and 1837, respectively.

Significance of the Southeast Asian publications

To expose the Chinese to a modern world

Through the publications, the missionaries delivered the Chinese people from isolation and ignorance about global affairs. Overseas study in Europe and the United States had not yet become popular in the first half of the nineteenth century; therefore, these firsthand accounts of the Western world were studied by the Chinese scholars to conduct their research. For instance, Wei Yuan referred to the articles in the *Eastern and Western Monthly Magazine*, *A Brief History of the United States of America*, and *A General Account of Trade* to compile the *Illustrated Gazetteer of the Maritime Countries* (*Haiguo tushuo* 海國圖說). Liang Tingnan and Xu Jiyu also cited information from *A Brief History of the United States of America* in writing *On the United States Circuit* and *A Short Account of the Maritime Circuit*, respectively.

To foster the publishing industry in China

Journal publication in China did not exist in China before the coming of the Protestant missionaries. Most of the propagation materials in ancient China, such as the imperial gazette (*dibao* 邸報), were issued by the government to announce any new policies. The *Chinese Monthly Magazine* and the *Eastern Western Monthly Magazine*, the pioneers of modern Chinese journalism, influenced the publication of Chinese periodicals in the second half of the nineteenth century. To name a few, these magazines included the *Chinese Serial* (*Xiaer guanzhen* 遐邇貫珍) in Hong Kong, the *Chinese and Foreign Weekly* (*Zhongwai xinwen qiri lu* 中外新聞七日錄) in Ningbo, the *Universal Miscellany* (*Liuhe congtan* 六合叢談) and the *Chinese Scientific Magazine* (*Gezhi huibian* 格致匯編) in Shanghai, and *The Peking Magazine* (*Zhongxi jianwen* 中西見聞).[38]

The missionaries also introduced Western printing methods to China. Lithography, invented by Alois Senefelder (1771–1834), an Austrian playwright, was first applied by W. H. Medhurst in his publication of the Chinese School Book in 1828. Medhurst's press in Batavia published several Chinese books by lithography as well, such as the *Comparative Chronology of East and West*, *An Annotated Catechism on the Teachings of Jesus*, *A Complete Discourse on*

Theology (*Shenli zonglun* 神理總論), A *Harmony of the Gospels* (*Fuyin tiaohe* 福音調和), and the *New Testament*. Lithography was introduced to Guangzhou and Shanghai in 1833 and 1842, respectively.

Another Western printing method introduced to China was lead letterpress printing. Metal printing types had been invented by the Chinese in ancient times, but only copper types were relatively popular, while tin and lead sorts were almost unused.[39] Lead letterpress printing, on the contrary, had been widely used in the West and it was introduced to China by the missionaries. Simultaneous to Morrison's compilation of the *Chinese Dictionary*, Peter Perring Thomas and several printing workers started making Chinese lead types at the request of the British East India Company, Macau office. A German improved Thomas' types and produced the second set of lead types after a decade. The new lead types were greatly improved as the workers prepared only half-sized types that would be combined into a complete Chinese character. For instance, in printing the characters " 碗 ," " 婉 ," and " 豌 , "the workers carved the smaller sized " 石 ," " 女 ," and " 豆 ," as well as the character " 宛 ." Fewer types were required in printing because these types were reusable to form other characters, but improper fixing of words resulted in untidy typesetting. This German set of lead types was purchased by the American Presbyterian Church in 1836.

The Anglo-Chinese College and the Morrison Education Society School

In the letter about the establishment of the Ultra Ganges Mission, Morrison also requested a response from the London Missionary Society about a free Chinese school in Malacca. Morrison's suggestion was welcomed by the London Missionary Society, the East India Company, and the British government, who all donated to the founding of the school. Morrison donated 1,000 British pounds as well. W. Milne was appointed as the head of the school. The church school was renamed as Anglo-Chinese College after its opening in 1818.

The "Proposal of the Establishment of the Anglo-Chinese College in Malacca" stated clearly the aim of the school, the curriculum, teachers, school facilities, and admission information (see appendix). The Anglo-Chinese College aimed to equip students with knowledge in Chinese and English culture and to arouse students' interest in Christianity. Chinese and English were the media of instruction. There were two libraries collecting Chinese and English books. Teachers included Western Protestants and the local Chinese. The Anglo-Chinese College admitted

European and American male students recommended by the Protestant churches, students subsidized by European universities, and local boys.[40] Simultaneous to the establishment of the secondary section, three elementary schools that used Hokkien dialect as the medium of instruction were established in 1818. In 1831, four primary schools whose medium of instruction was Malay were opened. There were also two independent schools for girls and women.

Fig. 3.5 The Anglo-Chinese College in Malacca

The school admitted only seven students in its opening year. The number of students had a continuous increase: 11 students in 1821, 17 in 1823, 30 in 1827, and 70 in 1835. There were 200 students in the Chinese primary schools in 1831. From 1818 to 1843, when the school was relocated to Hong Kong, there were seven principals and they all belonged to the London Missionary Society (refer to table 3.4).

Table 3.4 The first seven principals of the Anglo-Chinese College

Name	Duration of the term of service
W. Milne	1818–1822
James Humphreys41	1822–1824
D. Collie	1824–1828
S. Kidd	1828–1832
Jacob Tomlin42	1832–1834
John Evans43	1834–1840
James Legge44	1840–1843

Unlike traditional elementary Chinese schools that taught mainly characters and moral standards, the curriculum of the Anglo-Chinese College covered a wide range of subjects, including English, Chinese, mathematics, astronomy, geography, and religion. The school used the textbooks published by the Malacca Press. The classification of students according to their academic standards was different from the "large-class teaching" in traditional Chinese schools (See appendix).

Representative graduates of the Anglo-Chinese College were numerous (refer to table 3.5).

Table 3.5 Representative graduates of the Anglo-Chinese College

Name	Place of origin	Period of study	Achievements
Leung Fa	Guangdong	1820–1821	Scholarship in Theology The first Chinese Protestant evangelist and minister
Yuan Dehui	Sichuan	1823–1827	Interpreter-clerk of the Court of Colonial Affairs Assistant of Commissioner Lin Zexu
John Henry Moor	Macau	1825–1827	Editor of the *Singapore Chronicle* and the *Singapore Free Press*
William C. Hunter	The United States	1825–1827	Partner of Russell & Company Author of the *Bits of Old China*
J. R. Morrison	Macau	1827–1830	Son of Robert Morrison Secretary of the Superintendent of the Trade Translator during the signing of the Treaty of Nanjing
			Chinese Secretary of Henry Pottinger, the first Governor of Hong Kong Member of the Hong Kong Legislative Council
Hoh Fuk Tong	Guangdong	1840–1843	The first Chinese clergyman
Song Hoot Keam	Malacca	1840–1843	Continued study in Scotland after graduation Teacher in the Singapore College

(Cont'd)

The relocation of the Anglo-Chinese College to Hong Kong was first raised by J. Legge in 1842, Principal of the school at this time. The Principal found that Hong Kong, already a British colony by this time, had a larger Chinese population and closer ties with China than the Strait Settlements. These were all favorable conditions for evangelic missions in China. Both the school and the printing house were thus moved to Hong Kong in 1843, and the school was renamed as The Theological Seminary of the London Missionary Society in China. Due to limited employment opportunities in the religious sector for the graduates and the outbreak of the Taiping Uprising that threatened the political stability in Southern China, the college suspended its operations in 1856. The school site in Central was reserved for the Government Central School, later the Queen's College. While the college was closed down, the printing press continued its business to publish Chinese *Bibles* until it was acquired by Wang Tao and Wong Shing in 1870. From 1843 to 1856, the Anglo-Chinese College admitted 85 students.[45]

After the death of Robert Morrison in Macau in 1834, missionaries in Macau suggested the establishment of the Morrison Education Society and a subordinate school in memory of Morrison. This idea was welcomed by the Western residents in Guangzhou and Macau. With the help of the American Consul, the first meeting of the society was held on September 28, 1836. Lancelot Dent, a British merchant, was elected as the President. During the meeting, the committee also formulated a constitution which stated the aim of the society of improving the educational standards of the Chinese through the establishment of schools, the admission qualifications, the structure of the teaching team, the teaching method, the choice of textbook, and the management of the school library.[46]

Prior to the formal opening of the Morrison Education Society School in November 4, 1839, in Macau, the society entrusted several missionaries to organize preparation classes for the local students, who would be taught basic Chinese and English characters. In the early stage of the school, there were only six students — age 11 to 16. Samuel Robbins Brown, an American missionary, was the only foreign teacher of the Morrison Education Society School.[47] Brown, a man with profound knowledge and patience in teaching, exempted the students' school fees and provided free accommodation and commodities. With the excellent management of Brown, the school had a satisfactory development in its early stage. The number of students admitted had a stable increase. It admitted six more students in 1840, and 16 more in 1841. Up to 1844, there were 32 students, though 15 students had been dismissed due to misbehavior. According to Brown, the relationship between the teachers and the youngsters was cordial:

> The objects proposed in the constitution of the Morrison Education Society, have been before me in every arrangement. It is not merely a *teaching* society, but an *educational* society, which aims at the training of the entire man, on physical, intellectual, and moral levels. With these ends in view, I have assigned half of each day to Chinese, and half to English studies, beginning at 6 in the morning and closing at 9 at night. Thus eight hours are given to books, and from three to four to exercise and recreation in the open air…They mingle as if they were family, and we try to treat them as if they were sons, and we encourage them to be familiar with us and confident in us as their best friends. They are present with us in the morning and evening devotions of their own choice; and in short, we seek to make them feel that they are at home, and to give them the education of a Christian home.[48]

The school was relocated to Hong Kong in November 1842, on a nameless site situated between Wong Nai Chung and Happy Valley. With the opening of the school, the area was renamed as Morrison Hill (in present-day Wan Chai) in memory of Morrison. The school employed several more teachers, but five students dropped out rather than attending school in Hong Kong because they were too young to study overseas. The school business declined with Brown's return to the United States and E. C. Bridgman's transferal to Shanghai, and it was formally closed in 1850 due to a lack of funding.

The curriculum of Morrison Education Society School was comprehensive. Subjects taught in English included astronomy, geography, history, arithmetic, algebra, geometry, elementary engineering, biology, chemistry, music, and English language. The Four Books, the *Book of Changes*, the *Book of Poetry*, and the *Book of History* were taught in Chinese. Missionaries were responsible for the teaching of English subjects, while Chinese teachers were employed. The school used authoritative reference works as textbooks, such as *The History of England* by Thomas Keightley, instead of the published textbooks of the Morrison Education Society.

The 11-year operation of the school nurtured a few graduates, but several of them were notable figures in the late-Qing period (refer to table 3.6).

Table 3.6 Representative graduates of Morrison Education Society School

Name	Period of study	Occupation	Achievements
Yung Wing	1840–1847	Politician Educator	• The first Chinese student in the United States • The first Chinese graduate of The Yale University • Initiator of the educational mission to the United States for the poor boys • Supporter of the 1898 Reform and the 1911 Revolution
Huang Kuan	1840–1847	Doctor	• The first Chinese student in United Kingdom • The first Chinese graduate of the Edinburgh University • The first Chinese doctor of Western medicine
Wong Shing	1841–1847	Publisher Politician	• An English teacher in the Shanghai Institute for Dialects • Translator of *The China Mail* • Publisher of the *Chinese and Foreign Gazette, The Chinese Mail*, and the *Universal Circulating Herald* • The first Chinese Justice of the Peace in Hong Kong • The second Chinese ex-official member of the Hong Kong Legislative Council • Ex-official member of the Sanitary Board of Hong Kong
Tong King-sing	1842–1848	Entrepreneur	• Chief-comprador of the Jardine Matheson company • President of the China Merchants' Steam Navigation Company • Introduction of the shareholding system in China's modern enterprises • Administrator of the Chinese Engineering and Mining Company

Church schools apart from the Anglo-Chinese College and the Morrison Education Society School were established by W. H. Medhurst, Samuel Milton, and E. C. Bridgman, but these schools had limited success.

Fig. 3.6 Portrait of Yung Wing, the first Chinese stundent in the United States

Western Medicine and the Ophthalmic Hospital

Providing medical service as a method to proselytize was not an alien concept to the Chinese. As early as the Later Han Dynasty, Daoist priests Zhang Heng and his grandson Zhang Lu attracted followers by offering spells that they claimed were effective in curing any disease. Nestorian Christians, who penetrated into China during the Tang and Yuan Dynasties, attempted to start their evangelic missions through medical service. Jesuits in the Ming and Qing Dynasties also translated reference works of Western medicine and pharmacy reference works into Chinese.

The dissemination of Western learning was suspended due to the banning of Christianity by the Qing court, but Western medicine was preserved in Guangzhou and Macau, the only authorized trading port and the Portuguese sphere of influence, respectively. With Western residents came Western doctors. The British East India Company employed Western doctors to be stationed in Guangzhou and Macau since 1770. These doctors, including Thomas Arnot,

Thomas Hutton, Alexander Pearson, John Livingstone, and Thomas Richardson Colledge, had no knowledge of the Chinese language and medicine, but they were still visited by the Chinese, who had seen the effectiveness of Western medicine. It can be evidenced by the vaccination against cowpox to thousands of Guangzhou children by Dr. Pearson in 1805.[49] In the same year, Dr. Pearson published *The Extraordinary History of a New Method of Inoculation Discovered in the Kingdom of England* (*Zhongdou qishu* 種痘奇書, translated into Chinese by Sir George Thomas Staunton). It was the first reference work on vaccination against cowpox and the prevention of smallpox in China. The clinic in Macau established by Dr. J. Livingstone and Morrison had 300 patients who visited after its opening in 1820.

The background of the establishment of the Ophthalmic Hospital was laid in 1920, when Dr. J. Livingstone discovered that eye problems most plagued his Chinese patients. Dr. Livingstone, Morrison, and the newly arrived Dr. T. R. Colledge, opened an ophthalmic hospital in Macau, which aimed to provide eye treatment to the poor. It was reported that approximately 4,000 patients were cured from 1827 to 1832. They later opened another special clinic for eye and foot diseases in Guangzhou.

The works of the trio laid a foundation for Peter Parker (1804–1889), an American missionary and a Doctor of Medicine from Yale in 1834.[50] He was dispatched to the East after his graduation. He first arrived at Guangzhou, and he soon departed to Singapore in August 1835, where he cured mainly the overseas Chinese and learned Chinese. He returned to Guangzhou after one month, preparing for the establishment of the Ophthalmic Hospital, which was formally opened on November 4, 1835. Located in San Tau Lan Street (present-day Shibafu in Guangzhou), the hospital was commonly referred to as San Tau Lan Hospital by the locals. The three-story hospital was originally a property of Ewo Hong. The first floor was the warehouse, the second floor was the reception, and the third floor was the operation room and wards. Dr. Parker introduced the management of the Western hospital in the Ophthalmic Hospital: first, all patients should register on their first visit; second, the hospital should record the case history of the patients; third, the officers should classify the problems into various diseases for a more efficient diagnosis. The Ophthalmic Hospital provided medical service for not only eye problems, but also various diseases. For instance, a 13-year-old girl visited the hospital for a big sarcoma on her face in 1836. Dr. Parker thus arranged for a surgery for the girl.

Fig. 3.7 Portrait of Dr. Parker, founder of the Ophthalmic Hospital

The Ophthalmic Hospital had a stable development. During the first quarter, there were 1,195 patients, with 925 male and 270 female. Having found the hospital too small to handle the growing business, Dr. Parker rented a neighboring building, also from Ewo Hong, to be the new wing. The Ophthalmic Hospital was regarded as the former Canton Pok Tsai Hospital because of a tablet "Pok Tsai Hospital" which hung in the entrance of the new wing. The number of patients in 1837 reached 2,152, which was double the previous year's number. The rising popularity of the Ophthalmic Hospital was due to the perceived usefulness of Western medicine.

To solve the problem of the absence of doctors and the lack of a subsidy, Dr. Parker, T. R. Colledge, and E. C. Bridgman published an article "Suggestions for the formation of a Medical Missionary Society" in the *Chinese Repository* in 1836, aiming to raise the Western readers' concern of medical missions in China (refer to appendix).[51] The issue was well responded to, and a group of missionaries and merchants met on February 21, 1838. The meeting was presented by Dr. Colledge, Dr. Parker, E. C. Bridgman, William Jardine, J. R. Morrison, Alexander Anderson, and 10 others. They decided to establish a Medical Missionary Society of China, presided over by Dr. Colledge. The committee soon started fund-raising after its establishment. Up to May 1838, 9,300 silver dollars were raised. The operation of the Ophthalmic Hospital was suspended due to the outbreak of the Opium War in 1839. In November 1842, Dr. Parker returned to Guangzhou from the United States to resume his business.

The modern history of China witnessed a prolonged conflict (mainly on an ideological sense) between Chinese and Western medicine. However, Guangzhou and Macau saw limited boycott of Western medicine. It was described in a news article in 1840:

> Among the businesses of us (the Westerners), only medical service caught the Chinese fancy and confidence. Patients came from various provinces to Guangzhou, and they thanked us after being cured. The Chinese government had acknowledged the popularity of Western medicine, but they did not ban it.[52]

The reasons of the acceptance of Western medicine from the Chinese commoners were obvious: first, Western medicine cured quicker than Chinese herbs, which aimed at culturing a strong body instead of killing the virus immediately. Thus there was a need for a longer time to demonstrate the usefulness of Chinese medicine. Second, the Ophthalmic Hospital collected no medical fee. Third, Dr. Parker and his team focused on cures more than preaching which aroused little to no hostility from the Chinese.

Even several Chinese scholars saw Western medicine's appeal. Commissioner Lin Zexu, for instance, visited Dr. Parker in 1839 to be treated for his inguinal hernia but he was also open to the idea of curing his addiction to opium. Western medicine may not have been able to completely rid him of his addiction but it could, and did, cure his hernia.

4

Chapter

After the Opening of China

Because of the closed door policy of the Qing court, evangelic missions before 1842 were based in Southeast Asian cities such as Malacca and Singapore, which were actually too far away to influence China. The turning point came with China's defeat in the Opium War. According to the Treaty of Nanjing, Hong Kong was ceded to England as a colony, while Guangzhou, Fuzhou, Amoy, Ningbo, and Shanghai were opened as treaty ports. Having secured the freedom of movement, the missionaries relocated their bases to China.

Features of the Southern Ports

Scattered along the southern coast of the Chinese empire, Hong Kong, Guangzhou, Fuzhou, Amoy, Ningbo, and Shanghai had large populations, prosperous economies, and flourishing culture that prepared the cities for the dissemination of Western learning. Despite the similar socioeconomic backgrounds of these treaty ports, their features resulted in a distinct academic development and eventually Shanghai emerged as the center of Western learning in China.

Hong Kong, a small village in the Southern tip of China, developed as a British trading port instead of a cultural center. The British government had no plan to encourage any cultural activities in the small island and its distance to the hinterland added to the difficulty in developing itself as the center of Western learning. Fuzhou, the only city that had not been occupied by the British during the Opium War, was alienated from Western culture. Disdain to foreigners was commonly witnessed among various social classes, though the missionaries had mastered the Fuzhou dialects during their stay in Southeast Asia. Villagers had no respect to the British ambassadors because of their "informal" and casual behaviors. The local governors initially refused to allow any entrance of foreigners, designating decayed houses as the ambassadors' residences and an old temple as the British embassy after negotiation.[1] In response to such unfavorable conditions the British government almost withdrew from the development of Fuzhou, but the disruption of the tea transportation from the Wuyi Mountain to Guangzhou and Shanghai due to the outbreak of the Taiping Uprising saved the port from abandonment. Tea exported from Fuzhou to Europe reached 15,739,700 pounds in 1855, and amounted to 40,972,600 pounds in 1856 — 34.8 percent higher than the export volume of tea of Guangzhou. Despite the increasing trade volume, Western learning had never flourished in Fuzhou. Amoy, located in the south of Fuzhou, was important only in the trading of sugar, Chinese goods, and coolie laborers. Gulangyu, an island off the coast of Amoy, was the home to embassies and foreigners' residences. The unpopularity of Western learning in Amoy was also due to the limited communication between the Fujianese and the foreigners, who seldom left the island. Missionaries in Amoy were scarce as well — only seven out of 34 foreign residents were missionaries according to the population statistics in 1855. The remaining residents were merchants and ambassadors.

Ningbo had been one of the most flourishing trading and cultural cities in the lower Yangtze area ever since the Tang Dynasty. Named as Mingzhou in ancient times, it was the first stop for the Japanese ambassadors and traders who departed from Kyūshū Island. Its cultural development had begun since the Song Dynasty, when Wang Anshi and Zeng Gong, the great scholar-officials, promoted universal education during their terms of appointment in Ningbo. It remained the sole authorized port of the Sino-Japanese trade during the Ming Dynasty. It was also the home to the influential merchant group, the "Ningbo gang," as well as the largest private library, the Tianyi Library. The cultural and commercial tradition of Ningbo had prepared the city to emerge as the hub of Western learning, yet the Ningbo merchants found limited opportunity to expand their business in the over-developed Ningbo. These merchants left Ningbo for Shanghai, which had been a small county in the Songjiang Prefecture prior to its opening. Their arrival injected fresh momentum to the city, laying the foundation for its rise as the largest Chinese city as well as the center of Western learning.

Guangzhou, the only authorized port of foreign trade in the Qing Dynasty, became less influential after the opening of China and it was replaced by Shanghai as the first trading port since 1853. The Cantonese had acquired experience in how to deal with foreigners, but they had also developed a sense of xenophobia that resulted in a greater resistance to any business expansion of the Westerners. George Lanning, a principal of a Shanghai foreign school in the late Qing period, recalled the fierce image of the Cantonese:

> Not only were the two languages (Shanghainese and Cantonese) as wide apart as two European tongues, but the natural characteristics were equally separated. Where the Cantonese was aggressive, his Shanghai contemporary was peacefully complaisant. The southerner was a radical: the native of Wu a conservative. Shanghai had long since been reconciled to the *de facto* native government: Canton was ever ready to intrigue and rebel. When dealing with the foreigners, the Cantonese was stand-offish at best, and had on many occasions shown active antipathy, particularly since the war, while the Shanghai man, though not impulsively pro-foreign, was at least willing to meet friendly advances half way.[2]

Hosea Ballou Morse, an American officer in the Imperial Maritime Custom Service in late Qing China, also compared Guangzhou and Shanghai:

> At Shanghai, the other important centre of foreign trade and residence, other conditions prevailed. There full security was enjoyed by foreigners, and they were free to visit without molestation the country round about, the only limitation being that they should be able to return within the same day.[3]

Shanghai had a more shallow tradition of Sino-foreign communication than Ningbo and Guangzhou. It also had a smaller population of overseas Chinese than Fuzhou and Amoy. However, the city had an advantageous geographical location. Situated in the mouth of the River Yangtze, Shanghai was highly accessible from both the inland and the capital. Moreover, Shanghainese were more moderate for the foreigners to get along with them. All these factors contributed to the rise of Shanghai as the residence of Westerners as well as the center of Western learning in China.

The dissemination of Western learning was in these ports mainly through the publication of books and journals, as well as the establishment of schools by the missionaries.

Hong Kong and Guangzhou: a New Page of Dissemination of Western Learning

The population of Hong Kong had a stable growth after its opening. The small island had a small population of 7,450 in 1841, yet it increased to 12,361 after a year, and it reached 119,321 in 1861. The rising population, which was caused by the influx of Chinese and the arrival of Westerners, accelerated the transformation of Hong Kong from a fishing island to a Europeanized metropolis. The London Missionary Society relocated its Far East headquarters from Malacca to Hong Kong. Churches were found in various parts of the Victorian City, such as the Queen's Road, the Central Market, the Mid-Levels, and as far as Cheung Chau Island. Several of these historical churches are still there now, including The Chinese Union, Basel Mission, and Berlin Missionary Society. Missionaries who had been active in Southeast Asia moved to Hong Kong for either temporary or permanent settlement as well. To name a few, they were K. F. A. Gutzlaff, John Lewis Shuck[4], Issachar Jacob Roberts, S. R. Brown, E. C. Bridgman, B. Hobson, W. Lockhart, William Charles Milne, D. Abeel, William Jones Boone, Walter

Macon Lowrie, and William Henry Cumming. The missionaries spared no effort in organizing schools in Hong Kong. For example, the Anglo-Chinese School, the Morrison Education Society School, the Wang Ngai College (1842) by Shuck, the Baptist Girl's School (1843) by Madam Shuck, the Kung Li School (1843) of the American Board of Commissioners for Foreign Missions, the St. Paul Boys' College (1843) and the Diocesan Girls' School (1860) of the Anglican Church, and the Ying Wa Girl's School (1846) of the London Missionary Society.

Publication of religious materials and scientific titles began in the British colony following the relocation of the Malacca Press of the London Missionary Society. Missionaries planned for the editing of *The Bible* (Chinese edition) and the publication of religious materials since August 1843. The author had made statistics of the Western publications in Hong Kong from 1843 to 1860. Among the 60 titles, 37 belonged to religious brochures, such as the *Important Doctrine of Resurrection* (*Fuhuo yaozhi* 復活要旨), the annotated *Genesis* (*Chuangshizhuan zhushi* 創世傳注釋), *A Short Biography of Joseph* (*Yuese jilüe* 約瑟紀略), and the annotated *New Testament*. The remaining 23 titles included textbooks, dictionaries, annals, and journals that mentioned Western science and culture. Representative non-religious publications would be introduced in the followings publications.

Sino-Western Almanac

Published annually from 1843 to 1865, the *Sino-Western Almanac* (*Huafan hehe tongshu* 華番和合通書) documented important political, economic, social, and religious affairs in China and the West according to both the Chinese and Gregorian Calendars. It also attached maps and a list of the treaty terms between the Qing court and the Western powers. Dyer Ball, an American missionary, served as the chief editor of the almanac from 1843 to 1853, and from 1858 to 1859.[5] John Booth French took up the editing during 1854 to 1857. And the issue of the almanac fell to Daniel Vrooman since 1860, a missionary from the American Board of Commissioners for Foreign Missions.

Chinese Serial

Financed by the Morrison Education Society and printed by the Anglo-Chinese College Press, the *Chinese Serial* (*Xiaer guanzhen* 遐邇貫珍) had published 33 issues from September 1853 to May 1856. W. H. Medhurst, Charles Batten Hillier, and James Legge had been the publishers of the journal, but most of the work fell to Wong Shing, who was responsible for copywriting, translation, and general publication affairs. Medhurst founded the journal to enhance Sino-Western cultural exchange and to establish a cordial relationship between the East and the West.[6]

Fig. 4.1 ***Chinese Serial*** **published by the Anglo-Chinese College Press**

一千八百五十三年八月朔旦　第壹號

遐邇貫珍

香港中環英華書院印送

每號收回紙墨錢十五文

Fig. 4.2 Portrait of James Legge, publisher of the ***Chinese Serial***

This journal published articles of a wide range of topics, including Chinese and Western science, geography, politics, astronomy, calendar, medical science, commerce, journalism, and religion. Articles on humanity subjects included "The Rise of the Western World (August 1853)," "A Short History of Hong Kong (August 1853)," "The Origin of Western Trade (October 1853)," "The Political Institution of the United Kingdom (October 1853)," "A Short History of Hawaii

(November 1853)," "A Short History of the United Kingdom (September 1855)," and "The Political Institution of the United States (February 1854)." Articles on Science included "On Topography (September 1853)," "The Production of the Fire Turbine (September 1853)," "On Comets (October 1853)," "On the Spinning of the Earth (December 1853)," "On Geology (March 1854)," "A Complete Discourse on Biology (November 1854)," and "On Psychology (November 1855)."

The Anglo-Chinese College Press issued 3,000 copies of the journal. The 15-cent magazine was marketable in Mainland China, attracting people from various social classes. The journal, however, had only a few Chinese readers in Hong Kong.[7]

Complete Books on Mathematical Method

Compiled by Edward Theophilus Moncrieff during his teaching in the St. Paul Boys' College, the *Complete Books on Mathematical Method* (*Suanfa quanshu* 算法全書) taught basic arithmetic, fractions, decimal fractions, and ratios. It was also attached with sample questions. This book was published in 1852, two years after Moncrieff's arrival in Hong Kong. It was the first Western mathematics textbook published in Chinese.

New Treatise of Geography

The 19-page *New Treatise of Geography* (*Dili xinzhi* 地理新志) was published in 1855 by Wilhelm Lobscheid, a British missionary working in Hong Kong and Guangzhou since May 1848. This book mentioned the structure of the earth and its spinning, the changing day and night, and Spain and Portugal. It also included non-geographical discussion such as the doctrine of Buddhism and the production of the fire turbine. Lobscheid criticized previous geography reference works as uninformative in the preface, but it seemed that he also failed to provide better explanations.

Elementary Lessons in the Circle of Knowledge

Elementary Lessons in the Circle of Knowledge (*Zhihuan qimeng shuke chubu* 智環啟蒙塾課初步) was compiled by J. Legge during his teaching in the Anglo-Chinese College. Written in both Chinese and English, the 55-page textbook mentioned a wide range of subjects, including biology, political affairs, trade, environment, catering, and 24 others. This book was first published in 1855, and it was reprinted in 1864. The book was later introduced to Japan as a textbook and was published in 1867 by Edo Kaibutsusha.

For other non-religious titles published in Hong Kong, refer to table 4.1.

Table 4.1 Non-religious titles published in Hong Kong (1843–1860)

Publishing year	Book title	Author	Page number
1851	*The Encyclopedia of China and the United Kingdom*	J. Legge	9
1855	*Essential Notes for Cantonese Learners*	John Chalmers	33
1857	*Thousand Character Text*	W. Lobscheid	—
	A Primer in Verse		17
1858	*Notes about Migration to the United States*	J. Legge	18
1859	*Anglo-Cantonese Dictionary*	J. Chalmers	161
1860	*Idioms in the Four Books*	W. Lobscheid	31

Missionaries' activities, such as the publication of religious booklets, the opening of schools, and the provision of free medical service, were witnessed in Guangzhou, already an evangelic base in China before its formal opening. Despite the Chinese' hostility to foreigners after the opening of Guangzhou, the missionaries flocked to the city to expand their business. B. Hobson established the Kum-le-fow Hospital in 1848 with the assistance of several Chinese converts, such as Leung Fa, Liang Guichen, Lu Tingshan, and Zhou Qintang. Andrew Patton Happer (1818–1894) from the American Presbyterian Church also established a boys' school and a girls' school in 1850 and 1853, respectively. This was the beginning of modern education in Guangzhou.[8]

From 1843 to 1860, the missionaries published 42 titles of Chinese books and journals. There were 29 religious titles, such as *On the Crucifixion of Jesus Christ* (*Yesu ding shizijia lun* 耶穌釘十字架論), the annotated *Matthews*, the selected *Holy Bible*, and the annotated *Acts of the Apostles*. Several of the science titles published in Guangzhou would be introduced in the following publications.

A Brief Discourse on Geography

Published in 1859 by George Pierce, the 33-page *A Brief Discourse on Geography* (*Dili lüelun* 地理略論) included basic knowledge of world geography. Pierce, the Chinese representative of the British Methodist Church, compiled the book with reference to the *Universal Geography* (*Dili quanzhi* 地理全志) by W. Muirhead.

A Short Discourse on Astronomy

A Short Discourse on Astronomy, together with *A New Discourse on the Human Body* and *Natural Philosophy and Natural History* (*Bowu xinbian* 博物新編) were the three most representative works of B. Hobson. The 25-page book included 26 chapters that covered a wide range of topics of celestial operations and astronomical phenomena, such as the structures of various planets, the comets, the satellites, the movement of the Sun and the Earth, the eclipse, and the tides. This book was significant in three aspects: first, it introduced the latest developments of Western astronomy up to 1840s — for instance, the discovery of the Uranus in 1781 by Herschel and Neptune by Le Verrier in 1846. Second, it recognized the achievements of Copernicus and Galileo. Unlike the Jesuit missionaries in the late Ming Dynasty who avoided introducing the concept of heliocentric, the Protestant missionaries explained the solar-center theory systematically. They also openly criticized the Church's persecution to the astronomers.[9] Third, it opposed superstitious belief of the Chinese. The comet was commonly considered as a symbol of drought or war to the Chinese, yet Hobson explained the shooting star was actually influenced by solar radiation. Hobson also emphasized Chang's the goddess of Moon, her companion woodcutter Wu Gang, and the Jade rabbit were only imaginary residences of the Moon in the Chinese mythology. Published in 1849, this book was the first astronomy publication in modern China.[10]

Fig. 4.3 *Natural Philosophy and Natural History* and its Japanese edition

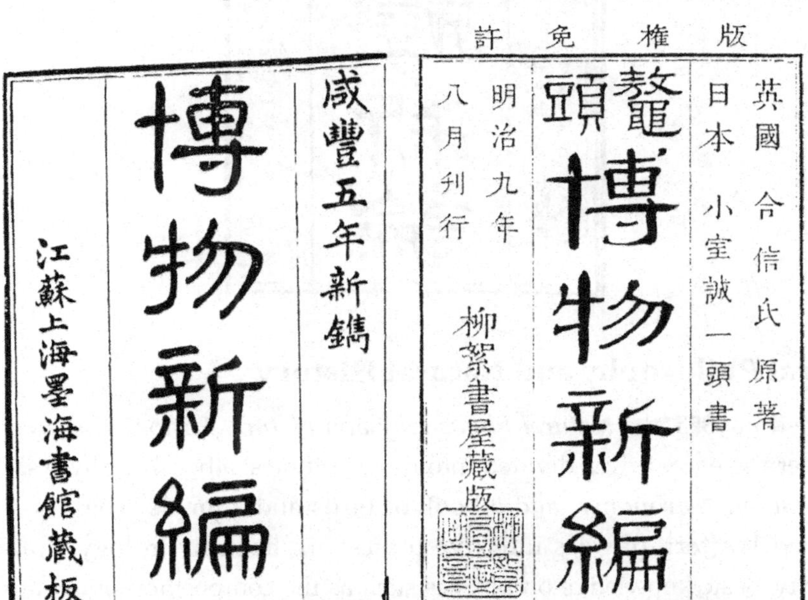

A New Discourse on the Human Body

Published in 1851, the 99-page *A New Discourse on Human Body* was the first Chinese reference work on Western anatomy. This book had three volumes that explained bones and muscles, organs, veins, and nerves. It attached diagrams of the the digestive system, respiratory system, circulatory system, urinary system, endocrine system, nervous system, and the reproduction system.

Western medical knowledge had been introduced to China through Western Views on the Human Body by J. Terrenz in the late Ming period. The book by Terrenz, however, had limited influence due to the unpopularity of Western medicine among the public. The publication of *A New Discourse on the Human Body* in 1851, when the Chinese had been familiar with Western medicine, had greater success, particularly in Guangzhou, where the citizens were used to visit Western hospitals and clinics. Feng Ye, the Governor-general of Guangzhou, copied eight diagrams from the book and posted them in his office. He also reprinted the book and distributed it to the local citizens for free.[11]

Fig. 4.4 ***A New Discourse on the Human Body***

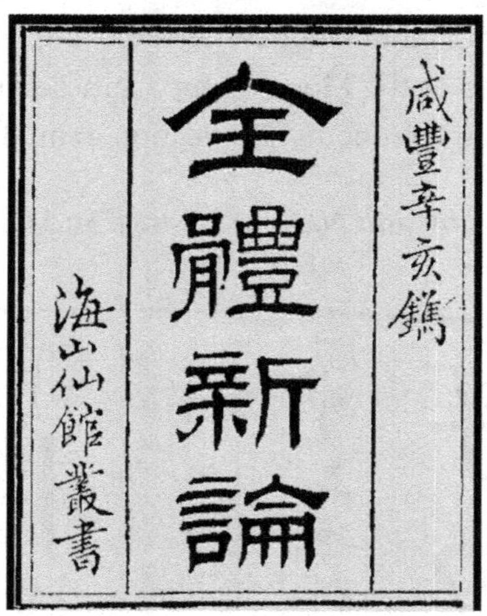

Natural Philosophy and Natural History

Published in 1855, the *Natural Philosophy and Natural History* was a collection of Western science. It was divided into three volumes: a book of physics, *A Short Discourse on Astronomy*, and a book of birds and animals. The first volume classified Western physics into five topics: air, heat, hydrology, optics, and electricity. Basic knowledge on physics such as the composition of air, the law of conservation of energy, the concept of gravity, the features and the application of heat energy, the composition and combination of water, the mirage, the reflection of light, the transmission of electricity, and the 56 elements were introduced. It also clarified the superstitious belief of will-o'-the-wisp, which was traditionally regarded as the ghostly fire to the Chinese. The third volume explained commonly seen animals in China, including monkey, elephant, hippopotamus, tiger, leopard, dog, bear, horse, camel, whale, and eagle. It also mentioned the latest research achievements of zoology in the West, such as the classification of animals.

Not all the knowledge in the *Natural Philosophy and Natural History* was new to the Chinese. For instance, Ji Xiaonan, the greatest scholar of the reign of Qianlong, had already realized that the will-o'-the-wisp was due to the interaction between phosphorus from corpus and the air.[12] However, the publication of the book still aroused a general interest in conducting scientific experiments. Xu Shou, a technician in the Anqing Arsenal, had a test on friction and produced a small steam machine.[13]

Fig. 4.5 Portrait of Xu Shou, a technician in the Anqing Arsenal and a late Qing scientist

Hobson's collection was popular not only in China, but also in Japan. The Japanese scholars considered the collection Western classics and studied the books in detail. *A New Discourse on Human Body* was translated by Ishikuro Atsushi and published by the Seigendō in 1874. *Natural Philosophy and Natural History* was translated by Komuro Seiichi and published by Ryūjo shooku in 1876.

Other non-religious titles published in Guangzhou included the *Selected Ancient Teachings* (*Guxun zuoyao* 古訓撮要, 1856) by Hobson, *On Chills and Enterocele* (*Lun faleng xiaochangshan liangzheng* 論發冷小腸疝兩症, 1859) and *On Special Illness* (*Qizheng lüeshu* 奇症略述, 1860) by John Glasgow Kerr, and *Good Medicine for Household* (*Jiayong liangyao* 家用良藥, 1860) by I. J. Roberts.

Fuzhou and Amoy: the Early Days after Opening

Fuzhou and Amoy, the two major cities in Fujian Province, were home to the majority of overseas Chinese in Southeast Asia. Prior to the opening of China, the Fujian natives flocked to Malacca, Singapore, Batavia, and Manila to strive for a better job and thus a better life. They were the first group of Chinese that the missionaries encountered. Through the establishment of Chinese schools that used the Hokkien dialect as the medium of instruction, the missionaries acquired experience in the command of the dialect and in getting along with the Fujian natives. Being confident to secure a foothold in Fuzhou and Amoy, the missionaries soon arrived at the Fujian cities for evangelic missions after the Opium War.

Fuzhou was formally opened on July 3, 1944. The first foreign visitor to Fuzhou after its opening was Stephen Johnson, a missionary of the American Board of Commissioners.[14] During 1846 to 1852, Johnson pioneered the establishment of the Fuzhou diocesan, laying a good foundation for latter evangelic missions. Following Johnson's arrival, several American missionaries also started working at Fuzhou. These missionaries included Judson Dwight Collins, Robert Samuel Maclay, Justus Doolittle, Lyman Birt Peet, Caleb Cook Baldwin, William Welton, and S. Livingstone Baldwin.

J. D. Collins (1822–1852), who belonged to the Methodist Episcopal Church, was dispatched to China after his graduation from the Michigan University. After arriving at Fuzhou in February 1846, he cooperated with Moses Clark White, another missionary of the Methodist Church, to establish a boys' school. Collins soon returned to the United States due to poor health.

R. S. Maclay (1824–1907), also a missionary from Collins' church, opened a boys' school in 1856 and the Yuying Middle School in 1859. During 1872 to 1881, Maclay was dispatched to Japan to assist the evangelic missions. After returning to Fuzhou, he established the Anglo-Chinese College (Heling), which had nurtured numerous celebrities including Lin Sen, the third President of the Republic of China; Hou Te-pang, a chemist and a member of the Chinese Academy of Sciences; Chen Daisun, an economist and the head of Department of Economics of the Peking University; and Chen Jingrun, a mathematician and the inventor of the Chen's Theorem. Maclay also published four religious publications.

J. Doolittle (1824–1880) of the American Congregational Church arrived at China in 1850.[15] He and his wife established boys' and girls' boarding schools — the latter Foochow College and the Wen Shan Girls' School (also Ponasang Girls' School). From 1853 to 1858, Doolittle published 25 titles of religious materials and science books—the most publications among his colleagues in Fuzhou. His representative work, the *Social Life of the Chinese* (*Huaren de shehui shenghuo* 華人的社會生活), helped readers understand the life in Fuzhou during the early days of the opening of the country.

L. B. Peet had worked in Singapore since 1839 before arriving at Fuzhou in 1847. He published four religious publications in the Fuzhou dialect up to 1860. *The New Testament* (in the Fuzhou dialect) amounted to 207 pages in its revised edition and was influential in the city. C. C. Baldwin, who arrived at Fuzhou in 1848, also published four religious booklets written in the Hokkien dialect. W. Welton (1817–1858), who belonged to the Church Mission Society, arrived at Fuzhou in May 1850. Before leaving Fuzhou to Shanghai in 1856, Welton opened a pharmacy and a clinic, as well as published two titles — *On the Prohibition of Opium Smoking* (*Quanjie yapian lun* 勸戒鴉片論) and *The New Testament* (in Fuzhou dialect). S. L. Baldwin (1835–1902), a missionary of the Methodist Episcopal Church, arrived at Fuzhou in 1858 and returned to the United States in 1861. During his brief stay at the city, he founded a journal, *Chinese Recorder* (*Jiaowu zazhi* 教務雜誌). His wife opened a girls' school in the city as well.

Table 4.2 Non-religious titles published in Fuzhou (1843–1860)

Publishing year	Book title	Author	Page number
1853	*On the Prohibition of Opium Smoking*	J. Doolittle	10
1854	*Catechism of Astronomy*		23
1855	*Discourse on Ma-tsoo-po*		6
	On the Hanshi and Ching Ming Festival		6
	On the Watchmaker Analogy		10
1856	*On the Prohibition of Opium Smoking*	W. Welton	10
	Brilliant Opinion on Gambling	J. Doolittle	7
1857	*Additional Law on Business*		—
	The Encyclopedia of China and the West		36
	A Brief Explanation of the World Map		2

(Cont'd)

Publishing year	Book title	Author	Page number
1858	*Disquisition on Human Nature*		6
	Disquisition on Slander		3
	The Causes of Poverty of the Chinese		3
	Disquisition on Filial Piety		6

Source: Lin Liqiang 林立強, "Meiguo chuanjiaoshi Lu Gongming yu wanqing Fujian shehui" 美國傳教士盧公明與晚清福建社會 (An American Missionary Justus Doolittle and the Society in Fujian in the Late Qing Period), Doctor diss., Fujian Normal University, 2004.

Before the formal opening of Amoy on November 2, 1843, missionaries D. Abeel and W. J. Boone had established a base on Gulangyu Island, preparing for latter evangelic activities. Having mastered the Hokkien dialect during their stay in Southeast Asia, the two American missionaries selected Amoy as their destination. W. H. Cumming, another American, arrived at Amoy in January 1844. Boone soon returned to the United States due to personal reasons, while both Abeel and Cumming settled in Amoy. Abeel and Cumming successfully befriended with Xu Jiyu, the Administration Commissioner of the Fujian Province. Xu, a man with profound knowledge, soon realized that China's defeat in the Opium War was a result of its prolonged isolation towards the Western world. The coming of Abeel and other missionaries opened Xu to global affairs, helping Xu to complete his representative *A Short Account of the Maritime Circuit*. Xu frequently visited Abeel, asking him about world history and geography. Abeel was patient in explaining the global situation to Xu, showing him world maps labeled with Chinese names of places. Abeel also presented several religious booklets to Xu, but he soon found that Xu was more interested in current affairs than the "truth of the heaven."[16] Xu particularly described his learning from Abeel:

> In the 23rd year of the reign of Daoguang, [I] was appointed to a station in Amoy. [I] encountered an American David Abeel, an experienced and knowledgeable man of the Western country. [Abeel] can command the Hokkien dialect. [He] brought a map, which was drawn in detail. Unfortunately, [I] am illiterate, soI traced about ten maps, visiting Abeel to ask about those maps. [I] had a basic idea on the names of the countries, but [I] cannot remember all of them in detail due to limited time.[17]

Xu also mentioned Cumming in his book, appreciating his profound knowledge and the establishment of the hospital.

Fig. 4.6 Portrait of David Abeel, a missionary active in Fujian

Fig. 4.7 Portrait of Xu Jiyu, the Governor-general of Fujian

The opening of Amoy attracted several other missionaries who had been working in Hong Kong and Southeast Asia. Elihu Doty (1809–1864), an American who left Borneo for Amoy, published several religious materials in the Amoy dialect, such as the *Gospel of John* and the *Thirteen Village Sermons* (*Xiangxun shisanze* 鄉訓十三則). He also compiled the *Anglo-Chinese Manual of the Amoy Dialect* (*Fanyi yinghua xiakang yuhui* 翻譯英華廈腔語匯) — the first dictionary that Romanized the Amoy dialect. William Chalmers Burns (1815–1868), also an American, came to Amoy from Hong Kong. He published *The Pilgrim's Progress* (*Tianlu lichen* 天路歷程) and the *Collections of the Selected Psalm* (*Shenshi hexuan* 神詩合選) in Amoy in 1853. He later moved to Shanghai and Niuzhuang to continue his evangelic missions. John Stronach (1810–1888), who belonged to the London Missionary Society, arrived at Amoy in 1844. During 1847 to 1852, he visited Shanghai, attempting to preach to the Fujian immigrants in Shanghai. He returned to Amoy in 1853. His brother, Alexander Stronach (1800–1878) was also dispatched to Singapore, Hong Kong, and eventually Amoy. In 1850, he established the Anglo-Chinese College (Amoy) that admitted local Chinese students for free.

During 1843 to 1860, missionaries in Amoy published 13 titles. Apart from the *Anglo-Chinese Manual of the Amoy Dialect* by E. Doty and the *Phonetic Transcription of the Amoy Dialect* (*Xiamenhua pinxie shu* 廈門話拼寫書, 1852) by John van Nest Talmage, the remaining 11 titles were religious booklets. Although Amoy had the least amount of publications among the five treaty ports, the significance of the establishment of th relationship between Xu and the missionaries on the dissemination of Western learning should not be underestimated.

Ningbo: The Chinese and American Holy Classic Book Establishment

Daniel Jerome MacGowan (1814–1893) was the first missionary who stepped on the soil of Ningbo after the city's formal opening on January 1, 1844. The physician-missionary of the American Baptist Church had no understanding of both local dialect and customs. MacGowan's early days in Ningbo were difficult, until he rented several rooms in the north of the city as both residence and clinic. Edward Clemens Lord (1817–1887), also from the Baptist Church, was dispatched to Ningbo to assist MacGowan. He moved MacGowan's clinic to Hongqiao Bridge, where was closer to the local settlements.

In addition to provide medical service, missionaries established schools for the local children. Mary Ann Aldersey, a British citizen who arrived at Ningbo from Batavia, established the Ningpo Girls' Academic in 1844. The first girls' school in China which taught Chinese language, English, mathematics, needlework, and religious studies. The school had almost no students because girls did not need to be educated under the traditional Chinese belief. With Aldersey's painstaking persuasion, the school admitted 15 girls in 1845, and the number of students reached 40 in 1852. Aldersey moved to Australia for the rest of her life due to illness, while the Ningpo Girls' Academic later combined with another girls' school of the American Presbyterian Church. The Presbyterian Church also opened The Ningpo Boys' Academic in 1845 with the help of Divie Bethune McCartee,[18]

W. A. P. Martin, John Livingston Nevius and his wife. Both the number of students admitted in the girls' and the boys' schools had a stable increase, and the schools successfully converted more than a half of the Chinese pupils.[19]

If publication were the highlight among the evangelic activities in Ningbo, The Chinese and American Holy Classic Book Establishment (*Huahua shengjing shufang* 華花聖經書房) would have been the highlight among the presses.[20] Established in September 1845 by Richard Cole, a man with experience in printing, and a missionary of the American Presbyterian Church, The Chinese and American Holy Classic Book Establishment published 105 books and magazines — the second highest number of publications among the treaty ports.

The Chinese and American Holy Classic Book Establishment originated from the Presbyterian Press in Macau, whose scale was too small to deal with the increasing missionaries of the church. Having found Macau also too small for the press to expand its business, the Presbyterian Church moved the press to Ningbo. Cole and his wife brought along the printing types purchased from the Singapore Press of the London Missionary Society. After arriving at Ningbo, the Cole couple started preparing for the opening of the new press. Cole even produced another set of copper printing types. The management of the press lied in the publishing committee formed by Presbyterian missionaries. The first committee, which lasted from 1845 to 1847, was formed by Cole, W. M. Lowrie,[21] and Michael Simpson Culbertson.[22] Following Cole's resignation, the second committee was formed by Augustus Ward Loomis[23] and D. B. McCartee. The third committee was organzied after Loomis' return to the United States due to unsatisfactory health. Moses Stanley Coulter,[24] President of the third committee, died on December 12, 1852 in Ningbo. The management fell to Richard Quarterman Way.[25]

Among the 105 titles published by The Chinese and American Holy Classic Book Establishment, 86 titles were religious materials, including the philosophy, rituals, and history of Christianity, and a collection of psalms. The remaining 20 titles covered a wide range of subjects, such as astronomy, geography, history, economy, customs, moral education, and language. Several non-religious titles published by the Sino-American press will be discussed in the following section.

Reference works of navigation

The 35-page *Navigators' Golden Needle* (*Hanghai jinzhen* 航海金針), the work of D. J. MacGowan, was published in 1853. This book, whose target readers were the Chinese fishermen according to the preface, included basic knowledge about typhoons. It also included plenty of diagrams. *A Manual of Compass* (*Zhinanzhen* 指南針) was compiled by Thomas Hall Hudson and was published in 1849. Hudson (1800–1876), the first missionary of the British Baptist Church visiting China, published 14 titles. *A Manual of the Compass* was the only non-religious book among his publications.

Reference works of astronomy

Compiled also by MacGowan and published in 1852, the *Plate of the Solar Eclipse with Explanation* (*Rishi tushuo* 日食圖說) recorded the solar eclipses on December 11, 1852, as seen from Beijing, Shanghai, Ningbo, Fuzhou, Amoy, Guangzhou, and Hong Kong. *An Encyclopedia for Safety Adventure* (*Ping'an tongshu* 平安通書), an annually published reference work for Ningbo fishermen, included information on navigation and astronomy, such as the solar system, sundials, the eclipses, climate, tides, and the Western calendar. This book also introduced the latest development on Western astronomy, for example, Le Verrier's discovery of Neptune as the eighth planet of the solar system in 1846.[26] This book was widely quoted in Wei Yuan's *Illustrated Gazetteer of the Maritime Countries*, one of the earliest Chinese works on the geography of the modern world.

Another informative work was the *Exploration of a World Map* (*Diqiu tushuo* 地球圖說) by R. Q. Way. Published in 1848 and reprinted in 1856, this geography treatise covered a wide range of topics, including the structure and the spinning of the earth, the continents, the oceans, Asia, Europe, Africa, Australia, and Americas. It also contained diagrams of the countries' flags, steamships, trains, and various rare animals. *The Exploration of a World Map*, written by a Westerner, was supposed to be a more reliable account of the West. It was thus frequently quoted in the *Illustrated Gazetteer of the Maritime Countries* and widely used as a textbook in Japan.[27]

Catechism of Astronomy (*Tianwen wenda* 天文問答) was published by A. P. Happer, an American missionary stationed in Guangzhou who had his book printed in Ningbo, as the city had already emerged as the publication center of the Presbyterian Church since 1840s. This book, written in a question-and-answer format, had 22 chapters and 20 questions in each chapter. The chapters covered: on the structure of the earth; on the division of zones; on the spherical shape of the earth and its status as a planet, on the objects in the sky; on the waxing and waning of the moon, its glow, and the lunar eclipse; on the solar eclipse and the day-and-night change; on the calculation of years and months; on the sun and the appearance of the rainbow; on rain and the emergence of rivers; on clouds and dews; on the sun and the wind; on the benefits of wind; on the benefits of the sun; on gravity; on the attraction force of objects; on the measurement of the attraction force; on the six natures of objects;[28] on the elements of objects; and on the benefits of studying.

This book not only introduced knowledge about astronomy, but it also covered information of geography and physics. This book, together with *A Short Discourse on Astronomy* by B. Hobson, was one of the earliest reference works of modern astronomy in Chinese. Explanations about the structure of the universe, the law of gravitation, the causes of the eclipses, and the formation of wind, rain, and comets enlightened both the Chinese scholars and the public.

This book was also credited for the use of simple language to explain difficult scientific knowledge. For instance, the incompatible nature of objects was written as:

> Question: What is the first nature of an object?
> Answer: It is incompatible.
> Question: Is there a needle inside the paper if we stab a needle into the paper?
> Answer: No. The needle is in the crack of the paper.
> Question: Why the needle and the paper are not at the same area?
> Answer: It is because of the incompatible nature of the needle and the paper. Therefore, no needle is on paper, and vice versa.[29]

The compiler also used needles and trees, stones and water, and air and water inside a bottle as examples to demonstrate the incompatible nature of objects.

Miscellaneous reference works

There were only two history titles published in Ningbo — the *Narrative Record of the Countries of the World, Past and Present* by K. F. A. Gutzlaff and the *Selected Narrative Record of the Countries of the World* (*Wanguo gangjian* 萬國綱鑒) by D. B. McCartee. Gutzlaff's work was a reprinted version based on the first edition published in Singapore in 1838, while McCartee's work, published in 1850 with 132 pages, was an excerpt from Gutzlaff's work.

Published by Henry V. Rankin in 1857, the 92-page *A Guide to Ningbo Dialect* (*Ningbo tuhua chuxue* 寧波土話初學) was the only teaching material of language published in Ningbo. This book introduced Chinese geography and history in the Ningbo dialect with Romanized phonetic transcription — seemingly a manual for missionaries to Ningbo. Rankin (1825–1863), a missionary from New Jersey, the United States, was dispatched to China in 1848. He soon started his evangelic mission after arriving at Ningbo in August 1849. He was skilled in translating and compiling religious materials in Ningbo dialect, such as *The Truth of Gospel* (*Fuyin zhendi* 福音真諦) and the *Collection of the Odes* (Zhanmeishi 讚美詩).

Compiled by D. J. MacGowan and published in 1851, the 62-page *Philosophical Almanac in Chinese* (*Bowu tongshu* 博物通書) was divided into three sections: "The Three-word Primer of the True Interpretation" that explained Christian teachings by Confucian doctrines, the main content that introduced the nature of electricity and the operation of the telegraph (with 44 diagrams), and the Gregorian calendar. This book began with an advertisement of his clinic:

> MacGowan, a Western doctor, resided in the Aihua Hall — outside the North Gate of Ningbo, Zhejiang Province. [MacGowan] preached and encouraged people, provided medical service and medicine, and hated harmful opium the most. Feel free to visit me for any assistance.[30]

MacGowan compiled this book to introduce the Western communication method, as he considered the telegraph essential for both government operation and daily use. This book was the first reference work on the telegraph in Chinese.

MacGowan also issued the *Chinese and Foreign Gazette* after May 1854, a biweekly magazine with four pages per issue initially and then a monthly journal since 1856. MacGowan established the *Chinese and Foreign Gazette* to broaden people's horizons and to admonish people to abandon any bad habit. Articles of the magazine covered a wide range of topics — from current affairs to religion, science, and literature. Following MacGowan's departure from Ningbo, the publication of the *Chinese and Foreign Gazette* fell to Elias B. Inslee, a missionary from the American Presbyterian Church who started working in Ningbo from 1856 to 1861.

Other non-religious titles published in Ningbo during 1843 to 1860 included *Six Talks on Gambling* (*Dubo minglun liujiang* 賭博明論六講 , 1847) by W. Milne, [31] *Six Talks on the Abandonment of Opium Smoking* (*Yapian liujie*, 1847) by I. Tracy,[32] *On Lying* (*Lun shuohuang* 論說謊 , 1848) by D. B. McCartee, *On the Worship of Ancestors during the Ching Ming Festival* (*Qingming jisao fenmu lun* 清明祭掃墳墓論 , 1848) by T. H. Hudson, and *The Pilgrim's Progress* (*Luren risheng* 旅人入勝 , 1855) by Robert Henry Cobbold.[33]

Shanghai: Rolling in the Sea of Ink

Shanghai formally opened on November 17, 1843 — the earliest among the five treaty ports. The northern-most port city, Shanghai was also deeply influenced by Western culture.

The city was originally a small county at the tip of the Yangtze River prior to its opening. It was less developed than the neighboring Ningbo, and it was not as brilliant as the picturesque Suzhou and Hangzhou. To the foreigners, however, these conditions meant more freedom from the local government and less resistance from the local residents. The number of foreigners registered in Shanghai reached 26 in 1843, and it increased to 50 in the next year. The foreign population had a drastic rise in the following decades. In the British and the American concessions alone, there were 569 foreign residents in 1860. The influx of foreigners was also evidenced by the number of foreign banks in Shanghai.

Missionaries were the earliest group of foreign visitors in Shanghai. Gutzlaff, the one who had travelled to plenty of coastal cities in China, visited Shanghai in 1831. Highly fascinated by the city, Gutzlaff, together with Hugh Hamilton Lindsay, the Secretary of the British East India Company, sought to establish a trading partnership between the United Kingdom and China. It was rejected by the Shanghai Circuit Intendant, who referred to the foreigner as a "barbarian" in his letter. Feeling humiliated, Gutzlaff argued with the Chinese governor, but the dispute ended with unsettled.

W. H. Medhurst and W. Lockhart (1811–1896) of the London Missionary Society were the earliest visitors to Shanghai after its opening. They were pioneers at introducing Western learning to Shanghai, directing the city towards the path of modernization. Medhurst had been working in Southeast Asia for more than two decades and had attended a seminar about the Chinese translation of The Bible in Hong Kong before heading to Shanghai. He arrived at the city in December 1843, settled outside the East Gate, relocated the Batavia Press to Shanghai, and renamed it as the London Missionary Society Mission Press (*Mohai shuguan* 墨海書館, literally "the press of the sea of ink"). W. Lockhart from Liverpool, the United Kingdom, worked as an intern in two hospitals in Dublin and London. After his graduation in 1833, he returned to Liverpool. He joined the London Missionary Society as a physician-missionary, and he was sent to China with Medhurst. The duo sailed along the African coasts, across the Indian Ocean, arriving at Batavia. Only Lockhart departed Southeast Asia two months later, heading to Macau, and taking over Dr. Parker's hospital. He returned to Batavia to help Medhurst after the outbreak of the Opium War. Lockhart arrived at Dinghai at Chusan, an offshore archipelago from Shanghai, after the British occupation of the island in 1840. He soon opened a hospital in Dinghai, providing free medical service. Following the British retreat from the Chusan Archipelago in the end of the Opium War, Lockhart headed to Macau, where he married Catherine Parkes. He visited Hong Kong after its concession to the United

Kingdom, helping in a hospital of the Medical Missionary Society of China. He returned to the Chusan Archipelago in June 1843 to resume the hospital's operation. He planned to move the hospital in Dinghai to Shanghai, which he found a more important port than the insular city. Approved by the London Missionary Society, the hospital in Dinghai was closed and a new hospital was opened in Shanghai in mid-February 1844. The new hospital, which was located near to the South Gate initially and was relocated to the north of the city, was the present-day Renji Hospital.

Following Medhurst and Lockhart, considerable missionaries flocked to Shanghai, including W. J. Boone, A. Wylie, W. C. Milne, J. Edkins, B. Hobson, J. Stronach, J. L. Shuck, Solomon Carpenter, William Muirhead, Tarleton P. Crawford, R. H. Gobbold, Griffith John, and others. These missionaries opened churches, established hospitals and schools, and published journals, making Shanghai the center for evangelic missions and the dissemination of Western learning.

Located in Medhurst's house outside the East Gate, the London Missionary Society Mission Press was the most influential organization of Western learning before 1860. The first floor of the two-storey building was the printing area, while the second floor was the residence of Medhurst. The annual rent of the building was 250 dollars. The press was moved to a 13.31-hecter site which originally belonged to Xu Caizhang on the Shandong Road in the British concession (also referred to as Maijiajuan by the locals). The annual rent of the site was 1,954.6 dollars.[34] Situated next to the Renji Hospital, the brick-and-wood building faced south and was 63 inches long and 33 inches wide. There were also various plantations that decorated the area with European elements.[35] The new press started its business in August 1846.

Most of the printing tools and machines that were transported from the Singapore Press via Hong Kong and Chusan Archipelago were damaged by flooding. Medhurst, his Dutch assistant William Veloberg, and a Chinese assistant Qiu Tiansheng thus did repairs for three months. There were three sources of the Chinese character types: the one casted by S. Dyer of the London Missionary Society, the one produced by the Indian Baptist Church at the request of K. F. A. Gutzlaff, and the one made in Berlin. Medhurst, who soon found that the types were inadequate for printing, hurried to carve 6,000 more big types and 25,000 small types. Having collected more than 100,000 types up to 1847, the press thus stopped making any types and it purchased the types from the Anglo-Chinese College Press since 1850 when necessary. The London Missionary Society Mission Press eventually started printing in summer 1844.[36] It printed 710,000, 222 million, and 263 million pages in 1844, 1845, and 1846, respectively. However, the old printing machine that required manual operation soon proved insufficient to meet the increasing demand of books. The press thus requested that the London Missionary Society purchase a new rotary printing press, which arrived at Shanghai in August 1847.[37] Most of the rotary printing machines were operated by manual or steam energy, but the one that the press used was a cow-pull device. The types were copper-made while the ink was a mixture of animal glue and kerosene.[38] With the use of the new printing machine, the London Missionary Society Mission Press printed 338 million pages within half-a-year — more than double the previous publication.

Medhurst was the first Director, the main contributor, and even the only worker of the London Missionary Society Mission Press during its early days of opening. Among the 17 titles published in the first three years, 16 titles were compiled by Medhurst. The arrival of a group of missionaries of the London Missionary Society to Shanghai since 1846 assisted in the running of the press. W. C. Milne, son of W. Milne, compiled religious materials published by the London Missionary Society Mission Press and assisted Medhurst in the translation of *The Bible*.[39] J. Stronach, who departed Amoy for Shanghai in May 1847, also assisted Milne in the translation of *The Bible*. After the translation *of The Old Testament* in 1853, he returned to Amoy. A. Wylie, who arrived at Shanghai on August 26, 1847, was particularly dispatched to China by the London Missionary Society to manage the press.[40] Works done during his stay in Shanghai, including the publication of *The Bible* and the translation of The Sequel of *Euclid's Elements and the Discourse on Astronomy* with Li Shanlan, was influential to the Chinese academic development.[41] W. Muirhead, who arrived in Shanghai together with A. Wyile, stayed in the city for the longest time and published the most books among the missionaries.[42] During his 53-year stay in Shanghai, he published 39 Chinese titles and three English titles, religious titles, *Universal Geography, and A General Gazetteer of the Great Britain* included. It seemed that he did not participate in the translation of *The Bible*. J. Edkins assisted Medhurst in his compilation of religious materials and management of the books after his arrival at Shanghai on September 2, 1848.[43] During his stay in the London Missionary Society Mission Press, he published both religious and scientific titles, including *The Correct Meaning of Buddhism* (*Shijiao zhengmiu* 釋教正謬), *A Summary of Christianity* (*Yesu jiaolüe* 耶穌教略), and *An Elementary Treatise on Mechanics* (*Zhongxue* 重學). He succeeded the post of Director of the London Missionary Society Mission Press after Medhurst had returned to the United Kingdom in 1856. He had been moved to the north prior to his return to Shanghai as a translator of the Customs.

In addition to the assistants from the London Missionary Society, the press employed Chinese scholars to cooperate with the missionaries in the translation of books. These scholars included Wang Changgui, Wang Tao, Li Shanlan, Guan Sifu, Zhang Fuxi, and others. They recorded the oral translation by the Westerners and edited the manuscripts. The London Missionary Society Mission Press was introduced in Guo Songtao's diary on March 15, 1856:

> Next, [I] visited the London Missionary Society Mission Press. Medhurst, a Western missionary, addressed himself as the Old Man of the Sea of Ink. The front-part of the building was a small chapel, while the inner room stored abundant books. Below the two windows were found two spheres — the celestial globe on the right and the globe on the left. Mr. Medhurst had an enormous amount of publications. Scholars who assisted Medhurst in his editorial works included Li Renshu from Haiyan and Wang Lanqing from Suzhou. Li, a man with profound knowledge, was an expert in trigonometry. Wang, who had an open mind, had a good character. [I] also found the *Compendium of Arithmetic* written by Wylie. Mr. Wylie, with a common appearance, was an expert in mathematics. Moreover, Edkins, a man with solid knowledge, was employed by Medhurst to manage the books.[44]

Most of the publications of the London Missionary Society Mission Press were Chinese titles. Among the 210 Chinese books, religious materials occupied a large proportion. The publication of the 33 non-religious titles began after the translation of *The Bible* in 1852. These titles, mainly edited by A. Wyile, B. Hobson, and W. Muirhead, covered a wide range of subjects, including astronomy, geography, botany, mathematics, physics, and medical studies. The press also published English books, which were written by Medhurst in the early days of operations. These titles included the Chinese Dialogues, the English and Chinese Dictionary, and others. Below are introduced several non-religious titles published by the London Missionary Society Mission Press.

Compendium of Arithmetic

Published in 1853 by A. Wylie, the two-volume *Compendium of Arithmetic* had 127 pages. The aim of the compilation was included in the preface of the book:

> I travelled to China from the Far West to preach the teachings of Jesus Christ. I also studied several subjects. Therefore, I compiled this book, the *Compendium of Arithmetic (with two volumes)*, to teach the students

in the school. Studying the easy topics first is similar to babies' learning to walk — from crawling to walking, and to running eventually. The publication of this book teaches only the crawling part. For runners, refer to the books of algebra and calculus.[45]

Compendium of Arithmetic, as suggested by its title, introduced elementary mathematical knowledge. Volume one explained arithmetic, fractions, and decimals, while volume two taught about ratios, roots, and logarithms. This book covered topics that were unmentioned in the *Essentials of Mathematics* published during the reign of Kangxi. However, the use of Arabic numbers and several arithmetical signs were unseen. This book was considered the most useful elementary reference work of Western mathematics. Liang Qichao praised the book as "a convenient guide for enlightenment,"[46] while Wang Tao borrowed the book from Gong Xiaogong to study mathematics on his own.[47] It was also adopted as a textbook for elementary schools.

The Sequel of Euclid's Elements

Published in 1857, the 401-page *Sequel of Euclid's Elements* included the remaining nine chapters translated by A. Wylie and Li Shanlan (the first six chapters were translated by Ricci and Xu Guangqi in the Late Ming period). Li recalled the translation process in the preface of the book:

> [I] arrived at Shanghai in 1852 to resume the unfinished works of Ricci and Xu (Guangqi) with a Westerner, Wylie. Mr. Wylie, an expert in astronomy and mathematics, was also experienced in Chinese. We started our works in June 1, translating a sample question daily. Work had been suspended due to my sitting for the civil examination, the outbreak of revolts, and my provision of corvée labor. The translation lasted four years.[48]

Hang Yingbi, a scholar from Songjiang, financed the publication of *The Sequel of Euclid's Elements*.[49] The printing plates, however, were destroyed during the wars of the Taiping Uprising. Li Shanlan visited Zeng Guofan, the governor-general of Jiangsu and Jiangxi by that time, stating the academic value of the book and seeking for assistance in its publication.[50] Amid a wave of expectation, *The Sequel of Euclid's Elements* was published in 1856. The classic of ancient Greek mathematics was completely introduced to China with the cooperation of Chinese and Western scholars, and the collaboration of the government and intellectuals. Having received the book, Wang Tao studied it night-and-day carefully and recommended the book to his friends. Wang also recognized the achievements of A. Wylie and Li, the translator of the sequel:

> Algebra was an important subject in the West. Since Ricci's arrival in China and the translation of the book with Xu Wending, the teaching was understood. The original book had fourteen volumes, so that [the incomplete translation] was regrettable. Mei Dingjiu indicated the final eight volumes were the essentials of the book...Now, a Western scholar Wylie and Li from Haining, feared not the obstacles and resumed the translation. [Their] achievements were comparable to Ricci and Xu.[51]

Elements of Algebra

Published in 1858, the 203-page *Elements of Algebra* was co-translated by A. Wylie and Li Shanlan with reference to the *Elements of Algebra* completed in 1835 by the British mathematician Augustus de Morgan (1806–1871). This book explained basic algebra, simultaneous equations, the law of index, logarithm and its application, and sequences. The translated edition featured the use of Chinese mathematical terms and signs. For example, the symbol " ⊥ " instead of the plus sign to denote addition, the character *tian* (天 , the sky) means the X-variation, the character *di* (地 , the earth) represents the Y-variation. The concept of imaginary numbers was introduced as well. For mathematical signs that had no Chinese correspondence, such as "√," " ∴ ," " ∵ ," and "∞," Western symbols were kept.

Elements of Analytical Geometry and of Differential and Integral Calculus

Published in 1868, the 298-page *Elements of Analytical Geometry and of Differential and Integral Calculus* was co-translated also by A. Wylie and Li Shanlan with reference to the work of the American mathematician Elias Loomis (1811–1889). Volumes one to nine of the book mentioned algebra and geometry, volumes 10 to 16 introduced calculus, and the last two volumes explained integrals. This book was the first reference work of advanced mathematics that established the translation of mathematical terms, such as coefficient (*xisu* 系數), function (*hansu* 函數), sequences (*jisu* 級數), constant (*changsu* 常數), variant (*biansu* 變數), differential calculus (*weifen* 微分), and integral (*jifen* 積分). Liang Qichao in his *Bibliography of Western Knowledge* commented on the content as "very difficult." And according to a missionary, Hong Rengan, King Gan of the Taiping Kingdom regime, was particularly interested in the *Elements of Analytical Geometry and of Differential and Integral Calculus*.[52]

Popular Treatise on Mechanics

Published in 1858, the 14-page *Popular Treatise on Mechanics* was translated by A. Wylie in oral and recorded by Wang Tao. This book began with the definition of gravity:

> The concept of gravity explains an extensive range of phenomena. Gravity, which is generated from the center of the earth, is found in every object. An object with a large volume and a higher mass is heavier, while an object with a smaller volume and a lower mass is lighter. The earth, which is larger than any objects on the planet, attracts all the objects to the core of the earth. The revolution and spinning of the planets, the flow of water and air, and the actions of humans, are all related to gravity...[One] will never master the use of machines if [one] cannot understand the concept of gravity.[53]

This book covered a wide range of topics, including the origin of the study of mechanics, sub-branches such as dynamics, statics, fluid mechanics, pneumatics, the lever theorem, the application of windlass and pulley, and concept of helix, and the relationships between mechanics and the earth, and mechanics between the gravity. It also included the research achievements of previous Western scientists, such as Archimedes, Galileo, Christiaan Huygens (1629–1695) the inventor of the pendulum clock, Newton, and Watt. This "simple yet clear"[54] reference work of mechanics was so significant that Wang Tao compiled this book in his *Collections of Western Learning* (*Xixue jicun* 西學輯存).

An Elementary Treatise on Mechanics

Published in 1859, the 226-page *An Elementary Treatise on Mechanics* was co-translated by J. Edkins and Li Shanlan with reference to the work of William Whewell (1795–1866). The translation of this book coincided with the translation of *The Sequel of Euclid's Elements*. As recalled by Li, "[I] translated the geometry book in the morning and the mechanics reference work in the evening. [The projects] lasted for two years and ended simultaneously."[55]

Li planned to publish the book after the completion of translation in 1855, but a fire in the Songjiang press suspended the printing. The book was reprinted in 1865 in Nanjing and several other places.

Record of the Solar Eclipse on November 1 in the 2nd Year of the Reign of Xianfeng

This record, originally published in the *North-China Herald*, contained the information about the solar eclipse on November 1, the 2nd year of the reign of Xianfeng (December 11, 1852) seen at various cities in China, including Beijing, Shanghai, Ningbo, Fuzhou, Amoy, Guangzhou, and Hong Kong. J. Edkins compiled the statistics and diagrams of the astronomical phenomena and published this record in Shanghai. This record was also translated in Ningbo by D. J. MacGowan (entitled as the *Plate of the Solar Eclipse with Explanations*).

Discourse on Astronomy

Published in 1859, the 361-page *Discourse on Astronomy* was co-translated by A. Wylie and Li Shanlan. This book, a translated work of the *Outlines of Astronomy* by John Herschel, was the third astronomy treatise that introduced to China since the publication of *Catechism of Astronomy* and *A Short Discourse on Astronomy* in 1849. Most of the topics that the book introduced, such as the structure of the earth, surveying, geology, celestial graphs, the apparent paths of the sun and the moon, motion of the planets, comets, perturbation, the elliptic orbit, stellar patterns, star clusters, the calendar, universal gravity, light, and sunspots, had been mentioned in the previous astronomy works. Only the translated terms had some variation. For instance, stellar, translated as *jingxing* (經星, the constant star) in *Catechism of Astronomy*, was renamed as *hengxing* (恆星, the fixed star), a term that is used at present. This book, a systematic reference work instead of an elementary manual, benefited the Chinese scholars who had been equipped with basic knowledge of Western astronomy. Its usefulness was irreplaceable.

This book included two prefaces written by A. Wylie and Li Shanlan, respectively. The two translators, based on their different academic backgrounds, had different concerns in their translation. Wylie traced the history of Western astronomy since the ancient time — from the geo-center concept of Ptolemy, the Tychonic system, and the heliocentric system of Copernicus:

> Back a very long time ago, Ptolemy claimed the earth as the center of the universe, with various layers of heaven surrounding the earth. Scholars who inherited Ptolemy's idea further suggested the presence of deferent and epicycle, complicating the theory. The astronomical devices of the latter generations were more precise, producing much accurate

> calculations that contradicted Ptolemy's observation. Copernicus thus raised a new theory, declaring the sun as the center with the earth and other planets revolving it. Tycho disagreed with Copernicus' idea, but [the idea] was proved trustworthy. Kepler, who concluded the three laws, confirmed Copernicus' idea. Newton moved a step further to studing Kepler's laws, making the heliocentric theory unchallengeable.[56]

Wylie also traced the development of various astronomical schools in ancient China, such as the spherical heaven, hemispherical heaven, and the shapeless universe, and compared the Chinese schools with the Western theories. According to Wylie, the resultant inaccuracy of Chinese astronomy theories lied in the imprecise and outdated devices. This conclusion was generally accepted by Chinese astronomers.

The development of Western astronomy was in fact a prolonged conflict between the Church and the scientists. Wylie, as a missionary, skillfully avoided responding to the challenge from the scientists. In introducing the ideas of Copernicus, Kepler, and Newton, the translator suggested the order of the universe lied in the power of the Creator:

> The Creator is omnipotent, omniscience, and omnipresence. Humans are tiny, but they benefit from the Creator. Our lives, our food and drink, and our clothes, are given by the Creator. To explain further, all the stars benefit from the Creator. I translated this book with Li, aiming to spread the message about the potency of the Creator and to arouse readers' interest to the observation of the sky.[57]

Wylie's preface demonstrated the reduced hostility of the Church towards science, but education as a method to proselytize was still practiced.

Li Shanlan also recognized the achievements of Copernicus, Kepler, and Newton in modern astronomy. His focus, however, lied in the Chinese scholars' discrimination towards Western astronomy. The heliocentric theory, which had been introduced to China during the reign of Qianlong through M. Benoist, had received harsh condemnation from the Chinese. For instance, Ruan Yuan, the author of the *Biographies of the Astronomers,* considered the theory of the movable earth as "heterodox."[58] Li spared no effort in criticizing the stubborn and ignorant astronomer, though he was also a respectable Confucian, arguing that those astronomers lacked precise observation while believing every teaching of the ancient classics. Through the preface, Li demonstrated the response from Chinese scholars towards Western astronomy, as well as his good characters as a scientist — independent thinking and truth seeking. Li Shanlan proudly presented his translation:

> There is no expert astronomer nowadays except me. The work I translated with Wylie is going to be published. The book will be considered as a classic by Chinese astronomers. Even Li Rui and Mei Wending would be astonished by my achievements.[59]

This book earned a high reputation in the academic circle in the late Qing period. Liang Qichao in his *Bibliography of Western Knowledge* suggested that readers "avoid hastily reading the book."[60]

The revised edition of the Discourse on Astronomy was published in 1874 by the Jiangnan Arsenal. Xu Jianyan the compiler included the new astronomy discoveries (up to 1871) in the book.

Fig. 4.8 Portrait of Li Shanlan and *Discourse on Astronomy*

Universal Geography

Published in 1854, the 365-page *Universal Geography* had 20 chapters. The author, W. Muirhead, referred to *A Short Account of the Maritime Circuit* by Xu Jiyu, the *Physical Geography* by Mary Somerville, *The Atlas of Physical*

Geography and the *Universal Geography* by T. Milner, and the *Elements or Physical Geography* by Hugo Reid. This book covered a wide range of topics of physical geography, such as the structure of the earth, the division of land and ocean, islands, mountains, earthquake and volcanic eruption, plateau, and oceans, several of which had been explained in the *Universal Miscellany*. In mentioning the countries, this book focused on the customs more than the history. France, for instance, was introduced as:

> The citizens have changing characters. [The men], always being combative, engaged themselves in clamor that disrupted discussions on politics. Unhappy faces never appear on the citizens who sing and dance for the whole day. The men and the women, regardless of their wealth, hesitate not to spend all of their money for glamorous clothes. [The citizens] are experienced in agriculture and craftsmanship, producing numerous devices such as watches and clocks. The scholars, who have undergone a painstaking learning process, are omniscience. Their works, similar to hearsay, contained evil ideas.[61]

The living condition in the United Kingdom was introduced as:

> [The citizens] are pure-minded, polite, and good at saving. The men are strong and the women are beautiful. Their multi-storey big houses are covered by tiles, coated by chalk, and decorated with wallpaper. The carpets are clean and collect no dusk. The clear glass windows are covered by curtains, making the rooms decorative. There is freedom of dating between the men and the women.[62]

Universal Geography was reprinted by The Chinese and American Holy Classic Book Establishment. It was also translated into Japanese and was reprinted by Sōkairō in 1858. Shionoya Tōin, a Confucian of the Edo Period who wrote the preface for the Japanese edition, found the book more systematic than the *Illustrated Gazetteer of the Maritime Countries* and more informative than *A Short Account of the Maritime Circuit* and praised the book as "a shortcut to the situation of the five continents."[63]

A General Gazetteer of Great Britain

Published by the London Missionary Society Mission Press in 1856, *A General Gazetteer of Great Britain* was translated from Thomas Milner's *The British*

Islands: Their Physical Geography and Natural History by W. Muirhead and edited by Jiang Dunfu. The first seven volumes traced the history of the United Kingdom — from its origin to the era of Queen Victoria. The last volume mentioned the current situation of the country, including the society, politics, culture, legal system, churches, taxation, education, military, agriculture, commerce, and geography. Having considered that the British political system might confuse the Chinese readers, Muirhead began his book with a general description of the existing political institutions in the preface:

> There are three political institutions in the world: first, absolute monarchy. The emperor exercises his sovereignty over rituals and war. The law protects the aristocrats instead of the lower class. Countries that practice absolute monarch include China, Russia, and France. Second, constitutional monarchy. Both the king and the people are subject to the law. Most of the European countries practice constitutional monarchy, the United Kingdom included. Third, democratic government. There is neither an emperor nor a king, but only a leader elected by the people. The term of service of the leader is limited. The United States is a democratic nation.[64]

Elements of Botany

Published in 1859, the 101-page *Elements of Botany* included 200 diagrams. The first seven volumes were co-translated by A. Williamson and Li Shanlan. J. Edkins took up the translation project from Williamson, who had returned to the United Kindom. This book was originally *An Outline of the Structure and Physiology of Plants* by J. Lindley. Volume one was an introduction, explaining the significance of the study of botany, the similarities and differences between plants and animals, and the geographical distribution of plants. Volume two explained the internal structure of plants. Volumes three to six mentioned the organs of plants, such as their roots, stems, leaves, flowers, and fruit. Volumes seven to eight introduced the classification of plants.

This book was the first translated work of modern botany in Chinese that explained the knowledge of Western botany systematically. To be specific, this book introduced the structures of plants that are visible only in the microscope, physiological function of the organs such as photosynthesis, transportation of nutrients by the stem, and gaseous exchange by the leaves, the classification of plants according to their production ways, and the distribution of plants in various latitudes.[65] The translation of the book was influential to the development of modern Botany in China and the establishment of scientific terms such as *zhiwuxue* (植物學 , Botany) and *ke* (科 , family).

The *Elements of Botany* was highly recommended as a manual of Western Botany. Liang Qichao in *A Research on Western Learning* praised the book:

> Zoology and Botany are the most useful scientific subjects that assist cattle rearing and cultivation. *The Elements of Botany* and *Illustrated Record of Plants* (*Zhiwu tushuo* 植物圖説) are the essential reference works.[66]

This book, considered as the most significant modern Botany reference work, was translated from Chinese to Japanese as *Elements of Botany: with Explanation from a Japanese Perspective* (*Shokubutsugaku wakai* 植物學和解) and *The Translated Elements of Botany* (*Shokubutsugaku shōyaku* 植物學抄譯) by Abe Gukuni and Tōi Tahara, respectively.

First Lines of the Practice of Surgery in the West

Compiled by B. Hobson and published in 1857, the 194-page *First Lines of the Practice of Surgery in the West* explained diseases and prescriptions from a Western perspective. "On Chinese and Western Medicine" in volume one was the first article comparing Chinese and Western Medicine. Hobson believed the reasons of the backwardness of Chinese medicine were several: first, Western doctors were required to sit in examinations while Chinese doctors studied on their own. Similar to the civil examination in China, Western doctors could not go into practice until passing the examinations. Second, Chinese doctors lacked training in anatomy. Chinese medicine, which emphasized the use of herbs, did not encourage the practice of anatomy, making the Chinese doctors unfamiliar with the complicated human body structure and even the shapes of the organs. Hobson also criticized the Chinese who refused to accept Western medicine by claiming their non-Western body structure inadaptable to Western medicine.

The publication of the *First Lines of the Practice of Surgery in the West* earned Hobson an enormous reputation from both the Chinese scholars and Western missionaries. W. Lockhart, also a physician-missionary, praised Hobson's work:

> This treatise, besides showing the benefits of surgical education, sets forth the entire subject of surgical practice, and is, like the former ones, well-illustrated. Perhaps this work may be regarded as the best of the series, as it is certainly the most adapted for direct utility. Immediately upon its

> publication people of all classes were eager to possess it, and doubtless, its rules for the treatment of various affections will be followed by many. The book will be one of frequent and studious reference, and will have a powerful influence in guiding many minds in their endeavours to aid those who hitherto in China have been left unattended to and reglected.[67]

And Wang Chi-min and Wu Lien-the, two physician-historians in the Republican Period, also highly recommended the book *First Lines of the Practice of Surgery in the West*.[68]

Practice of Medicine and Materia Medica

Published in 1858, the 117-page *Practice of Medicine and Materia Medica* was divided into two volumes. The aim of the publication was clearly written in the preface:

> Medical treatments included in the *Practice of Medicine and Materia* Medica were compiled and translated from European medical reference works. Returning to the United Kingdom soon, I have no idea on my second trip to China. Western merchants in Shanghai thus printed 1,000 copies of my titles, the *Practice of Medicine and Materia Medica* included, for distribution. The peaceful relationship between China and the West nowadays accelerates the cultural exchange. Essentials of Western learning that benefit the Chinese territory, such as medical science, should never remain as secret subjects.[69]

Volume one of *Practice of Medicine and Materia Medica* explained various diseases and their corresponding treatments, such as poor digestion and circulation of blood. Volume two introduced various Chinese and Western medicine.

Hobson, a man with profound knowledge and a medical expert, arrived at Shanghai in February 1857 at the request of the Renji Hospital to fill up the position of physician of W. Lockhart, who was on leave and returned to the United Kingdom. He left Shanghai in early 1859. His two-year stay, though short, already gained him a reputation from the Chinese scholars. Wang Tao, for instance, had his feet cured by Hobson:

> I had suffered from foot problems since 1856. Visiting doctors was useless. Cost spent on medicine made me penniless. Walking even for just a half-a-step distance was uncontrollable...until the Westerner (Hobson) took care

of me. Hobson, who had been working in Guangzhou, provided effective medicine for me. I was suddenly cured after a few months.[70]

Hobson's departure from Shanghai in late 1858 was regrettable to the Chinese scholars. Guan Sifu and Wang Tao presented two decorative Chinese fans and several books for the missionary, respectively. The Chinese also accompanied him to the pier on his departure day. Wang recalled the farewell in his diary:

> In the afternoon on October 4, the 8th year of Xianfeng (December 18, 1858), [we] paid farewell to Hobson at the Whampoa bund. Seeing his ship on the horizon, I knew that it was a valediction. Hobson, a medical expert, was honest and sincere, making him the best among the Western doctors. His five works, *Natural Philosophy and Natural History, A New Discourse on Human Body, First Lines of the Practice of Surgery in the west, Treatise on Midwifery and Diseases of Children* (*Fuying xinshuo* 婦嬰新說), and *Practice of Medicine and Materia Medica*, were precise yet insightful.[71]

Chinese Almanac

Chinese Almanac (entitled as *Sino-Western Calendric Treatise* before 1856), a calendar manual, included both science knowledge and religious teaching. It was published in Shanghai from 1852 to 1862 annually before its relocation of printing to Beijing. Generally, the average page number of each issue was 30. A. Wylie and J. Edkins had been the chief editors of the almanac. This book compared the Chinese and Western calendars, listed the tables of the eclipses and the equation of time, seasons, and climatic periods (*jieqi* 節氣), and introduced important world events and inventions. There were articles on the teaching of Christianity and basic science knowledge, such as the solar system, optics, nebula, and planets. The 1854 issue, for instance, explained that the "non-falling" of the moon was due to universal gravity.[72]

The publication of the *Chinese Almanac* received deserved attention from Chinese scholars. Wang Tao was invited by Wylie to write a preface for the 1859 issue, in which he traced the cause of the backwardness of the Chinese calendar:

> Both Chinese and foreign mathematics were not well developed in ancient times, but Western methods were found superior to Chinese methods nowadays. Why could it be? The answer lied in the conservativeness of the Chinese scholars, who blindly followed the old method without inventing any new technique. Sailing to the East, the Western scholars

> introduced the new methods to astronomers on the Chinese territory through the translation of books and clarifying the origin and the development of the calendar that benefitted the latter generations.[73]

Scientific Manual

Published in 1856, the 15-page manual was written in special phonetic symbols invented by T. P. Crawford (1821–1902) and his wife. Crawford from the Baptist Church arrived at Shanghai on March 28, 1852. He stayed in the city until 1858, when he returned to the United States due to sickness. In 1860, he resumed his journey to China, settling in Shandong until his return to America in 1900.

To explain his newly-invented phonetic symbols, Crawford even published the *Scripts of Shanghai Dialects* (*Shanghai tuyinzi xiefa* 上海土音字寫法) in 1855. The symbols, actually twisted Chinese characters, were strange and unrecognizable nowadays. However, these symbols seemed influential to the foreigners in Shanghai in late Qing period. Crawford's other titles written in these symbols were reprinted, helping the study of the evolution of the Shanghai language and scripts.

Universal Miscellany

Universal Miscellany, the first integrated monthly journal in Shanghai, began its publication on January 26, 1857.[74] The magazine covered a wide range of topics, including science, literature, news, religion, and trading of Shanghai. Contributors of the *Universal Miscellany* included A. Wylie, also the chief editor of the journal, J. Edkins, A. Williamson, W. Muirhead, and other missionaries. Wylie established the magazine to bridge the Sino-Western culture and to introduce Western learning to inland China:

> It had been fourteen years ago since we, the Westerners, sailed across 70,000 *li* to the East and seeking for a cordial relationship with China. Our citizens, who settled in Shanghai for years, had been familiar to the city and its surrounding areas through befriending with the Chinese scholars and commoners. Trading and preaching, however, were restricted in the five treaty ports. Chinese territories that saw no footprint of the Westerners were multiple. The Chinese on these unvisited lands communicated with a different dialect and had a distinctive habit. How could our teachings be understood by these outsiders? The method actually lied in the publication of books, spreading our messages

> through articles instead of oral communication. It would help break the isolation between the outsiders and the Westerners...The publication of the *Universal Miscellany* was an attempt to bridge the gap between the Chinese and Western worlds, to narrate the ancient and contemporary affairs, and to trace the historical vicissitudes.[75]

Among the 15 issues of this missionary-published journal there were found more articles about science than religion. Articles by W. Muirhead explained world geography, while essays by J. Edkins focused on Western culture, such as "Ancient Greece as the Origin of Western Literature," "Introductions to Poets in Ancient Greece and Rome," and "Biographies of Homer and Plato." It also welcomed local scholars to submit pieces of writings. Excellent articles by the Chinese included "Caesar the Extraordinary Foreigner" by Jiang Dunfu, "On the Forceful Emergence of China" by Han Yingbi, and "On the Anti-forceful Emergence of China" by Wang Tao. The publication of the *Universal Miscellany* was suspended in March 1858.

Table 4.3 Non-religious titles published in Shanghai (1843–1860)

Publishing year	Book title	Author	Page number
1847	*Seven Talks on the Abandonment of Opium Smoking*[76]	I. Tracy	5
1851	*Catechism to Science*	W. Muirhead	10
1855	*Introduction to the Shanghai Dialect*	Cleveland Keith	76
1857	*Primer for Kids*	Caroline Phebe Keith	87
1858	*Treatise on Midwifery and Diseases of Children*	B. Hobson	73
1860	*Primer for Enlightenment*	Madam Cunnyngham	83

This chapter studied the respective activities of the missionaries in the treaty ports. Most of these works played a pioneering role in the dissemination of Western learning in modern China. The Chinese and American Holy Classic Book Establishment and the London Missionary Society Mission Press were the first Chinese presses specialized in the publication of Western reference works. *Elements of Botany* co-translated by J. Edkins and Li Shanlan was the first reference of botany in Chinese. It was also the first time when the law of conservation of mass, the universal gravitation, and chemical elements were introduced to China. The translation of Chinese terms was established. Modern journals and magazines were issued. These publications played a significant role in enlightening Chinese scholar-officials. Wei Yuan extensively quoted from the *Exploration of a World Map* and *An Encyclopedia for Safety Adventure* in compiling of the *Illustrated Gazetteer of the Maritime Countries*. Xu Jiyu compiled *A Short Account of the Maritime Circuit* by referring to the Western reference works from D. Abeel. Li Shanlan, Xu Shou, Hua Hengfang, and Wang Tao became enlightenment philosophers of Western learning to China through translation and extensive reading of these newly published titles. These titles, which were translated into Japanese, influenced not only the Chinese scholars, but also the Japanese intellectuals.

Table 4.4 The introduction of Western titles (in Chinese) to Japan

Publishing date	Titles	Translator or publisher
1857	*A New Discourse on Human Body*	Mr. Echi
1858	*Universal Geography*	Sōkairō
	The First Lines of the Practice of Surgery in the west	Mr. Miyake from Tōjuen
1859	*Practice of Medicine and Materia Medica*	—
	Treatise on Midwifery and Diseases of Children	Heian tenkōdō
1860	*Popular Treatise on Mechanics*	Kōri Arai
	A Brief Discourse on the Earth	Mitsukuri Genpo
1861	*Discourse on Astronomy*	Rōka Fukudaie
1864	*A Brief Survey of the United States of America*	—
1867	*Elements of Botany*	Mitsukuri Genpo
	The Translated Elementary Lessons in the Circle of Knowledge	Edo Kaibutsusha
1868	*Natural Philosophy and Natural History (with Explanation)*	Omori Ichū
1870	*Elementary Lessons in the Circle of Knowledge*	Shōtsu Gakkō
1872	*Elementary Lessons in the Circle of Knowledge*	Uryū Hajimu
1873	*Elementary Lessons in the Circle of Knowledge: with Explanation from a Japanese Perspective*	Ishikawaken Gakkō
1874	*A New Discourse on Human Body (with Explanation)*	Ishikuro Atsushi
	A Brief Discourse on the Earth: with Explanation from a Japanese Perspective	Kansendō
1875	*A Brief Discourse on the Earth (with Explanation)*	Hōshūdō
	Elements of Botany: with Explanation from a Japanese Perspective	Abe Gukuni
	The Translated Elements of Botany	Tōi Tahara
1876	*Natural Philosophy and Natural History*	Komuro Seiichi

5

Chapter

Facing an Alienated World

The era from the publication of Robert Morrison's first Chinese book on Western affairs in 1841 to the signing of the Convention of Beijing after the end of the Second Anglo-Chinese War in 1860 witnessed the unprecedented advancement of Western powers into China. The firing from gunboats, the ceding of territories, the opening of ports, and the indemnity of the Western powers alarmed the "sleeping" Oriental Empire to face a threat that China had not faced for centuries. The narrower distance and the tighter bonds between the Oriental and Occidental worlds led China out of its prolonged isolation, although the Chinese were reluctant to be dragged into the new world.

The missionaries worked on another front, diffusing new kinds of knowledge through the translation of Western classics. They compiled and published Chinese books and journals in Southeast Asia cities and the treaty ports along the Chinese coast. The publication of 527 titles during this period demonstrated the Westerners' eagerness to break their ignorance towards the situation of the Far East, and it greatly astonished the Chinese, who had indulged only in the narrow world of literature and philosophy. It was the first time the Chinese scholars realized the presence of knowledge which was inexpressible by the Chinese language.

The new situation, new environment, and new knowledge, in return, propelled the Chinese scholars to learn what they regarded as useful knowledge to save the country. The school of "practical knowledge," represented by Lin Zexu, Wei Yuan, Liang Tingnan, and Xu Jiyu, studied world history, geography, and international affairs and, hoped to apply the knowledge to the reforms. The "truth-seekers," another group of scholars headed by Li Shanlan, Wang Tao, and Zhang Fuxi, focused on the learning of natural science.

The contributions of these historical figures were so well-known that little elaboration is required in this chapter. The author is concerned more about their achievements in the dissemination of Western learning in China.

Lin Zexu: Striving to Understand International Affairs

Prior to the appointment of Lin Zexu as the Commissioner of opium-banning in 1839, Lin, who had a similar background with the general scholars, lacked understanding of the world. He had a smooth yet just middling qualification and career compared to his colleagues since he had attended college and acquired a degree before joining the government as the Governor of Jiangsu and being promoted to the Governor-general of Hunan and Hubei. It was actually his characteristics of earnestness, practicality, and creativity that distinguished him from his colleagues and made him one of the most decisive officials in the mid-Qing period.

His good working attitude could be illustrated from two incidents during his terms of office in Jiangsu: first, the improvement of the cropping schedule. Double cropping had never been practiced astride along the Southern bank of the Yangtze River before Lin's arrival at Jiangsu. Having compared the climate and soil condition of Jiangsu to his hometown, Fujian, where double cropping was commonly adopted, Lin was confident at being able to increase the yields of the lower Yangtze province through the abandonment of single cropping. This proposal, however, faced strong opposition from the local gentry, who firmly upheld their traditional farming practice. Through a series of successful experiments, Lin overcame all the opposing views. Second, the reform of the disaster-relief method. Lin invited scholars to take up fund-raising and distribute materials to prevent officials from embezzling funds. These green scholars, unlike the shrewd officials, were unfamiliar with the way of corruption yet they were eager to earn the public trust. They thus spared no effort to help the victims. Lin's reforms were shown to be enormous successes. The public even composed a piece of prose, "The Song of Disaster Relief," to remember Lin's contributions. These two attempts demonstrated Lin's consciousness, practicality, and sense of innovation that freed him from the binds of outdated customs.

Lin arrived at Guangzhou in March 1839 as the Commissioner of opium-banning. Before his dismissal in May 1841, he was also promoted as the Governor-general of Guangdong and Guangxi Provinces and the Person-in-charge of the Sino-British diplomatic affairs. The commissioner had little knowledge about the Occidental empire and the current international situation in his early days in office, regarding China a "celestial empire endowed with invincible might and martial prowess." Trading was nothing more than "a mark of favor to the foreigners (*Jiahui yuanren* 嘉惠遠人)" that occupied the country's economy for only a little proportion. Once China prohibited the export of tea and herbs, no foreigners could survive. Officials sharing the same view with Lin were found everywhere, but the commissioner, facing the advancement of the Western naval fleets, soon realized the importance of understanding the actual strength of both the opponents and the country to prevent lagging behind from world affairs.

Lin's attempts to understand foreign affairs were several: first, Lin recruited talents who were familiar with foreign affairs. He discussed politics with Liang Tingnan and Zhang Weiping. He employed Yuan Dehui, a Sichuan citizen and a graduate of the Anglo-Chinese College in Malacca who had mastered Latin,

Chinese, and English and had been a translator of in the Court of Colonial Affairs for decades before the Opium War. Another assistant of Lin was Liang Jinde, son of the first Chinese missionary Leung Fa and who had been baptized by Robert Morrison in 1823. Liang studied English and Christianity with E. C. Bridgman, and he was employed by a Western company in Guangzhou as a translator for Guangzhou after his graduation from the Morrison Education Society School in Macau. In addition to the assistants above, Lin also hired a young man who had stayed in the United States for a few years, two cooks who had worked in foreign restaurants and a doctor with working experience from the Ophthalmic Hospital established by Dr. Parker.

Second, Lin learned from foreign visitors in China about the foreign situation. He grasped every opportunity to befriend foreigners, asking the missionaries, businessmen, captains, and editors who visited Humen for his destruction of opium about the circumstances of the United States. Lin also understood the process of the production of opium and situations of foreign countries including the United Kingdom, the United States, and the Ottoman Empire from the physician of an English ship. He also sought help from Dr. Parker to translate part of *The International Law* and a letter from the British King.

Third, Lin organized the translation of English books and newspapers. Once arrived at Guangzhou, the commissioner started filing the newspaper articles from several English newspapers, such as *Canton Press*, *Canton Register*, *Singapore Free Press*, and other newspapers from Bombay (Mumbai), Bangladesh, and London in chronological order. The collection of these newspaper clippings was published as the *Macau Newspaper*, and the copies were either kept by the commissioner or submitted to other officials in Beijing. Another title of Lin was the *Gazetteer of the Four Continents* (*Sizhouzhi* 四洲志), a selected translation from the masterpiece of Hugh Murray, the 1500-page *Encyclopedia of Geography* (London, 1834). It covered essays on the history and geography of major countries in Asia, Africa, Europe, and the Americas, such as Thailand, Burma, India, the Ottoman Empire, Portugal, Spain, the Netherlands, France, Italy, Gemany, Austria, Poland, Switzerland, Greece, the United Kingdom, Ireland, Russia, Prussia, and the United States. The United Kingdom and the United States had the most informative description among the mentioned countries. These articles, amounting to over 87,000 words, were classified and compiled into the *Illustrated Gazetteer of the Maritime Countries* by Wei Yuan.

Gazetteer of the Four Continents was the first world geography reference work translated by the Chinese. Many of the names and concept of foreign affairs were unheard of to the Chinese translators, who thus transliterated these terms according to Chinese characters. For example, "president" was transliterated as *bolexiling* (勃列西領), "senate" as *xiye* (西業), "election" as *iliduo* (依力多), and "senator" as *xinaduo* (西那多) — too odd to be understood and be useful to present-day scholars.[1] *The Law of Nations* (*Geguo fali* 各國法例) by the famous Swiss jurist Emerich de Vattel (1714–1767)[2] was translated with the help of Dr. Parker and Yuan Dehui. The book was a select translation of the English version by Joseph Chitty that included the terms of wars, blockade, and embargo.[3] *Chinese: An Overview of the Chinese Empire and Its People* was written by John Francis Davis, a *taipan* of the British East India Company in Guangzhou and also later the second Governor of Hong Kong. Its English edition was published in London in 1836 and was translated into Chinese by Commissioner Lin, as he found the British perspective towards Chinese issues interesting to study.

Lin's efforts provided much valuable knowledge for the Qing court to understand the international situation, to be familiar with international practice, and to formulate corresponding measures on diplomacy. His introduction to world geography and international law also played a positive role in broadening people's horizons. Another significance of Lin's contribution was to direct the "sleeping" empire and its arrogant subject people out of ignorance of global affairs. Lin, though a scholar trained with traditional knowledge and an official serving the absolute monarch, forecast the future of the kingdom with scrupulous insight before the arrival of the "unprecedented" transition. Unlike his colleagues who blindly stuck themselves to old patterns, Lin's adaptability was exceptionally rare in history. Lin also opened the trend of studying world affairs in Chinese academia. The friendship between Commissioner Lin and Dr. Parker also had an epochal significance. Most of the Chinese scholar-officials, indoctrinated to avoid staying with foreigners — to be specific, barbarians — did not see the appeal of Western learning. Lin, on the contrary, had no discrimination towards both Westerners and their knowledge. He particularly appreciated Dr. Parker's opening of the Ophthalmic Hospital and regarded it as a benevolent act.

Lin's behavior was actually a response to the slogan of "acquiring foreign technology to subdue foreigners (*Shi yizhichangji yi zhiyi* 師夷之長技以制夷)" proposed by Wei Yuan — a complex mentality of scholar-officials in the transitional period who wanted to catch up with the development of the advanced nations while preserving their national dignity simultaneously.

Liang Tingnan: Sensing the Impending Transformation

Among the scholars of Western learning in the reign of Daoguang and Xianfeng, Liang Tingnan (1796–1861) was the representative of the Guangdong area. Liang Tingnan, also named as Liang Zhangran, whose pseudonym was the Master of the Tenghua Pavilion, was born into a scholarly family. He was provided with an education in Classical Studies in his adolescence by his father and uncle but he shifted to the study of textual interpretation after several failed attempts to pass the imperial examination. Although he lacked the talent in the writing of the eight-legged essay, an indispensable skill for success in the examination, he made remarkable research achievements in literature, history, poetry, drama, and tonality. Liang's early works, the *Collections of Songs of the Tenhua Pavilion* (*Tenghuating quhua* 藤花亭曲話) and the *History of the Southern Han State* (*Nanhanshu* 南漢書), however, were irrelevant to the study of Western learning.

His passing of the civil examination in 1834 and his participation in the translation of *A Conspectus of Guangdong's Coastal Defense* (*Guangdong haifang huilan* 廣東海防匯覽) at the invitation of Lu Kun, the Governor-general of Guangdong and Guangxi Provinces, constituted the turning point of his career and his study.

Having witnessed the constant harassment of coastal China by the British troops and their raid of the Whampoa Harbor in Guangzhou, and using his editorial experience and his strong sense of patriotism, Liang attempted to raise the Chinese people's concern about the West, and to develop his own understanding of the Western powers. He was appointed as Chief Editor of the Guangdong Customs in 1838 to compile the *Gazetteer of the Guangdong Customs* (*Yue Haiguan zhi* 粵海關志). Through the compilation of a reference work of the busiest custom of handling negotiation between China and the Western countries, Liang obtained a clear understanding of the West. For instance, Liang supported the opinion of the five continents, though the so-called authoritative reference work, *The General History of Institutions and Critical Examination of Documents of the Qing Dynasty* (*Qingchao wenxian tongkao* 清朝文獻通考), had labeled such a concept as ridiculous. Liang could even indicate the location and basic information of several European countries in the book:

> Italy is located in the middle of the Mediterranean Sea. It has had no communication with China since the past. Matteo Ricci, the Westerner who arrived at China during the reign of Wanli of the Ming Dynasty, was a citizen of the country…It was a peninsula with high mountains and

fertile soil on the Northern part of the territory, with numerous cities. The six largest cities include Roma, Venice, Milan, Napoli, Genoa, and Firenze.[4]

Portugal is situated at the Westernmost edge of Europe. The sea-facing country was divided into five circuits and it witnessed commercial ships from various parts of the world. Representative local products included fruits, velvet, fishes, and red wine.[5]

England, located in Western Europe, was once a subordinate of the Netherlands. Once getting more affluent, it soon confronted the Dutch, occupying North Africa to emerge as a strong kingdom. This country that is approximately 50,000 *li* away from Guangdong produces wheat, fruits, soy bean, and tin…The city where the king resided was named London.[6]

China's humiliated defeat in the Opium War astonished the Qing court and the Chinese, triggering the Chinese scholars, particularly Liang, to conduct research on the West. Two years after the signing of the Treaty of Nanjing, Liang published four titles on current affairs: *On the United States*, *The Difficulties of the Introduction of Christianity to China* (*Yesujiao nanru Zhongguo shuo* 耶穌教難入中國說), *Discourse on Vassal States Sending Tribute to Canton* (*Yuedao gongguo shuo* 粵道貢國說), and *An Account of London* (*Lanlun oushuo* 蘭侖偶說).

Fig. 5.1 ***An Account of London*** **and** ***On the United States***

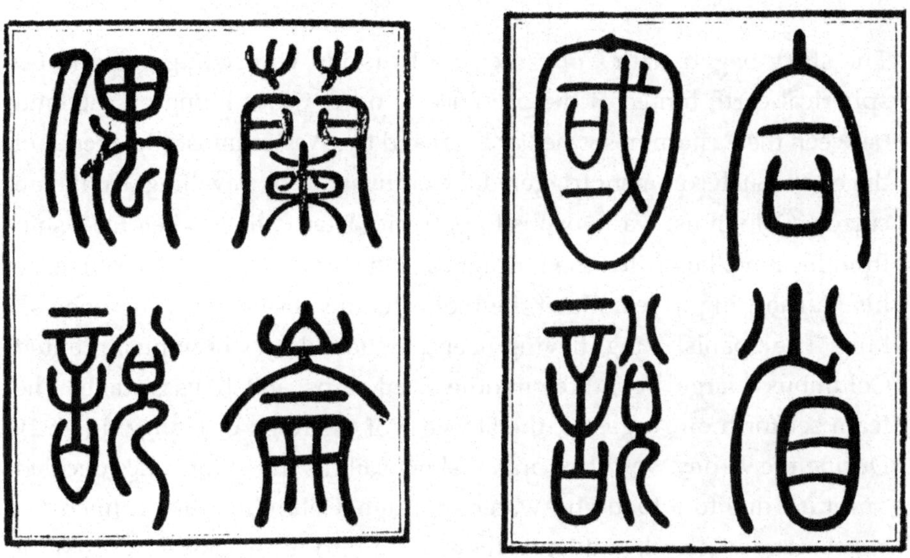

On the United States

Published in 1844, *On the United States* was the first Chinese-compiled set of books about America. The first volume began with the basic geographical concept of the West and the Americas, the discovery of America by Columbus, the successful circumnavigation by Magellan, the British colonization of North America, and the Anglo-French conflict over the American colonies. Liang spared several paragraphs to clarify the translation terms of the United States, as he found the variation of terms had confused most Chinese people, who regarded *meilijian* or *amakleigaak* (America), *heshengguo* (the United States), and *faakeigwok* (the country with a flowering flag) as three different countries. He explained:

> The Canton residents addressed the United States as *faakeigwok* as they saw the flowering flags hung on the American commercial ships. The Americans, on the other hand, regarded "the United States of America" as the formal name of their country...*Amakleigaak* was a transliteration of the term Amerigo, the captain who claimed to have discovered the new land himself...*Meilijian*, also a transliteration of America, was a mixed pronunciation of Cantonese and other Chinese dialects...And *Heshengguo* indicates the combination of various states as a country.[7]

Liang preferred the use of "*Heshengguo*" instead of the two other terms as the official translation of the United States, as he stressed the uniqueness of the federation system of the country more than its location. Liang also spared a large paragraph to relate Columbus' discovery of the Americas:

> The story began with Copernicus, a Prussian whose suggestion of a spherical earth hinted at the presence of other tribes living on the land between the Easternmost (the Far East) and the Westernmost (the Iberia) of the earth. Such comment triggered the enthusiasm of travelling. An Italian citizen, Columbus, was anxious to prove it. After failing to beg for a ship from his king, he visited the Portuguese king, who also refused to finance his journey. Eight years later, he requested a subsidy from the Spanish king. The Spanish king, having been persuaded by Columbus, granted Columbus a large ship, three middle-sized ships, and 100 assistants. The team set forth on August 3, the 5th year of the reign of Hongzhi (1492). During the 90-day westward and offshore sailing, the sailors once decided to return due to a food and water shortage. Columbus thus calmed his assistants down and, suddenly, they saw a bird in the sky — a signal of

> a coast nearby. Delighted, the sailors thus prepared for the landing. The land that they arrived at was America...Columbus and his team stayed for five months before returning to Europe.[8]
>
> Three years after Columbus' journey, another Italian captain, Amerigo Vespucci, followed the route of Columbus. [Amerigo] stayed for months in the nameless wild land, which was named as The New Land and later America.[9]

Liang even mentioned the mysterious Bermuda triangle, saying that in the windless Bermuda archipelago lives an evil that sinks nearby ships.[10]

The second volume traced the War of Independence of the United States, various institutions established after the foundation of the country, and the Westward expansion of the Americans. The election of the President and the composition of the legislative bodies were clearly elaborated:

> The United States has a President assisted by the Vice President, as the head of the nation. Elected by the people, the President has a four-year term of office, after which the people would choose another candidate. Those popular Presidents can serve the second term with enough votes, but the total length of term should not exceed eight years. Below the President were members of the Upper House, with two representatives per state. The Lower House, institutionally below the Upper House, was composed of a few representatives from each state...There were 52 members of the Upper House, whose term of office was six years.[11]

The focus of *On the United States* was the political system. The author demonstrated not only his particular concern on the separation of powers, but also the change of government through election:

> The judiciary officials were responsible only for judgments according to the law. The duty of the discussion for state affairs rested with the members of the houses, who were not granted the right of judgment...The President cannot decide the affairs on his own before the discussion in the parliament.[12]

Law had been the core value of the people ever since the establishment of the country. The people formulated laws prior to the election of the head of state. The leader would be elected after a certain number of years even if he had an excellent performance record during his term of office. Such a practical method prevents the dictatorship of the President.[13]

Liang was indeed such a studious and thoughtful scholar that he satisfied not only those wishing for more explanation on the American system, but he also went a further step to explore the invention of the democratic system by the United States, a former colony under the governance of the absolute English king:

> Too distant to establish full control over the United States, the United Kingdom allowed the American people to govern on their own. The loose domination and the dissociation between the colonial power and the people was a result of the long-term autonomy. The American people would be satisfied to have a simple life with only the making of money and the invention of devices. Because of their geographical distance with other countries and the lack of ambition to trigger any political conflicts, the Americans established an unprecedented peaceful environment.[14]

The third volume introduced a wide range of topics, including religion, language, publications, newspapers, libraries, weddings, funerals, dining, clothing, residence, industry, agriculture, local products, and the aboriginals, in a topically arranged genre. The 26 letters of the English alphabet were annotated with Chinese characters pronounced in Cantonese, for example, the letter "B" as *bei* (碑), "Q" as *kiu* (翹), and "Z" as *si* (思).[15]

In compiling *On the United States*, Liang employed considerable reference works, including *Miscellaneous Records of the Jiwen Mountain Studio* (*Jiwen shanfang zaji* 寄味山房雜記) by Ye Zhongjin, *Maritime Records* (*Hailu* 海錄) by Xie Qinggao, *Enlightenment on the Heaven and the Earth* (*Gaohou mengqiu* 高厚蒙求) by Xu Chaojun, and the *Gazetteer of the Guangdong Customs, and also A Brief History of the United States of America,* the most quoted book.

Fig. 5.2 E.C. Bridgman and *A Brief History of the United States of America*

An Account of England and An Account of London

Published in 1846, the 13,000-word *An Account of England* traced the historical vicissitudes of England over the past millennium and the customs of the residents of the British Isles. *An Account of London*, based on the content of *An Account of England* with slight changes on word choice and a new chapter on the social system, was actually a revised edition of *An Account of England* instead of an introduction to the British capital.[16]

Volume one of *An Account of London*, similar to the original work, traced the 1,000-year history of England — from the history of a Roman province to the conquering of England by William I, the formulation of the Great Charter, the Glorious Revolution, and the Industrial Revolution. Liang particularly focused on the dynastic changes, the achievements, and shortcomings of several rulers, and the diplomatic relationship of England and other countries. The English Civil War from 1642 to 1651, for instance, was introduced as:

> King Charles I succeeded the throne in the 42nd year of the reign of Wanli (1614). The notorious king paid no attention to people's livelihoods, triggering a nationwide revolt. The parliament was prorogued and tax collection was suspended. The king attempted to wage war against France, yet his reputation was too low to mobilize the troops. And the navy returned to England with no achievements. In the 4th year of the reign of Shunzhi (1647), [Charles] recruited another army (the Scottish) to conquer the rebels. His people confronted Charles, and the king was executed. Since then, England has been under the protectorate of a group of notable gentry (the Commonwealth) who acclaimed themselves the reformers.[17]

Volume two explained the geography of the United Kingdom, the situation of the shires and the development of British colonies in North America, India, and Southeast Asia. Liang also clarified that the various translation terms of the country, such as *yingjili* (英機黎 , English), *yingguili* (英圭黎 , English), *yingchili* (英吃黎 , English), *yingjili* (英吉利 , English), *yinglun* (英倫 , England), and *buliedian* (不列顛 , Britain) carried the same meaning.

Volume three introduced various institutions of the United Kingdom, such as the parliament, composition of the army and navy, taxation system, postal system, and the insurance system. Both the parliament and insurance systems were new to the Chinese and Liang paid particular effort to explain them:

> The triennially elected Parliament was a place for the officials and people to discuss political matters. No ministers and judicial officers were invited to join the meeting. Military affairs would be discussed as well. No action would be taken before the approval by the Parliament. Legislation, the appointment and dismissal of officials, taxation, and the issue of money would be decided by the Parliament members before passing the issues to the Cabinet.[18]
>
> Merchants paid an insurance fee to the guild after evaluating their goods. Generally, the guild had a full compensation from their insurance fee for any sinking of ships, while the merchants would get half compensation for a total loss of goods. The company also insures residences against destruction, and also rich men who would leave compensation as alimony for their wives.[19]

Volume four covered an extensive range of topics on socioeconomic affairs, including the Anglo-Chinese trading relationship, the opium issue, the situation of London, customs of the British people, their clothing, hairstyle, dining, weddings, funerals, court etiquette, religion, property inheritance, law and punishment, measurement, coinage, charity organizations, education institutes, and local products. The book had an informative description of the British education system:

> Students aged from seven to 18 studied four humanity subjects in the elementary schools: maxims of the ancient sages, history of various nations, literature, and writing of articles. Once passing the examination, students entered the secondary school, where they studied science and philosophy. Those excellent students would be recommended to the university, where they were free to choose their specialties. There were four main streams of study in the university: medical studies, government and politics, legal studies, and education. Students who passed the oral defense would be granted the qualification.[20]

The operation of ships, trains, and steam engines were also introduced in detail:

> Fueled by hot water, the steamship sailed as fast as the wind. It was used as a mail delivery system initially, and it was later used in the army... Transporting goods with the train was economical in human and animal

resources, time, and cost. However, the road must be flattened before laying the rail. Steam energy was also used in weaving.[21]

Discourse on Vassal States Sending Tributes to Canton

Published in 1844, *Discourse on Vassal States Sending Tribute to Canton* included both China's vassal states in East Asia and the Western powers. Actually, never had a European country established a tributary relationship with China, but these countries were included in the account as Chinese, long indoctrinated by the belief of the "heavenly kingdom" and ethnic-center, regarded all its trading partners as its tributary states. The list of the "vassal states" of China was long enough to cover the six volumes, with the first two about Siam (present-day Thailand), the third about the Netherlands, the fourth about Spain, Portugal, France, and Italy, and the last two about the United Kingdom. The narration, arranged in a chronological order, documented the tributary gifts and China's rewards to these states.

This book traced not only the Sino-foreign trading situation, but it also covered the history and custom of the "vassal states," as well as important events in the history of East-West communication, including the evangelic mission of Ricci in China, and the voyage of Zheng He in the early Ming Dynasty.

Discourse on Vassal States Sending Tribute to Canton was a highly reliable account of the foreign countries as considered from several aspects: Guangzhou was the only authorized port of China before its opening. People in the southern city, Liang included, witnessed the frequent arrival of foreign traders. Moreover, this book was a first-hand account of Liang, who had been working in Guangzhou for years and had compiled the *Gazetteer of the Guangdong Customs*. Nobody other than Liang was more familiar with the Sino-foreign trade before the Opium War than Liang, making him the most suitable narrator of such a topic.

The Difficulties of the Introduction of Christianity to China

Published in 1844, *The Difficulties of the Introduction of Christianity to China* widely covered the doctrines of Christianity, its dissemination to China, and the resistance to the Western religion among the Chinese people. In exploring the difficulties for Christianity to enter the Chinese society, Liang compared the Western religion with Buddhism, a religion which originated in India that became highly influential in China following the unrest of the Six Dynasties. He indicated that Buddhism attracted only the lower classes, who took the advantages of tax-exemption on monks. Most of the scholars found the Buddhist teachings of a total withdrawal from the secular affairs and *tapas* (spiritual suffering) were too harsh to practice. The conversion of some ancient scholars to Buddhism during their later years was nothing more than a search for tranquility and calmness. Theoretically, Christianity, which required respect to God and the good behavior of a convert, was more humane and practical. However, Liang continued to point out that the reasons for the failure of Christianity to challenge the domination of Confucianism among the upper Chinese class were several: first, Confucianism had a long history since the ancient times. Second, the resurrection of Jesus was too mysterious to believe, while doomsday, an evidence of the truth of the *Book of Revelation*, was not witnessed even a millennium after the death of the Christ. Actually, the inaccessibility of Christianity to the Chinese society was a complicated issue. The Chinese, on the one hand, were highly vigilant to the violent and rampant spread of the religion after the signing of a series of unequal treaties that protected any missionary activities. On the other hand, the Chinese scholars were confident to resist any intrusion of the "heterodox" belief by upholding the glorious traditional Chinese culture.

China could no longer shut the door against the ever-changing global situation. China, being forcefully dragged into the new world order, was exposed to various political, economic, and cultural problems. The intellectuals, who were trained to be the future leaders of the country, were anxious to seek for a solution. Liang's compilation of these four titles may provide a substantial and clear solution to such a predicament. Liang Tingnan, a native Guangdong person, and his fellow villagers were the first group of Chinese who witnessed the advancement of the British troops. His firm support to fight against the enemy and the eagerness to awake his compatriots out of ignorance was demonstrated not only in the defense of the Guangzhou city during the Opium War, but also the compilation of these four titles. *Discourse on Vassal States Sending Tribute to Canton* provided a perspective from an insider towards the trading issue — the root cause of the Opium War. *On the United States*, which gave a detailed account on the relatively new nation, demonstrated his excellent judgment to this country — neither Sinicized nor Europeanized. The unique political institution of the United States was too astonishing to him that he could not wait to introduce it to his compatriots. *The Difficulties of the Introduction of Christianity to China* showed the scholars' deep concern to the challenge of Western religion posed to the Chinese traditional belief. Liang particularly conducted research on the

United Kingdom, the most powerful European power and also the arch-rival of China at this time, through the publication of *An Account of London*.

Xu Jiyu: the Oriental Galileo

Xu Jiyu (1795–1873) had similar experience to many successful Chinese scholars: sitting in the provincial examinations, passing the imperial examination, and getting the degree of advanced scholar — a qualification equivalent to a doctoral degree in the West. His career in the court began with his appointment as the Circuit Intendant, and he was later promoted as the Provincial Administration Commissioner and the Provincial Governor. However, Xu had his name remembered in history neither because of his education background nor his brilliant career, but due to his compilation of the *A Short Account of the Maritime Circuit*, the first and the best geography reference work in the mid-Qing period that demonstrated the scholar's anxiousness to learn the new knowledge within 150,000 words.

Xu Jiyu, also named as Xu Jiannan (pseudonym Songkan), was born in a scholarly family in Wutai, Shanxi. His father, Xu Rundi, passed the examination of the *jinshi* degree in the same year of Xu's birth and was once a Secretary of the Grand Secretariat and the Sub-prefectural Magistrate. Rundi, a studious and perseverant man who lived a simple life and stayed away from corruption and bribery, was a gentleman in the official community. Xu Jiyu inherited the excellent character from his father, particularly the desire to pursue study. Xu passed the provincial and imperial examinations at the age of 19 and 30, respectively. Having scored the highest in the latter examination, Xu was appointed as the Hanlin Bachelor of the imperial academy, and he was later promoted as the Junior Compiler of the Hanlin Academy, the Investigating Censor of Shaanxi, and the Prefect of Xunzhou, Guangxi. He was in his tenure as the Circuit Intendant in Fujian responsible for also the defense of Zhangzhou during the Opium War.

The transferal of Xu from inland to the coastal Fujian Province was a turning point of both his career and study that offered him the opportunity of firsthand contact with the emerging Western influence. As a studious and thoughtful scholar, Xu started questioning the underlying cause of China's defeat in the Opium War. It seemed impossible for such a historically strong nation to have lost to remote and "barbarian" countries, while Amoy, equipped with 400 cannons and 7,000 soldier stations, also failed to resist the raid by only 30 ships of the "rebels." He soon sensed the problem was China's arrogance and ignorance towards the outside world. He thus began to understand the global circumstances. In a letter to his Shanxi friend written in early 1842, Xu concluded his impression of the English people, saying that they were the most powerful tribe among the "Red Hair" who lived 7,000 *li* away from China. The United Kingdom occupied over ten ports along the coast of the Atlantic, India, and Southeast Asia, possessed advanced cannons, warships, and a mighty navy, and sustained its economy through trade instead of territorial expansion.[22] Most importantly, Xu indicated that the root cause of British eastward advancement was to seize the Chinese ports for trade. Xu might have acquired such accurate information on the United Kingdom from his fellow officials, citizens of Amoy, and the new publications.

Xu accelerated his study of the rest of the world after the end of the Opium War, making use of every possible opportunity in his spare time to read books, to visit the Westerners, and to conduct research. All this work was in preparation for the publication of his famous title, *A Short Account of the Maritime Circuit*, in 1848.

In compiling *A Short Account of the Maritime Circuit*, Xu referred to three kinds of reference material: first, Chinese documents, such as the official histories, *An Account of Luzon* (*Luzon jilüe* 呂宋紀略) by Ye Qiangyong, *Record of Things Seen and Heard about the Maritime Countries* (*Haiguo wenjianlu* 海國聞見錄) by Chen Lunjong, and *On the Advantages and Disadvantages of the Countries and States of the Empire* (*Tianxia junguo libingshu* 天下郡國利病書) by Gu Yanwu. Second, Chinese books published by the Jesuits missionaries, including the works of Ricci, J. Aleni, and F. Verbiest. Third, the interview record of the foreign visitors in Fujian.[23] Xu, a high-ranked provincial official who visited the Westerners in person, was rare yet commendable circa the Opium War, when China had just been opened and people still judged anything foreign from a conservative perspective.

Xu befriended and interviewed several Westerners during his stay in Fujian, including D. Abeel, W. H. Cumming, George Tradseent Lay, and Rutherford Alcock and his wife. Among these interviewees, Abeel influenced Xu the most in his study of Western affairs. The first meeting of Xu and Abeel began in January 1844, when Xu, the Provincial Administration Commissioner of Fujian, presented at a diplomatic meeting in Amoy. Abeel, the interpreter in the meeting, was impressed by Xu's raising of insightful questions on world geography. Abeel tried to answer all the questions, and he suggested a second meeting with Xu, in which he would bring along an atlas for Xu's convenience to understand the locations and boundaries of the countries. Delighted to accept Abeel's suggestion, Xu soon arranged for the next discussion — a long-cherished dream and a rare opportunity of proselytization to Abeel. The dedicated missionary prepared a package of geography and religious books, the *New Testament* included, for the meeting, but the Chinese official's interest lie in the map rather than the *Holy Bible*, though he also perused these religious materials. Xu met Abeel several times during his business trip to Amoy in February and May in 1844. He grasped the opportunity to consult Abeel for his compilation of *A Short Account of the Maritime Circuit*. Abeel recalled the half-day meeting in May:

> He is as free and friendly, as it is possible for him to be. That he has gained considerable knowledge is very evident; but he is far more anxious to learn the state of the kingdoms of this world, than the truths of the kingdom of heaven. The maps he has constructed are by no means accurate. He aims more at obtaining general ideas of countries — the size, political importance, and commercial relations, especially with China — than at tracing the lines of latitude and longitude, and thus fixing the exact position of places. England, America, and France have been subjected to a more careful examination than the other countries of the world.[24]

Xu's meeting with W. H. Cumming also began in 1844, but it was a bit later than the meeting with Abeel. Cumming, a physician-missionary who opened a hospital in Amoy with another missionary James C. Hepburn, was mentioned in *A Short Account of the Maritime Circuit* for his familiarity of Switzerland.

The conversation between Xu and G. T. Lay in July 1844 was another significant event in both the history of Sino-Western cultural communication and an unofficial meeting between the Chinese and the British high officials. Lay, an English missionary and naturalist, was dispatched to China in 1836 as the Agent of the Anglican Church. He was promoted as the first English consul in Guangzhou due to his excellent performance as the interpreter of Henry Pottinger during the post-Opium War negotiation. At the time when Xu was working in Amoy, Lay was acting as the British Consul of Fuzhou. Xu, who was responsible for diplomatic affairs of the province, helped Lay settle in the south of Fuzhou city. Having mastered the Chinese language before visiting China, Lay encountered no language barrier when chatting with Xu. Through the three discussions with Lay, Xu learned much geography and politics of the Middle East. Xu mentioned the memorable conversations with "Lay the British official" in *A Short Account of the Maritime Circuit*, showing his respect to the foreign official.

Xu also established a cordial relationship with R. Alcock, the English Consul who was stationed at Fuzhou since March 1845. The Alcock couple spared no effort to help Xu compile his masterpiece. Alcock presented a globe to the Chinese official, while his wife sketched a world map, indicating the sphere of influence of the United Kingdom, France, and Russia with different colors.[25] Xu's learning efforts brought him remarkable success. By the end of 1845, his profound knowledge on world geography and international affairs was not only championed in Chinese academia, but it also astonished Westerners. Smith, an American who visited Fuzhou during the end of 1845, recalled his impression of Xu:

> Of all these officers of the local government the acting governor of the province (Xu) far exceeds the rest in the varied extent of his information and liberality of his views. In the reference that has already been made to him in the case of the full toleration of foreign religions, it has been seen that he is far in advance of the generality of his countrymen. In his intercourse with the British consul, he has alluded to the more prominent events of modern European history, and shown his general acquaintance with the whole cycle of European polities; as for instance, the difficulty of governing Ireland on account of popery, the revolt of Belgium from Holland, the separation from Britain and Spain of their colonies in North and South America, the ambitious career of Napoleon, and his closing defeat at Waterloo. He also seems to have heard of the excitement in England consequent on the discussion of the Maynooth grant. For hours together he will converse on geography, and he has pasted the Chinese names over an expensive American Atlas presented to him by one of his subordinate officers from Canton.[26]

A Short Account of the Maritime Circuit had 10 volumes, with enough informative content to cover an overall account of the earth, the five continents, and the five oceans, two about Asia, three about Europe, one about Africa, and two about North and South America.

Compared with other geography titles published circa the Opium War, *A Short Account of the Maritime Circuit* featured Xu's selection of useful reference works. Xu, instead of compiling all the previous works and the interview reports, analyzed the data carefully, discarded any unreliable record, and organized all the content with his own words. Once he found that his knowledge was contradictory to the map from Mrs. Alcock, Xu soon wrote to her for confirmation. Moreover, the content of the book was informative but the wording was irredundant. With the aid of illustrations, the globe, the latitudes and longitudes, the Northern and Southern hemispheres, the poles, and the geography and history of over 80 countries were systematically introduced, helping readers to have a comprehensive understanding about the world. No unnecessary textual inquiry was found. The description of both the continental and maritime countries made the book more outstanding than the *Record of Things Seen and Heard about the Maritime Countries*.

Another feature of *A Short Account of the Maritime Circuit* was the focus on practical knowledge and the author's awareness of current affairs. Understanding the strength of Western powers was the most urgent task for the Chinese scholars to prevent a second defeat in war. Therefore, nearly half of the content was the introduction of the United States, the United Kingdom, France, the Netherlands, and other European colonial powers — the biggest threat to the Chinese domination in East Asia. The author particularly focused on the narration of the military strength and their political institution of the Western powers. For instance, the British parliamentary system was carefully studied:

> The parliament in London has two houses: the house of the aristocrat and the house of the commoners. The house of the aristocrat is composed of noblemen and clergymen; the house of the commoners is composed of elected intellectuals. When there are any political affairs, the king issues an edict to the Prime Minister, who would then inform the noblemen to hold a meeting, to refer to ordinances, and to decide the practicality of the policies. Once finished, [the aristocrats] refer the cases to the Lower House, who would make the final decision. Without the approval of the Lower House, the policy would not be implemented.[27]

And the federation system of the United States was explained:

> After acquiring the American territory, Washington informed his subjects that to pass the right of governance to only one's descendants was against common sense. It was better to choose a virtuous man to be the leader of the state. [Washington] divided the American land into 26 parts under the leadership of one Governor and one Vice Governor, who had a four-year term of office. The Governor can continue his second term if the fellow people found the Governor an eligible candidate; otherwise, the Vice Governor would replace the Governor. [The people] will vote for other parties if there is no suitable choice of persons...Both present officials or common people are qualified to be recommended. The retired governors had the same social status with commoners. Among the 26 Governors there is an elected President, who stayed in the capital to respond to diplomatic and military affairs.[28]

George Washington, who retreated from his post after the end of the term of service, was praised as "an incredible man" by Xu:

> He was an uncommon man. He conquered more rapidly than Shing (Chen Sheng) and Kwang (Wu Guang), and in courage he was superior to Tsaon (Cao Cao) and Lew (Liu Bei). Seizing the two-edged sword of three cubits long, he opened the country 10,000 *le* (*li*). He then refused to receive a title, or to secure one for his posterity, preferring to establish an elective administration. Patriotism to be commended under the whole heaven! Truly like the three dynasties (The Three Kingdoms Period, 220–280)! In administering the Government he fostered virtuous customs, and, avoiding war, made his country superior to all other nations. I have seen his portrait. His countenance exhibits great mental power. Ah! Who would not call him an uncommon man![29]

Never had a Chinese leader, except the legendary emperors Yao and Shun, passed the right of governance to non-descendants or relatives. The "generosity" of Washington shocked Xu, who particularly highlighted the sentence of "Patriotism is to be commended under the whole heaven!" — an ideal political practice to the Chinese intellectuals.

A Short Account of the Maritime Circuit soon became an essential reference work to the Chinese scholars after its publication. Wei Yuan quoted nearly 40,000 words of the book when revising his *Illustrated Gazetteer of the Maritime Countries*. Wang Tao also highly recommended the book for its tracing of the historical vicissitudes, the rise and decline of various nations, and the ever-changing global situation.[30] Reformist leaders Kang Youwei and Liang Qichao also benefitted much from reading the book. Kang read the book during his journey to Hong Kong, where he was astonished by the Western architecture, the clean and well-managed roads, and the law and order. He was inspired to have a better understanding of the Western powers after reading Xu's masterpiece.[31] Liang, having failed in the provincial examination, returned home via Shanghai, where he bought a copy of *A Short Account of the Maritime Circuit* from the market. Not until his perusal of the book did he understand the existence of the five continents.[32] He also recognized the pioneering role of the book on the enhancement of the understanding of the Chinese towards world geography.[33] Zhang Yilin, the education minister in the early Republican Period, recalled his learning of the study of George Washington from Xu's book.[34] Much impressed by the deeds of the first President of the United States, he was eager to visit the country and to have a firsthand study of the democratic system. Yan Xishan, a fellow villager of Xu who had neither the chance to study overseas nor to attend school in his adolescence, regarded the book as the only key for him to access the Western world.[35] Huang Qingcheng also recommended the book in the geography section of his *A Shortcut to Enlightenment* (*Xunmeng jiejing* 訓蒙捷徑).

Even the government and the Chinese diplomats found the book indispensable. It was reprinted and financed by the Ministry of Foreign Affairs. It was made one of the textbooks in the Imperial Foreign Language Institute. It was widely consulted by Zeng Guofan, the chief person-in-charge of China's modernization reform, on policy-making. Guo Songtao and Xue Fucheng brought along the book on their diplomatic trips to Europe during the early 1870s.[36] Xue even planned to compile the sequel of the book, but it was left unfinished.

Fig. 5.3 A Portrait of Guo Songtao, the Qing diplomat

A Short Account of the Maritime Circuit also received much attention from Western intelligentsia after its publication. The September and October issues of the *North-China Herald* used two long articles to comment on this book. These articles began with a biography of Xu. The editor highly appreciated Xu's objectivity in mentioning Christianity and Westerners, and his active role in changing the Chinese perception of Westerners as being rude and irrational.[37] W. A. P. Martin, delighted with Xu's appreciation of the first American president, presented a stone tablet, with the paragraph inscribed with "the uncommon man" to the Washington Memorial Hall.[38] Xu, though having more interest in geography, also introduced world history, politics, the judicial system, taxation, and religion. Most of this content was new to the Chinese, particularly the principle of the presumption of innocence that contradicted the "presumption of guilty before trial" in the Chinese legal system.

This book was widely circulated in Japanese academia as well. The Japanese edition, which was published in 1861 and reprinted several times, featured a colored world map, names of historical figures and places expressed in both Japanese and English, and the adoption of the Japanese era titles. It was also an important reference work for the Japanese reformists to initiate the modernization movement.[39]

While the book was a great hit, the career of Xu benefitted nothing from his masterpiece. Ironically and dramatically, Xu was downgraded from the position of the second-ranked Governor of Fujian to the fifth-ranked Vice Minister of the Office of Imperial Stables in 1851, and he was dismissed in the next year.[40] It was believed that the power struggle in the court resulted in the downfall of Mujangga, Xu's supporter, and the decline of Xu's clique. Xu was accused by the opposing clique for not holding a firm attitude towards the foreigners during negotiations, and expressing disrespectful opinions in his *A Short Account of the Maritime Circuit*. The so-called "rebellious narration" was actually a twisted interpretation from his political enemies, who amended the quotation of "Germany was the mainstay of the imperial power of the Western territory" into "Germany was the mainstay of the imperial power of the world" in the memorial submitted to the Emperor. Even the authoritative *New York Times* doubted that Xu's dismissal was a result of the publication of *A Short Account of the Maritime Circuit*:

> Till within a quarter of a century, the study of barbarian annals has been one of the most dangerous branches of learning a Chinese could pursue; and a candid geographer (Xu Jiyu) has dared the fate of Galileo.[41]

When Westernization became an irreversible trend in China 13 years after Xu's dismissal, the banished minister was re-appointed to serve in the Ministry of Foreign Affairs and the Imperial Foreign Language Institute because of his profound knowledge of Western affairs, yet he was already in his declining age at the time.

On October 21, 1867, at the American embassy in China, Berlingame represented the American government and presented a portrait to Xu. For the details of the ceremony, refer to the article "America in China" from the *New York Times* in the appendix. The meeting should have been a grand event in the history of Sino-American diplomacy, yet it was never recorded in Chinese historical accounts.

Wei Yuan: One Publication and One Conclusion

Among the mid-Qing scholars who specialized in geography, Liang Tingnan was born and grew up in Guangdong, thus having a firsthand contact with foreign affairs. Xu Jiyu was a provincial high-ranked official in Fujian, who was responsible for maritime defense and diplomatic negotiation. Wei Yuan (1794–1857), on the contrary, was neither born nor worked in the coastal area; however, with his strong sense of "statecraft," he managed to compile the *Illustrated Gazetteer of the Maritime Countries*, a masterpiece comparable to *A Short Account of the Maritime Circuit* of Xu Jiyu.

Wei Yuan, also named Wei Moshen, who was born in the isolated region of Shaoyang, Hunan. Similar to the general Chinese scholars, Wei attended local traditional college and sat the civil examination at an early age. His concern for social issues sprouted after his participation in the imperial examination in Beijing, where the Hunan villager was exposed to life in a metropolis. After failing in the examination, Wei travelled the rest of China, making friends with several intellectuals, such as Lin Zexu, Gong Zizhen, and Bao Shichen.

Illustrated Gazetteer of the Maritime Countries was undoubtedly the most representative work of Wei Yuan, yet it was not his only publication. *The Collected Essays about Statecraft of the Qing Dynasty* (*Huangqiao jingshi wenbian* 皇朝經世文編), compiled in 1825 at the request of He Changling, the Provincial Administration Commissioner of Jiangsu, was the first title of Wei Yuan. The 120-volume collectanea included articles completed before the reign of Daoguang on various topics, such as academic development, politics, administration, taxation, rites, military, law and punishment, and public works. Through the compilation of this collection, Wei strengthened his understanding and awareness of social issues which inspired his further research on the West.

His first direct encounter with foreigners came with the outbreak of the Opium War, during which he participated in the defense of Zhejiang. Based on the oral confession of an English captive, he acquired a better understanding of the overseas kingdom and he compiled his second title, *A Brief Record of England* (*Yingjili xiaoji* 英吉利小記). China's humiliated defeat in the Opium War had badly shaken the confidence and morale of Wei who wanted to contribute to the country. Once Lin Zexu invited him to compile an updated geography reference based on his *Gazetteer of Four Continents* in 1841, he did not hesitate to accept the request.

The first draft of the *Illustrated Gazetteer of the Maritime Countries*, with 50 sections included, was finished in 1842. In the following decade Wei kept revising and adding information, enlarging the book to 100 sections in the 1852 edition. The book featured a strong sense of statecraft as was reflected in its preface:

> What is the purpose of the present work? Its purpose is to show how to use barbarians to fight barbarians, how to make the barbarians pacify one another [to our advantage], and how to employ the techniques of the barbarians in order to bring the barbarians under control…In ancient times those who succeeded in driving off the barbarians knew the enemy's position as clearly as if it were spread out upon their own desk or carpet; they were informed of the enemy's condition as intimately as if the enemy were dining or sleeping with them.
>
> Note: Wei Yuan 魏源 , *Haiguo tuzhi* 海國圖志 (Illustrated Gazetteer of the Maritime Countries). Translated by K. C. Liu. In Wm. Theodore de Bary and Richard Lufrano ed., *Sources of Chinese Tradition* 2 (New York: Columbia University Press, 2000), 209-210.

Wei added two sections, "On Maritime Defense" and "A Summary of Maritime Defense," in addition to the introduction of the history, politics, and economics of various countries of the world — a different approach compared to other geography treatises at the time. Wei particularly spent 15 sections to describe the principles, production, and operation of the Western steamship, cannon, bomb, fort, and torpedo. This content was irrelevant to geography, yet its inclusion demonstrated the strong sense of practical statesmanship of Wei.

Wei, a man with great political ambition, had an unsteady career. He did not pass the imperial examination until the age of 52, and he was appointed to be a low-ranked provincial official responsible for trivial matters. He was always sensitive to the root problem of China's weakness which he felt lied in the dictatorship that hindered effective communication between the ruling class and the subject people, yet his position as the magistrate offered him no chance to express his concern towards the decline of China. Wei's study of Western knowledge after the Opium War was not a blind worship of the Western democratic system, but it was actually an expression of his resentment towards the establishment.

Wei's appeal to the British parliamentary system was witnessed from the large section of the *Illustrated Gazetteer of the Maritime Countries*, indicating that no decision would be approved without the consent of the parliament. Even the king, who had the right on deciding military affairs (such as the dispatching of troops and concluding treaties) and socioeconomic issues (such as the amendment of ordinances, appointment of officials, increase of taxation, and the issue of coins) should allow the parliament to discuss the policies. The parliament was also responsible for monitoring various government departments, deciding the promotion or dismissal of the officials from the performance in the previous year. The right of the parliament, however, originated from the people instead of the aristocrats: "The parliament will pass any bill if the public finds it unproblematic, while the parliament will veto any bill if the public shows any negative response," according to Wei's description.

The federation of the United States, a completely different political institution to the autocracy of China, was highly praised in the *Illustrated Gazetteer of the Maritime Countries*. According to Wei, the strength of the United States lied not only in the leadership of strong statesmen, but the establishment of "the everlasting excellent institution." Wei particularly found the election of senate members and the governance by an elected president contributed to the high efficiency in policy-making.

Illustrated Gazetteer of the Maritime Countries and *A Short Account of the Maritime Circuit* by Xu Jiyu were the two most representative and influential geography publications in the mid-Qing period. Each title had its own merits according to Wang Tao: Wei's work featured wide coverage, while Xu's title was characterized by its conciseness. The comprehensiveness of the *Illustrated Gazetteer of the Maritime Countries* was evidenced by its long list of bibliography, which included both Chinese and Western reference works, as well as ancient and contemporary documents (refer to table 5.1 and table 5.2).

Table 5.1 Bibliography of the *Illustrated Gazetteer of the Maritime Countries*

Author	Title	Remarks
A. Vagnoni	*Treatise on the Composition of the Universe*	
Chen Lunjong	*Record of Things Seen and Heard about the Maritime Countries*	
D. B. McCartee	*An Encyclopedia for Safety Adventure*	The 1850, 1851, and 1852 issues
E. C. Bridgman	*A Brief History of the United States of America*	
F. Furtabo	*Explanation on the Celestial Spheres*	
F. Sambiasi	*De Anima*	

(Cont'd)

Author	Title	Remarks
F. Verbiest	*Illustrated Explanation of the Entire World*	
Hang Shijun	*Further Study of Christianity*	
Huang Kechui	*An Account of Luzon*	
J. Aleni	*Geography of Foreign Countries to China*	
Ji Xiaolan	*Random Jottings from the Cottage of Close Scrutiny*	
José Martinho Marques[43]	*A Study of Geography*[44]	The most referred reference work
	On the Earth and Astronomy	
J. R. Morrison, M. C. Morrison, and R. Morrison	*History of the Foreign Countries*	Wei claimed that the *History of the Foreign Countries* was composed by Morrison. Zou Zhenhuan believed the title involved joint efforts of R. Morrison and his sons.
K. F. A. Gutzlaff	*A General Account of Trade*	
	Eastern Western Monthly Magazine	
	Universal Geography	Published in Singapore in 1838
M. Benoist	*A Complete Map of the Globe*	
Ma Huan	*The Overall Survey of the Ocean's Shores*	
Nimaca Qishiyi	*Record of Things Seen and Heard in the Western Regions*	
Qian Daxin	*Collected Essays of the Qianyan Hall*	
R. Q. Way	*Exploration of a World Map*	• The 1853 edition • Wei miswrote R. Q. Way as a British
Wang Dahai	*A Desultory Account of the Malayan Archipelago*	
Wei Yuan	*A Brief Record of England*	
	Records of August Military Achievements of the Qing Court	
Xiao Lingyu	*On England*	
Xie Qinggao	*Maritime Records*	
Xu Jiyu	*A Short Account of the Maritime Circuit*	

(Cont'd)

Author	Title	Remarks
Xu Song	*Records of Waterways in the Western Region*	
Yan Sizong	*To Measure the Sea with an Oyster Shell in the Southern Ocean*	
Yang Guangxian	*An Exposure of Heresy*	
Yao Ying	*Journey to Tibet and the Southwest China*	
Yao Ying	*The Territory of England with Illustrations*	
Ye Zhongjin	*Brief Record of Occurences Relating to the English Barbarian*	
Yu Yonghe	*Journey across the Small Sea*	
Yu Zhengxie	*A Variety of Manuscripts Written in 1833*	
Zhang Yi	*On the Eastern and Western Oceans*	
Zhang Yuji	*Records of Macao*	

Table 5.2 Statistics of Citation in the *Illustrated Gazetteer of the Maritime Countries*

Title	Number of citation
An Encyclopedia for Safety Adventure	11
A General Account of Trade	14
A Brief History of the United States of America	24
Eastern Western Monthly Magazine	28
Exploration of a World Map	34
Universal Geography	57
A Study of Geography	91

Wei referred to considerable Chinese titles, yet he actually cited more from Western publications — amounting to 80 *percent* of the content, as he found it more appropriate to study the Western affairs from the narration of the Western authors.[45] For instance, by quoting from *A Brief History of the United States of America* by E. C. Bridgman, Wei successfully indicated the wrong description of the United States in the *Maritime Records,* which regarded the United States as an island to the west of England. Wei maintained that the territory of the United States was too large to be regarded as an island, stressing that the misunderstanding was a result of the carelessness of Xie Qinggao, the author of the *Maritime Records*.[46]

Wei, who considered the Western titles more reliable accounts, only consulted ancient and Chinese titles for any inconsistent description among the reference works. In determining the Chinese translated terms of Denmark, he made inquiries into *Gazetteer of Four Continents, A General Account of Trade, Eastern Western Monthly Magazine, A Map of the Myriad Countries of the World, A Study of Geography* (*Dili beikao* 地理備考), *History of the Foreign Countries* (*Waiguo shilüe* 外國史略), and other titles, clarifying that both *Lianguo* (嗹國), *Lianma* (嗹馬), and *Dali* (大尼) were the transliterated terms of Denmark, and such a misunderstanding was the result of territorial rearrangement during the Congress of Vienna in 1815.[47] Wei also attached more than 70 maps and 80 diagrams of various machines in *Illustrated Gazetteer of the Maritime Countries*.

Wei had never stepped foot out of Chinese territory, nor learned any foreign language. Therefore, he could rely only on the Western titles translated by the missionaries. The publications of the Jesuits missionaries were actually more widely circulated in the academic world than the newly published titles of the Protestant missionaries, yet a large proportion of the content of the *Illustrated Gazetteer of the Maritime Countries* was similar to the Protestant publications. Neither did Wei nor his biography in the official history mention the way that he acquired these Protestant publications, yet from the content of the *Illustrated Gazetteer of the Maritime Countries*, the tracing of his learning process was still possible.

Illustrated Gazetteer of the Maritime Countries received widespread attention in Chinese academia. Wei's proposal of "subduing the barbarian through the mastery of the technique of the barbarian" guided the Self-Strengthening Movement in China. Zuo Zongtang, the leader of the Self-Strengthening Movement responsible for inland defense, wrote a preface for the revised edition of the *Illustrated Gazetteer of the Maritime Countries*, showing his appreciation to Wei, his fellow villager. The introduction of the parliamentary and federal systems also directed the political modernization attempts in the turn of the nineteenth and twentieth centuries. Kang Youwei claimed that a significant proportion of his knowledge originated from Wei's title.

Wei's masterpiece was soon introduced to Japan after its publication, yet it was listed as a forbidden book by the Tokugawa shogunate, which prohibited any selling of the book under the fear that Wei's ideology would trigger the collapse of the seclusion policy and the outbreak of anti-regime revolts.[48] Another edition of the *Illustrated Gazetteer of the Maritime Countries* was also banned from circulation. The banning was lifted following the opening of Japan in 1854. With the declining reputation of the shogunate, scholars soon engaged in the translation and study of Wei's masterpiece, regarding it the key to the modern world. Seven out of the 15 imported copies were kept by the shogunate, while the rest were on sale. The Japanese publishers could not wait to reprint the book. Over 20 editions of the *Illustrated Gazetteer of the Maritime Countries* were published during 1854 to 1858. Similar to the situation in China, this book played an important role to ignite patriotic scholars' enthusiasm to initiate reform. Sakuma Shōzan, Yoshida Shoin, and Saigo Takamori, the leaders of the *Sonnō-jōi* Movement (尊皇攘夷, literally means respecting the emperor and rejecting the barbarian), developed their modernization theories through the reading of the *Illustrated Gazetteer of the Maritime Countries*.[49] However, it was pretty ironic that the Japanese scholars had a much better understanding of the essentials of Western learning than the Chinese reformers though they absorbed only the "re-imported" knowledge from Chinese publications.[50]

Li Shanlan, Wang Tao, Guan Sifu, and Zhang Fuxi: Pioneering the Introduction of Modern Science

Not all the Chinese scholars were interested in compiling books on Western learning like Lin Zexu, Liang Tingnan, Xu Jiyu, and Wei Yuan. Several of them contributed to the dissemination of Western learning through the translation of Western titles with the help of the Protestant missionaries — the method of "*xiyi zhongshu*." Such a translation method required the missionaries to have a basic standard of the Chinese language to explain the meaning of the Western titles. The Chinese scholars, on the contrary, needed not to be proficient in English, as their duty was to present the previously unheard ideas by using simple and clear words, making them understandable to the general Chinese populace. Even though several of these translators had been equipped with scientific knowledge, there was difficulty to digest the unheard of concepts and to invent new scientific terms in Chinese. The translators' contributions to the dissemination of modern science to China should be remembered.

Li Shanlan: Mastering mathematics after seven nights of meditation

Li Shanlan (1811–1882), also named as Li Renshu (pseudonym Qiuren), was highly respected in the history of translation and science in modern China. His multi-aspect achievements in mathematics, physics, astronomy, biology, and other fields had been well studied in other reference works. This chapter, therefore, concerned more the influence of Western learning on him and his attitude towards Western learning.

Li was born in Haining, Zhejiang in 1811, the year when Robert Morrison published the first Chinese book in Guangzhou. Zhejiang, the most literate province in the Chinese empire, had been deeply influenced by Western learning since the late Ming Dynasty and numerous scholars had been nurtured there, Li included. Surrounded by a strong atmosphere of study, Li exposed himself not only to the Confucian classics, but also mathematics. His mastery of the content of the *Nine Chapters on the Mathematical Art* (*Jiuzhang suanshu* 九章算術) and *Euclid's Elements* (the translated edition by Ricci and Xu) in the age of 10 and 15, respectively, demonstrated his talent in mathematics. Sitting on the top of a mountain and observing the celestial movements was another daily activity of Li. By the age of 35, Li had been a well-known author, with three titles on mathematics and astronomy: *Explanation of Secrets in Squares and Circles* (*Fangyuan chanyou* 方圓闡幽), *Revealing the Secrets of the Bow and Arrow Star* (*Hushi qimi* 弧矢啟秘), and *Exploration to Logarithm* (*Duishu tanyuan* 對數探源).

Li was undoubtedly qualified to participate in the translation of Western titles with the missionaries. He left his hometown for Shanghai, already a developed treaty port 200 *li* away from Haining, to pursue further study in science. His journey to Shanghai was mentioned in the *Chinese Scientific Magazine*:

> [Li Shanlan] visited the chapter of the London Missionary Society Mission Press in Shanlan, showing his publications to Mr. Medhurst, and asking Medhurst whether the Western academia had such learning. Wylie, who was working at the London Missionary Society Mission Press, found Li's works remarkable. He thus invited Li to translate the difficult Western mathematics and astronomy treatises.[51]

He had been working with A. Wylie, J. Edkins, and A. Williamson from 1852 to 1854 in the London Missionary Society Mission Press to translate eight titles, including *The Sequel of the Elements*, *Elements of Botany*, *Elements of Analytical Geometry and of Differential and Integral Calculus*, *Elements of Algebra*, *Discourse on Astronomy*, *An Elementary Treatise on Mechanics*, *Explanation on Conic Sections (Yuanzhui quxian shuo* 圓錐曲線說*)*, and *The Mathematical Writings of Newton (Nairui shuli* 奈瑞數理*)*.

Li pioneered not only the introduction of Western subjects, such as multivariable mathematics, classical mechanics, botany, and astronomy to China, but also the use of the newly invented scientific terms, most of which are still widely used in present-day Chinese academia, such as *weifenxue* (微分學 , differential calculus), *jifenxue* (積分學 , integral calculus), *fangchengshi* (方程式 , equation), *daishuxue* (代數學 , algebra), *zhiwuxue* (植物學 , botany), and *xibao* (細胞 , cell). His achievements other than translation included the compilation of *The True Explanation of Firearms* (*Huoqi zhenque* 火器真訣), a thesis on ballistics through mathematical analysis, the calculation of the area of the circle and the volume of a cone by definite integral — the so-called "conic technique (*jianzhuishu* 尖錐術)," and the conduction of research on power series.[52]

Actually, the difficulty that Li faced in translating various titles and inventing abundant new terms was unprecedented and unimaginable. Yet the largest obstacle of Li's studying of Western learning lied in the conservativeness of the public. Sitting in the imperial examination had long been regarded as the most appropriate path for scholars. Li, though he had also attended the provincial examination at 17, had never written the eight-legged essay and instead read Confucian classics after boycotting the examination. He had been criticized by his teacher for getting a higher score in mathematics than Classical Studies, and he risked accusation from the public of "changing the Chinese tradition by the barbarous culture (*yiyi bianxia* 以夷變夏)" through staying with the foreigners. Working with foreigners was already a rebellious act in the Chinese society, not to mention being friends with them. The general hostility and discrimination about staying with foreigners was evidenced from Li's picnic with J. Edkins in Hangzhou:

> I accompanied Edkins to travel in Hangzhou. Our trip to Mount Tianzhu was discovered by the General. Never had a Westerner been to Hangzhou at the time, so the public was astonished [by our travelling]. The General particularly asked the Governor of Yanhe. The Governor thus responded by forcing Edkins to return to Shanghai. Later I returned to my hometown.[53]

Strictly speaking, Li might not have been the first Chinese scholar to assist in the translation of Western science titles in the mid-Qing period, as the well written *A Short Discourse on Astronomy* by B. Hobson and the *Catechism of Astronomy* by A. P. Happer hinted at editorial works by Chinese assistants. Still, his pioneering role in the translation of scientific reference works was undeniable. With the prevalence of the Westernization movement, Li was employed as a teacher in the Imperial Foreign Language Institute.

Wang Tao: the Long Hair *Zhuangxuan*[54]

The multi-aspect achievements of Wang Tao were thoroughly studied in Chinese academia. Those people who conducted research in the history of thought classified Wang as the representative of the earliest modern reformist. Scholars who studied the history of journalism focused on the *Universal Circulating Herald* (*Xunhuan ribao* 循環日報) published by Wang Tao. Sinologues who were interested in the history of the Westward dissemination of Eastern learning found his cooperation with J. Legge in translating Confucian classics into English highly impressive. Historians specialized in the history of education recognized his management of the Shanghai Polytechnic Institution, which nurtured new types of intellectuals. Experts in political history investigated his support of the Taiping Uprising. However, his contributions in the introduction of Western science to China received too little attention that was worth more exploration.

The differences between Wang Tao and Li Shanlan in the career of translation were obvious. Wang, 17 years younger than Li, had started working in the London Missionary Society Mission Press since his teen years. Li, on the contrary, did not engage in translation until the age of 40. Wang had no foundation in Western learning before his arrival in Shanghai, while Li had been trained in mathematics and astronomy since his adolescence. Li, without any personal network, recommended himself to the missionaries to join the translation projects, while Wang was employed with the recommendation of his father, Wang Changgui, a helpful and knowledgeable assistant of W. H. Medhurst. Therefore, Li began his career as a translator with passion, while Wang merely treated the translation as a job inherited from his father. Fortunately, Wang made fast progress due to his intelligence and adaptability to new challenges, making great contributions to the introduction of Western learning. Despite these differences, both Wang and Li had remarkable achievements.

Too inexperienced to take up the work independently, Wang cooperated with missionaries to translate several titles (refer to table 5.3). He was an excellent observer and hard-working student who kept learning new knowledge. In addition to the translation of the scheduled titles, Wang also compiled three other titles during his spare time: *Explanation of Western Learning with Diagrams* (*Xixue tushuo* 西學圖說), *An Inquiry into the Beginnings of Western Learning* (*Xixue yuanshi kao* 西學原始考) — an addendum to the *Outline of New Studies in the Science* (*Gezhi xinxue tigang* 格致新學提綱), and *An Inquiry of the European Publications* (*Taixi zhushu kao* 泰西著述考), which listed the works of the Jesuits missionaries compiled in the Ming-to-Qing transitional period. These three titles, together with *A History of Astronomy of the Western Countries*, the *Popular Treatise on Mechanics*, and the *Record of the Sino-British Trade* (*Huaying tongshang shilüe* 華英通商事略), were published in the series of the *Six titles on the Collections of Western Learning* (*Xixue jicun liuzhong* 西學輯存六種). Studying these titles in detail, readers could found that most content was completed before 1860 — circa his working in the London Missionary Society Mission Press.

Table 5.3 Translated Works of Wang Tao

Translation partner	Title	Working years	Remarks
J. Edkins	*Chinese Almanac*	1853–1859	
	Outline of New Studies in Science	1853 and 1858	The book was later compiled in *An Inquiry into the Beginnings of Western Learning*
A. Wylie	*A History of Astronomy of the Western Countries*		
	Record of the Sino-British Trade	1857	The book was serialized in the *Universal Miscellany* (issue no. 2, 6-10).

A History of Astronomy of the Western Countries

The translation of the *A History of Astronomy of the Western Countries* began after a discussion between Wang and A. Wylie:

> I was fascinated by the words of astronomers since my teenage years, yet I found the words of the astrology and apocalypse unbelievable. Aged 20, I travelled to Shanghai, where I met a Westerner, Wylie. We spent our spare time editing books, and through inquiry, I learned a little about Western astronomy. One day, when I asked [Wylie] about the biography of the Western astronomers, Wylie showed me a book, talking and gesturing. I thus recorded his words, spending ten days to edit the manuscript. Since then, the history of astronomy of the Western countries has been well understood. And I was delighted and satisfied.[55]

This book traced the historical development of Western astronomy. It started with the celestial movement described in the *Old Testament*, it continued to elaborate the astronomical phenomena documented in the historical accounts of

Homer and Thucydides, and it was followed by the thoughts of representative astronomers in the West, including Ptolemy, Copernicus, Tycho, Kepler, Galileo, Newton, Laplace, and Herschel.

Wang, an astronomy amateur, was confident that his work, co-translated with A. Wylie, was the most authoritative Chinese reference work on Western astronomy. The translator compared the development of Chinese and Western astronomy, concluding that the backwardness of Chinese astronomy lied in the blind adherence to old theories and practice, while the Westerner always held a skeptical view towards previous opinions, striving to surpass the achievements of the precedents:

> There were numerous astronomy schools in Western academia. These schools had no conclusion until the proclamation of the heliocentric theory by Copernicus...Our China, on the contrary, firmly holds the traditional belief of a static earth. The moving of the earth was similar to the principle of sailing — the boatman sees the coast "moving backward" but it was actually the boat that moved.[56]
>
> Both Chinese and Western mathematics were far from accurate. Why do Western methods surpass the Chinese techniques nowadays? Generally speaking, it is due to the absence of creativity and innovativeness among the Chinese scholars.[57]

Wang, unlike Ruan Yuan, the author of the *Biographies of the Astronomers* who misunderstood that the Western astronomers supported both the geocentric model and the heliocentric theory and criticized the inconsistency of the astronomers, demonstrated his observation of the development of Western astronomical thoughts in *A History of Astronomy of the Western Countries*. However, it was pitiful that Wang did not go a step further to explore the cause of the Chinese to firmly believe the traditional belief, leaving the question to be answered by contemporary scholars.

An Inquiry into the Beginnings of Western Learning

An Inquiry into the Beginnings of Western Learning was a complete annalistic history on the development of Western science that listed all the major discoveries, inventions, events, and representative scientists. The annals covered the development of considerable fields of study, including mathematics, physics, chemistry, astronomy, geography, geology, biology, medical science, agriculture, philosophy, law, music, architecture, and art, from 2400 BC to 1874 within 30,000 words.

Table 5.4 Sections of *An Inquiry into the Beginnings of Western Learning*

Subject	Sections
Applied science	The invention of the telegraph; the production of tap, sewing machine, glasses, telescope, and glass; gilding
Astronomy	Calculation of the radius of the earth by the ancient Greeks; the making of armillary sphere; Ptolemaic system; Copernicus system; the Tychonic model; the discoveries of Uranus and Neptune and their satellites; the use of thermometer; the observation and discovery of the sunspots; the achievements of Galileo, Kepler, Laplace, and Newton
Biography	The process of understanding the human structure of the European; zoology and botany; the consumption of coffee and cigarettes of the Europeans; the invention of inoculation
Chemistry	The discovery of elements; the development of metallurgy
Fine art	The invention of oil painting; the biographies of representative musicians, poets, and literati men; the foundation of notable universities and museums in the West
Geography	Cartography; discovery of the Americas; the opening of new sea routes; the arrival of the Europeans at Australia and New Zealand; the exploration of the Arctic Ocean; the birth of modern geology
History	The history of Western philosophy since Socrates; the history of the legal system in the West; the emergence of parliament; the urban history of Paris
Mathematics	The history of algebra; the establishment of Calculus; the invention of logarithm; the popularization of Arabic numbers in the West
Physics	Mechanical theory of Archimedes; Classical Mechanics of Newton; the discovery of electricity; the nature of light; the pinhole camera model

The publication of *An Inquiry into the Beginnings of Western Learning* was significant for the late-Qing scholars who wanted to understand the classification of Western learning. It symbolized a transformation of learning: from a fragmentary accumulation of knowledge to a systematic absorption of knowledge.

Explanation of Western Learning with Diagrams

There was limited information about the compilation process of the *Explanation of Western Learning with Diagrams*. It was believed that the book was composed when Wang was serving as the assistant of J. Edkins in the editing of the *Chinese Almanac*. This book, attached with 31 annotated diagrams, covered mainly astronomical topics, including the structure of the Sun, the equator, the revolution of the planets, features of Mercury, Venus, Mars, Jupiter, Saturn, and Uranus, and axial precision. There were also a few sections on astrology, acoustics, optics, and the operation of telescopes. The book was also credited for using simple wording.

The profound knowledge of Li Shanlan might beat Wang, yet in the passion for advocating the learning of Western science, Wang indisputably gained an upper hand. Through translating Western titles, teaching in the Shanghai Polytechnic Institution, and the publishing of the *Universal Circulating Herald*, Wang provided a new direction for the development of Chinese astronomy: it no longer remained at the level of a superstitious astrology or learning to serve only the emperor.

Wang also criticized any old belief that he regarded as unconvincing. A majority of scholars believed that the section of "Investigation of things (*Gewu* 格物)" and "The Records of Examination of Craftsman (*Kaogongji* 考工記)" in the *Great Learning* (*Daxue* 大學) and the *Institutes of Zhou* (Zhouli 周禮), respectively, were lost and introduced to the West during the unrest in the Spring and Autumn Period. These two sections became the origin of Western science, mathmatics, and architecture according to the Chinese. To Wang, such a prevailing belief of the Chinese origin of Western learning indisputably helped pacify the arrogant conservatives while preventing enlightened scholars from being discriminated against by the public. However, after conducting research on the origin of Western astronomy, he found such comments too general to trace the development of Western learning and it would be a potential obstacle to the modernization of China in the long run. It was unquestionably true that several Western techniques, such as the production of gunpowder, paper-making, and the use of the compass, were introduced from China but the contributions of the Islamic scholars who re-introduced the Oriental learning to the West, and the European intellectuals who improved the techniques from the East, should not be understated. For instance, algebra, also named as the "Method from the East (*Donglaifa* 東來法)" by the late Ming scholars, originated from the Middle East instead of the Far East.[58] Actually, recognizing the strength of Western technique did not contradict the appreciation of the Eastern learning.

Guan Sifu: the forgotten translation talent

Guan Sifu (also called Guan Xiaoyi) was occasionally mentioned in history because of his father, Guan Tong (also Guan Yizhi), a representative literary man of the School of Tongcheng, or his teacher, Feng Guifen, the leader of the Self-Strengthening Movement. His achievement in assisting B. Hopson to translate the three Western medical titles — *First Lines of the Practice of Surgery in the West, Treatise on Midwifery and Diseases of Children*, and *Practice of Medicine and Materia Medica* — was always forgotten by scholars.

Guan inherited the tradition of study from his scholarly family and was influenced by the flourishing culture of his hometown, Nanjing. He was a holder of the *xiucai* degree (秀才 , literally means the "flowering scholar"), yet his pursuit of study was suspended by the outbreak of the Taiping Uprising, during which the long-haired troops conquered his hometown. Guan escaped to Wuxi, where he met J. Edkins. He followed the missionary to settle in Shanghai. Having shown his interest in medical study, Guan approached B. Hobson, discussing medicine with the physician-missionary. Guan's interest chimed perfectly with Hobson's profession, and the two scholars decided to translate the medical titles together. Actually, Guan was the first expert in both Chinese and Western medicine.

He was invited by E. C. Bridgman to edit *A Brief History of the United States of America*, which would be reprinted in 1861 under the title of the *Brief Survey of the United States of America*.[59] His excellent performance brought him another job from Bridgman, the translation of the *Old Testament*. However, Guan refused to take up the translation of the *Holy Bible* as he found it rebellious for a Confucian to spread the heterodox belief. His friend Wang Tao, who also helped the missionaries to translate part of the *Holy Bible*, advised his friend not to take the matter so seriously, saying that their works involved only the amendment of words instead of the judgment of the Christian teaching. However, Guan still found Wang's opinion unacceptable, claiming that he would never take part in the translation of the Christian materials in his lifetime as he found the job offensive to ancient sages.[60]

Zhang Fuxi: a beacon of the introduction of Western science

Zhang Fuxi, also called Zhang Nanping, was born in Guian, Zhejiang. He was highly influenced by his teacher, Chen Jie, once the Erudite of the Water Clock in the Imperial Board of Astronomy and the author of the *A Complete Treatise on Arithmetic* (*Suanfa dacheng* 算法大成) and astronomy section of the *Supplementary Gazetteer of Huzhou Prefecture* (*Bu Huzhou fuzhi* 補湖州府志), in the study of astronomy. He had already demonstrated his talent in science before his graduation through the compilation of the *New Illustrations and Explanations on the Calculation of Angles* (*Liangbian jiajiaojing qiu duijiao xinfa tushuo* 兩邊夾角徑求對角新法圖說) with his classmates, a well-explained thousand-word research report highly praised by his teacher. Zhang inherited his teacher's specialty in the study of comets and the eclipses, compiling two titles — *A Study of Comets* (*Huixing kaolüe* 彗星考略) and *An Inquiry into the Eclipses* (*Riyue jiaoshi kao* 日月交食考). And according to the *Biographies of the Astronomers*, Zhang had an excellent understanding on the epicycle of planets suggested in the Ptolemaic theory.

Zhang arrived at Shanghai in 1853 to work in the London Missionary Society Mission Press at the invitation of his friend Li Shanlan. His main duty was to assist in the translation of *On Light* (*Guanglun* 光論) and other astronomical and science titles. *On Light*, co-translated with J. Edkins, was the most representative title of Zhang. The translation was finished in 1853, but it was compiled in the *Collectanea of the Lingjian Pavilion* (*Lingjiange congshu* 靈鶼閣叢書) by Jiang Biao instead of being published as an individual title. The reference work, amounting to 6,000 words and attached with 17 diagrams, was the first translated title that discussed various topics of optics, including rectilinear propagation of light, reflection and refraction of light, the mirage, luminance, dispersion, spectrum, eyes and sight, and the color wheel. New concepts, such as "the beam of light (a direct travelling of light)" and the radiation of the ray, and new theories, like the inverse-square law of light and the law of reflection, were included.

Zhang's achievements in scientific research received good reviews from his colleagues and the public. Xu Youren, the Governor of Jiangsu and also a friend of Zhang, even composed a poem to remember his discussion with Zhang:

> Being an upright man for his whole life, he is similar to the ancient sages.
> Spending two decades to study astronomy, he learned the stars by heart.
> Completing a book on the comet, he opened the way for the Western methods.
> Bringing the book to the market at Wu, he fascinated the Governor of Jiangsu.[61]

Actually, Li Shanlan, Wang Tao, Guan Sifu, and Zhang Fuxi shared several similarities. In terms of their academic background, they had a tortuous path to the civil examination but they, apart from Wang, were equipped with basic science knowledge. None of the four scholars passed the examination of the juren degree — Li and Wang had attended the examination yet failed in it, while it was unknown whether Guan and Zhang had joined in the examination. All of them soon quit attending the examination due to different reasons: the family of Wang and Zhang were too impoverished to support their learning, the hometown of Guan was full of too much unrest, and Li gave up the writting of eight-legged essay for Western mathematics. And they occasionally engaged in the research of their particular specialties: Li studied mathematics, Guan was interested in medicine, and Zhang showed his talent in astronomy. The publications of Wang covered a wide range of topics as he had no particular field of study.

In terms of their personal characters, they were all resentful towards current affairs yet they lacked the chance to express their opinion. Failing to enter the establishment, they were nothing more than a group of insane scholars who indulged in alcohol and entertainment, fooled around with prostitutes, and screamed at the street whenever they liked–some acts commonly seen on frustrated scholar. Wang Tao also witnessed Li screaming alone in one night.[62] Scholars nowadays recognize their talent and achievements in the dissemination of Western learning, but they were discriminated against by the public for their strange behaviors. Actually, translators in the late Qing society had a low social status as only losers in the civil examination would downgrade themselves to work with foreigners.

And in terms of their birthplace, all of them were natives of the Lower Yangtze provinces, where a strong learning atmosphere and acceptance of Western learning had grown since the arrival of Ricci. It was also an area where enlightened Chinese scholars and amateurs of Western learning, such as Xu Guangqi, Li Zhizao, Yang Tingjun, Sun Yuanhua, Mei Wending, Wang Xichan, Jiang Yong, Luo Shilin, Xiang Mingda, Dai Xu, Chen Jie, Xu Youren, Zheng Fuguang, Cheng Enze, and Gu Guanggong, were nurtured. With the blowing of the "Western wind" since the late Ming period, scholars were exposed to science knowledge and the intellectual circle was prepared for the development of "practical scholarship."

A Limited Response from Society

The names of scholars who contributed to the research of world history and geography other than the aforementioned pioneers during the reign of Daoguang and Xianfeng were numerous: Xiao Lingyu, the author of *On England* (*Ji Yingjili* 記英吉利); Ye Zhongjin who composed the *Brief Record of Occurences Relating to the English Barbarian* (*Yingjiliguo yiqing jilüe* 英吉利國夷情紀略); Xie Qinggao, the author of the *Maritime Records*; He Dageng, the author of the *Discourse on England* (*Yingjili shuo* 英吉利說); Tang Yi, the author of the *Records of the English Navy* (*Yingjili bingchuanji* 英吉利兵船記); Yan Sizong, the author of the *Explanatory Remarks on Coastal Defence* (*Haifang yulun* 海防餘論); and Yao Ying, the author of the *Journey to Tibet and Southwest China* (*Kangyou jixing* 康輶紀行). These records, either a personal account or an oral report, introduced the situation outside the Chinese world from various perspectives.

In addition to the author of the Western titles, people who engaged in the dissemination of Western learning were numerous: Chen Xiutang, who provided editorial work to B. Hobson for his publication of *A New Discourse on Human Body*; Jiang Dunfu, Chen Cuiting, and Zhou Shuanggeng, who participated in the translation project of the London Missionary Society Mission Press; Xu Youren and Gu Guanguang, who discussed Western astronomy and mathematics with Li Shanlan and Zhang Fuxi; and Yung Wing, Wong Shing, and Yu Dehui, graduates of the church schools who assisted in the translation of Western titles.

Such a long list of scholars' names and publications seemed to suggest a widespread acceptance of Western learning in China in 1850s, yet the truth was the opposite: the influence of Western learning was limited to a few treaty ports, the only authorized cities in China where missionaries had the freedom of proselytization. Inland residents were still isolated from the arrival of new learning until the further opening of China. The difficulty in the dissemination of Western learning was added by the immature communication system. There was neither railway nor modern communication devices that strictly limited the speed and the scope of the diffusion of knowledge.

Another obstacle for the dissemination of Western learning was the mismatch between the disseminator and the receiver. Missionaries aimed at spreading the Christian teachings and the translators published titles of their specialties.[63] The learners, on the other hand, were neither interested in the Western religion nor realized the necessity of catching up with the global circumstance as a result of the long-term isolation of China. Knowledge taught in these publications remained at a superficial level to suit the readers' academic standards.

The exact amount of the published copies of the *Compendium of Arithmetic*, *An Elementary Treatise on Mechanics*, and other Western titles was unknown, yet the issue volume was imaginably low as evidenced from the limited social response to their publications. Even the *Eastern Western Monthly Magazine* and *The Church News*, two of the relatively popular journals in 1850s, published 600 and 500 copies per each issue, respectively.

Moreover, there were a few stories showing the ignorance and groundless prejudices of the Chinese towards Western affairs and Western people. Wang Zhongyang regarded that the Westerner were invisible under the Sun due to their blue eyes, and their long legs made it difficult for them to run.[64] Ye Zhongjin believed that all the Westerners were unable to shoot the target critically and to walk on the land because of their short-sighted eyes and small feet, respectively.[65] Borjigit Yuqian, the Governor-general of Guangdong and Guangxi, and Jin Yinglin, the Chief Minister of the Court of Judicial Review, also believed that the Westerners were vulnerable to attack because of their straight bodies and legs.[66] Liu Yunke, the Governor of Zhejiang, even regarded that tea was a necessity for the foreigners to survive. "Limiting the export of tea means to control the lives of the barbarians," according to Liu.[67] *The Management of Barbarian Affairs in Its Entirety* (*Chouban yiwu shimo* 籌辦夷務始末) also documented opinions that the foreigners suffered from blindness and constipation without Chinese tea and herbs.[68]

Actually, people awakened by China's defeat in the Opium War (like Lin Zexu) constituted only a minority of the intellectuals. Most of the scholars were still in a deep sleep, holding their security blanket — the unequal treaties that they considered a guarantee of eternal peace — and reading the quotations of the Confucian classics aloud, and glorifying their long-lived emperor. The debate on the establishment of the Imperial Foreign Language Institute in the early 1860s triggered by the conservative officials symbolized the general reluctance against Western learning. Actually, the influence of Lin Zexu, Liang Tingnan, Xu Jiyu, Wei Yuan, Li Shanlan, and Wang Tao were far from whipping up a revolutionary storm to overcome the stubbornness and arrogance of the Chinese officials.

Appendix

Article 1: "Suggestions for the formation of a Medical Missionary Society" by Thomas R. Colledge et al., published in the *Chinese Repository* (Dec 1836, page 370-373).

Viewing with peculiar interest the good effects that seem likely to be produced by medical practice among the Chinese, especially as tending to bring about a more social and friendly intercourse between them and foreigners, as well as to diffuse the arts and sciences of Europe and America, and in the end introduce the gospel of our Savior in place of the pitiable superstitions by which their minds are now governed, we have resolved to attempt the foundation of a society to be called the "Medical Missionary Society in China."

The objects we have in view in the foundation of a Society of this description are: 1st, That those who shall come out as medical missionaries to China, may find here those to whom they can apply for assistance and information, on their first arrival in the country. 2d, That by this means their services may be made immediately available, while, at the same time, they may be put in the way of learning the language for the purpose of fitting themselves to practice in parts of the country to which foreigners have not hitherto gained free access. 3d, We do not propose to *appoint* individuals to the work, but to receive and assist the medical men who shall be sent out by Societies formed for the purpose either in England or America. Being acquainted with the peculiarities of the case, our especial desire is to draw attention to the selection of men of suitable qualifications. 4th, We therefore propose to receive any sums of money which may be given in aid of this object, and to disburse them as shall be deemed expedient, until *the Society* be formed, so that the labors of those who engage in the cause shall not be retarded.

Individuals, subscribing fifty dollars, or upwards in one payment, shall be considered members for life; or fifteen dollars annually, members during the period of their subscription.

In further illustration of our view, we would be premise, that in order to the success of the object contemplated, those who engage in it must not receive any pecuniary *remuneration*: the work throughout must be, and appear to be, one of *disinterested benevolence*. It is indispensable that the men who shall conduct the institution be not only masters of their profession, and conciliating in their manners towards all classes, but *judicious* men — men thoroughly imbued with the spirit of *genuine piety*, ready to endure hardships, and to sacrifice personal comfort, that they may commend the gospel of our Lord and Savior, and so cooperate in its introduction among the millions of this partially civilized yet, '*mysterious*' and idolatrous empire — men willing to suffer the loss of all things for joys that await those who *for Christ's sake* do good on earth.

In addition to the *Ophthalmic Hospital* already established, other departments are equally needed, and each would fully occupy the time and talents of one medical person. Among these may be mentioned,

A Surgical department, for the treatment of cases requiring the interposition of the surgeon, as the removal of tumors, cure of ulcers, reduction of fractured and dislocated limbs, and the like.

A department for the Ear. A vast amount of good may be effected by curing the affections of this organ, which perhaps are as numerous as those of the eyes, or even more so. The man who shall publish a treatise in Chinese, accompanied by a statement of facts that shall correct the pernicious practice of barbers who introduce a shartp cutting instrument into the ear, by which violence is frequently done to this delicate organ, will deserve well of the Chinese nation, for it is a national evil.

A department for Cutaneous Aeffections. In no country in the world are diseases of this class more numerous and aggravated; and added to the misfortune of being thus afflicted, if the disease of the sufferer is *suspected* to be malignant and contagions, he is liable to be deprived of his liberty, and immured during the remainder of life.

A department for Diseases of Females. Daily experience has disclosed that these are very numerous, and in some instances exceedingly aggravated, and but little understood by Chinese physicians. And contrary to expectation facts have demonstrated that the seclusion, characteristic of the upper classes of Chinese females, does not restrain them from applying to foreign practitioners with the hope of relief from these calamities.

A department for the Diseases of Children. An inconceivable amount of suffering is endured by children in China, which in many instances might be avoided, but for the ignorance of parents and want of medical aid and advice. The merchants from distant provinces, who trade at Canton, are often attended by members of their families, and frequently have brought their children for medical treatment. We cannot suppose the fond parent will remain insensible to the obligations of gratitude when he returns to his own home, or fail to speak there of the *excluded foreigner* who has gratuitously restored his child to the blessings of health. We conceive there cannot be a more direct avenue to influence than will be presented in this department, and the impression may be far more enduring than that made in almost any other way; for while in the case of the aged, who received medicine from the foreigner, the remembrance may quickly depart with them; it may be otherwise in respect to the babe and the youth, who are, by the hand of charity, rescued from a premature grave, or from diseases which uncontrolled might extend through life.

Regarding it desirable that these several departments be established as soon as Providence shall prepare the way, and the men and means are provided, we would also recommend to Societies, while they are sending out medical persons, not to neglect to encourage pious and well-disposed young men to accompany them, with a view to becoming dressers and apothecaries, and to render themselves useful in the supervision of the internal concerns of the hospitals. Here it may be proper to repeat, and with the utmost emphasis, that all who engage in this work should be judicious *men, thoroughly imbued with the spirit of* true piety, *willing to endure hardships and to sacrifice personal comforts*.

We cannot close these suggestions without adverting to one idea, though this is not the place to enlarge upon it. It is affecting to contemplate this empire, embracing three hundred and sixty millions of souls, where almost all the light of true science is unknown, where Christianity has *scarcely* shed one genial ray, and where the theories concerning matter and mind, creation and providence, are woefully destitute of truth; it is deeply affecting to see the multitudes who are here suffering under maladies, from which the hand of charity is able to relieve them. Now we know indeed, that it is the 'glorious gospel of the blessed God' only that can set free the human mind, and that it is only when enlightened in the true knowledge of God that man is rendered capable of rising to his true intellectual elevation; but while we take care to give this truth the high place which it ought ever to hold, we should beware of depreciation other truth. All truth is of God; the introduction of medical truth into China, would be the demolition of much error.

In the vast conflict which is to revolutionize the intellectual and moral world we may not underrate the value of any weapon. As a means then to waken the dormant mind of China, may we not place a high value upon medical truth, and seek its introduction with good hope of its becoming the handmaid of religious truth? If an inquiry after truth upon any subject is elicited, is there not a great point gained? And that inquiry after medical truth may be provoked, there is good reason to expect: for, exclusive as China is, in all her systems, she cannot exclude disease, nor shut her people up from the desire of relief. Does not then the finger of Providence point clearly to one way that we should take with the people of China, directing us to seek the introduction of the remedies for sin itself, by the same door through which we convey those which are designed to mitigate or remove its evils? Although medical truth cannot restore the sick and afflicted to the favor of God; yet perchance, the spirit of inquiry about it, once awakened, will not sleep till it inquiries after the source of truth; and he who comes with the blessings of health may prove an angel of mercy to point to the Lamb of God. At any rate, this seems the only open door; let us enter it. Loathsome disease, in every hopeless form, has uttered her cry for relief from every corner of the land; we have heard it, and would and must essay its healing. A faith that worketh not may wait for other doors. None can deny that *this* is a way of charity that worketh no ill, and our duty to walk in it seems plain and imperative. We most confidently rely on the aid of the pious and benevolent in the accomplishment of this great work, and when the millions which compose this mighty empire shall feel the influence of true religion and civilization, when the light of Christianity shall take the place of the dark cloud of paganism, which now envelops them, then will be fulfilled, in its spiritual sense, the prophecy of Isaiah:

"The eyes of the blind shall be opened, and the ears of the deaf shall be unstopped; the lamp shall leap as an hart, and the tongue of the dumb sing."

(Signed.) T. R. Colledge, P. Parker, and E. C. Bridgman. *China, October 5th,* 1836.

Article 2: "General Plan of the Anglo-Chinese College, Forming at Malacca," in *The Indo-Chinese Gleaner*, October 1818, appendix page 1-3.

I. Name.

The Institution is to be designated *The Anglo-Chinese College*. This appellation is thought more appropriate than Academy, School, or any other name, which occurred when the plan was originally formed.

II. Object.

The object of the College is, — The *reciprocal cultivation of Chinese and European*

Literature, and the diffusion of Christianity.

On the one hand, the Chinese language and literature will be made accessible to Europeans: and on the other hand, the English language with European literature and science will be made accessible to the Ultra-Ganges nations, who read Chinese. These nations are, China, Cochin-China (Kochi, India), the Chinese colonies in the eastern Archipelago, Loo-choo (Ryukyu, present-day Okinawa, Japan), Corea (Korea), and Japan.

It is hoped, that this course of proceeding will finally have a favorable influence on the peaceable diffusion of Christian principles, and the general civilization of the eastern hemisphere.

III. What the college will afford to students.

1. The College will be furnished with an extensive Chinese Library, and a collection of all such European books as bear upon its object, viz. such as treat of the language, history, manners, &c. of the nations above mentioned.
2. There will be appointed European Tutors of the Chinese language, capable also of teaching European learnings; and native Chinese teachers. The European Tutors will be Protestants.
3. Accommodations in the College for a limited number of students, at rates hereafter to be mentioned. Those students who maintain themselves, may if they please lodge in the town, as is the case in Europe.
4. A Fund will be formed for the maintenance of poor native students.
5. To European students, the Chinese language will be taught, for such purposes as the students choose to apply it — to religion; to literature; or to commerce.
6. To native students, the English language will be taught, geography, history, arithmetic, and such other branches or learning or science, as time may afford, together with moral philosophy, and Christian theology, and Malay.
7. There is at the station an English and Chinese Press, which literary students may avail themselves of.

IV. Who will be admissible.

Persons of any nation of Europe, or of the Continent of America, belonging to any Christian Communion, bringing with them letters of respectable recommendations as to their moral habits, and the objects they have in view, will be admitted.

Persons from European Universities having travelling fellowships, Christian Missionaries, and persons belonging to Commercial Companies, or attached to

National Consuls, will be admitted.

Native youths of any of the above countries, who either support themselves, or who may be maintained by Christian Societies, or by private Gentlemen, who wish to serve them by giving them an English education. These native youths will not be compelled to profess the Christian religion, nor will they be compelled to attend Christian worship; they will, however, be invited to do so, and, the good order of the Institution will require their attendance on all Lectures given publicly.

V. Continuance in the college.

The period of continuance in the College, must depend on circumstances to be arranged hereafter.

VI. Resources.

The resources of the College will be — fees, paid by European or native students who maintain themselves, or are maintained by their patrons or friends and voluntary contributions.

VII. Management.

The management of the College and its funds, will be placed in the hands of a patron and trustees.

Any subscription, from two dollars and upwards, to the general purposes of the Anglo-Chinese College, or to any particular part of the plan, will be thankfully received in behalf of the object, by The Rev. W. Milne, *Malacca*, or by The Rev. Dr. Morrison, *China*.

October, 1818.

Article 3: *Accessory Contract* of the "Constitution of the Morrison Education Society," in *Chinese Repository* (Dec 1836, page 376-377).

By-laws — Section 1: Scholars.

1. Chinese youth of any age, of either sex, and in or out of China, may be received under the patronage of the Society; also schools, conducted in a manner approved of by the Trustees.
2. Whenever practicable, young children, six, eight, or ten years of age, will be preferred.

3. With the advice of the Trustees, and the approbation of the parents and guardians of children, they may be sent to the Straits of Malacca, to India, Europe, or America, for the purpose of completing their education.
4. If necessary, children may receive their whole support — board, clothing, books, tuition, &c., from the Society; but no reward or premiums will ever be given, expecting money or articles expressly designated for that purpose by the donors, unless by a special vote of the Society.

Teachers.

1. Tutors and Masters from Europe or America, or both, shall be employed permanently, so far as the means of the Society will allow.
2. Native Masters, of good character and acquirements, may also be employed.

Books.

3. The School books for teaching the children reading, writing, arithmetic, geography, and other sciences, shall always be the best that can be obtained, both in the English and Chinese languages.
4. The Scholars shall be furnished with the *Bible*, and with the instruction and aids to understand it, which are usually afforded in the best schools of Christendom; but the reception of its doctrines is not to be a test for the admission of scholars.
5. The Books belonging to the Society shall form a public library, and be styled the "Library of the Morrison Education Society."
6. This Library shall be under the immediate control of the Trustees, who shall take all suitable measures in their power to make it available to all the foreign residents and visitors; provided they do not expend for this purpose a sum greater than would be necessary to take care of the Library were it not open to the Public, it being supposed that for the sake of having such a Library, the foreign residents will be ready to bear a part of the expenses.
7. Rules for the regulation of the Library, sanctioned by the Trustees, shall be published, with a Catalogue of the Books, and a copy of the same be placed in the hands of all those who are admitted to the privileges of the Society and the Library.

Article 4: "America in China," in *The New York Times* (March 29, 1868).

The last official act of Mr. Burlingame in his capacity as Minister to China, was a very significant one. It was, as elsewhere recorded, the official presentation of a copy of Stuart's Washington to a Chinese writer who, twenty years ago, was sent into exile for his tribute to our great First President — an exile from which he seems to have been lately recalled to greater honors and rewards than ever, by the personal intercession of Mr. Burlingame. It was a wondrous sign of the times when so deep-dyed a criminal is restored to favor and crowned with laurels. Till within a quarter of a century, the study of barbarian annals has been one of the most dangerous branches of learning a Chinese could pursue; and a candid geographer has dared the fate of Galileo.

The writer in question was SEU-KI-YU, degraded from office and banished by a former Emperor "for eulogizing Washington in his works, *The Geography of the World and The Men of Note of Other Countries*," published we believe, in 1849, and for which the author suffered eighteen years of exile. One is interested to know what it was that was so treasonable in utterance. We are not without a key to explain what the published account makes mysterious.

In 1850 a Mr. Peet, an American missionary in China, sent to our country an account of a new Chinese geography, written by the Lieutenant-Governor of the Fuh-Chan (Fujian) province, and recommended by the Governor-General as trustworthy, despite its novelty. The idea of the Chinese beginning to study geography, was, of course, startling enough — and as many of them were not before aware that anything worth speaking of existed beyond the boundaries of the Flowery Kingdom, their own wonder may be imagined at seeing a book in ten volumes (or rather sections,) with matter enough to fill three about the earth's shape in general, and about Asia "outside of China" — four about Europe, two about America, one about Africa. It was something like a revelation to learn that the universe was not made for the use and behoof of the Celestials.

There were 42 maps, quite accurate, and and these, with all the information, were derived, of course, from "western men," and particularly from American missionaries. The whole time-honored Chinese system of geography was revolutioned by this Oriental Galileo. For example, he narrated the existence of a Southern hemisphere and a South pole, with "a second frozen ocean — it is a mistake," he said, "to suppose the equator to be the South Pole. Truly we ought to hear this explanation and believe it."

But we pass the geographical marvels, as though one of the offences of Seu-ki-yu according to the account just referred to, was published a Geography of the World, it was Men of Note, with its words about Washington that were the most "disloyal." Now, referring to this treatise we find in Mr. Peet's translations from it, a very curious account of the discovery and early history of America, and of our Republic, with chronology somewhat disregarded — the historic picture, with its "foreshortenings," reminding one of a Chinese drawing — but, in the main, the facts tolerably accurate. But its most marked feature is its vivid appreciation of Washington's character, to which, no doubt, the author's American acquaintances did patriotic justice. "When small he had great views both in regard to civil and military affairs, and excelled in strength and courage. Without arms, ammunition, or provisions, Washington stiulated his countrymen to action by a righteous spirit." Then, we are told, "while his army was often reduced a weakened, Washington's spirit was undiminished, and the English army became old." Here is the summing up of the character:

"He was an uncommon man. He conquered more rapidly than Shing and Kwang, and in courage he was superior to Tsaon and Lew. Seizing the two-edged sword of three cubits long, he opened the country 10,000 *le*. He then refused to receive a title, or to secure one for his posterity, preferring to establish an elective administration. Patriotism to be commended under the whole heaven! Truly like the three dynasties! In administering the Government he fostered virtuous customs, and, avoiding war, made his country superior to all other nations. I have seen his portrait. His countenance exhibits great mental power. Ah! Who would not call him an uncommon man!"

All this treason and heresy, this praise of barbarians, could hardly be palatable to the Chinese Emperor. According to the common rectangular maps in previous authority, China, the "Middle Kingdom," occupied the greater part of the habitable world; there was no Southern Hemisphere at all, and no Western Hemisphere. Other countries were only the fringes on the frozen oceans which surrounded China. To disturb this complacent theory comes a map in which China cuts a sorry figure, chronologies which overthrow Chinese reckonings, and such talk as this:

"Western men produce maps having a Southern frozen ocean. Why should Chinamen doubt, since their vessels have not gone a great distance, and since the Knang-tung (Canton) Province is the extremity of their country?"

As to Washington, to place him above the illustrious Tsaon and Lew could not, a score of years ago, be endured, nor to announce that, as Mr. Burlingame says, "he recalled the three dynasties whose serene virtues had shed their light along the ages for 4,000 years." But the exile has his reward. The act of our Government in sending over this peculiar memorial is one not only of appreciation, but of "poetical justice," and is a happy commentary on the words, "I have seen his portrait. Ah! He was an uncommon man." That such as official is now raised "near the head of the State to aid in controlling the affairs of 4,000,000,000 of people," is a significant token also of the influence of America in China.

Notes

Chapter 1

1. There is almost no in-depth study on this topic apart from Wang Yangzong's "A Brief History of the Translation College of the Jiangnan Arsenal (1988)" and the author's "A Brief History of the Translation College of the Jiangnan Arsenal (1989)".
2. Foreign Sinologues had the same questions about the limited study of the missionaries' works in China. Paul A. Cohen in his "Christian Missions and Their Impact to 1900" listed three main issues that needed further study: "First, a problem for the student of communication — how clear was the missionary's message? How intelligible were missionary compilations and to what extent did they say what their compilers intended them to say? Second, a problem for intellectual historians — what was the message? Missionary translators posed as transmitters of the best that Western civilization had to offer. Yet it was left for people like Yan Fu to translate Spencer, J. S. Mill and Montesquieu, while the most widely circulated of all missionary translations of secular works, Mackenzie (*A New History of Europe*), was a vulgar hymn to the conquests of science and the dogma of progress ... A third and final question: who got the message? How wide a readership, both social and geographic, did missionary writings have, and in what ways did patterns of readership change over the years?" John K. Fairbank ed., *The Cambridge History of China (Vol. 10: Late Ch'ing, 1800–1911)* (Cambridge: Cambridge University Press, 2008), 581.
3. Article VIII of the Anglo-Chinese Treaty of Tianjin (1858) stated that: The Christian religion as professed by Protestants or Roman Catholics inculcates the practice of virtue and teaches man to do as he would be done by. Persons teaching it, or professing it, therefore, shall alike be entitled to the protection of the Chinese authorities, nor shall any such, peaceably pursuing their calling, and not offending against the Laws, be persecuted or interfered with.
4. Yingkou, Chefoo, and Swatow replaced Niuzhuang, Dengzhou, and Chaozhou, respectively, as the designated ports.
5. Xu Weize's *Bibliography of Japanese-Western Knowledge* documented 567 titles (excluding religious works) of Western books up to 1899. There were 555 titles published during 1860 to 1899.
6. Xu Weize and Gu Xieguang's *Bibliography of Japanese-Western Knowledge (enlarged edition)* recorded 366 titles of books translated during 1900 to February 1902. Gu Xieguang's *Records of Translation* listed 533 titles of books translated during 1902 to 1904. Tam Yue-him's *Catalog of Translated Japanese Books in China* documented 617 titles of books translated during 1905 to 1911. Ma Tailai's *A Complete List of the Translated Works of Lin Shu* recorded 65 titles translated by Lin Shu that were not seen in the above catalogs. And Zhang Yuying's *Catalog of Books Published before 1911 Revolution* recorded 18 more titles of translated works. The total number of translated titles according to the above information is 1,599. However, due to the absence of a complete catalog, the actual number of translated books should be larger.
7. Li Hongzhang 李鴻章, "Fu Zhu Jiuxiang xueshi" 覆朱九香學使 (A Letter to Zhu Jiuxiang the Education Commissioner), *Li Wenzhonggong quanji* 李文忠公全集 (A Complete Collected Works of Li Hongzhang).
8. Gu Changsheng 顧長聲, *Chuanjiaoshi yu jindai Zhongguo* 傳教士與近代中國 (Missionaries and Modern China) (Shanghai: Shanghai People's Publishing House, 1981), 233.
9. Ma Zuyi 馬祖毅, *Zhongguo fanyi jianshi* 中國翻譯簡史 (A Short History of Translation in China) (Beijing: China Translation and Publishing Corporation, 1984), 247.
10. Robert K. Merton, "Science, Technology and Society in Seventeenth-century England," *Osiris* 4 (1938): 430.

11. Ibid., 455.
12. "Guangxuehui nianbao dishici" 廣學會年報第十次 (The 10th Annual Report of the Society for the Diffusion of Christian and General Knowledge among the Chinese), *Chuban shiliao* 出版史料 (Publication of Historical Materials), No. 2 (1991).
13. The Full name of the book was *An Outline of Translation of Books of the Jiangnan Arsenal* (*Jiangnan zhizao zongju fanyi xishu shilüe* 江南制造總局翻譯西書事略).
14. Sun Weixin 孫維新, "Taixi gezhi zhixue yu jinke fanyi zhushu xianglüe deshi hezhe wei zuiyaolun" 泰西格致之學與近刻翻譯諸書詳略得失何者為最要論 (Achievements and Limitations of the Recently Published Books of Western Science), Wang Tao 王韜 ed. *Gezhi shuyuan keyi* 格致書院課藝 (Textbook of the Shanghai Polytechnic Institute) (Shanghai: Tao Yuan, 1889).
15. Trigonometry was named "*baxian* 八線" in ancient Chinese mathematics. *Baxian*, literally means "eight lines," correspond the curves of sine, cosine, tangent, cosecant, secant, cotangent, versed sine, and covers.
16. Sun, "Taixi gezhi zhixue yu jinke fanyi zhushu xianglüe deshi hezhi wei zuiyaolun."
17. Ibid.
18. Located in the West Liyu Bridge in the Shaoxing County, the Guyue Library was a first opened private library in modern China. Its collection was amounted to 70,000 books.
19. Xu Weize and Cai Yuanpei had established a solid friendship in their young ages. They passed the examination of the degree of "recommended man" together in 1889, and they participated in the imperial examination together in the next year.
20. The term *jingji* originated from an ancient Chinese phrase "*jing shi ji min* 經世濟民" (literally, to administer the country and to help the people). Before the adoption of the term "*jingji*" for "economy," a Japanese term "*shiseigaku* 資生學" (literally means the study of aiding the livelihood) was used in Chinese translation. It can be seen in Liang Qichao's article "On the Benefits of Learning Japanese," where other Japanese imported terms for academic subjects can be found. It is stated that, "Books translated by the Chinese focused in *heigaku* (兵學, military) and *geigaku* (技學, technology) while leaving *seiji* (政治, politics) and *shiseigaku* (economics) titles unstudied."
21. The short poem "There is an overseas island ... where we sojourned for years and became depressed" seemed hinted the background of the authors as the "overseas island" is generally understood as Japan.
22. The author found two editions of the *Summary of Western Reference Works*. The first was published in Intercalary May 1 in the 29th year of the reign of Guangxu (1903) by the Tongya Shuju printed in Shanghai, while the second was published in March of the 30th year of the reign of Guangxu in Tokyo. In terms of authorship, formatting style, font style, and content, these two books were similar to each other. Only the note and preface written by Shen Zhaoyi that was included in the Shanghai edition was not seen in the Tokyo edition.
23. Zhu Xun 朱勛, postscript to the *Xinxue shumu tiyao* 新學書目提要 (Summary of Western Reference Works). Shen Zhaoyi 沈兆禕. *Xinxue shumu tiyao* 新學書目提要 (Summary of Western Reference Works). Shanghai: Shanghai Tongya Shuju, 1904.
24. It was renamed to China Christian Education Association in 1916.

Chapter 2

1. Representative research titles included Chen Yuan's "A Brief History of the Coming of Christianity to China" issued in *Truth Monthly*, no. 18 (1924); *The History of Chinese-Western Communication* (1934) by Xiang Da, *The History of European Cultural Dissemination into China* and *Collection of Historical Sources on Sino-Western Communication* (1977) by Zhang Xinglang; *History of Catholic Evangelic Missions in Sixteenth Century China* (1936) by Henry Bernard; *A Summary of the History of Evangelion of Catholics in China* (1938) and *A Summary of the Translated Works of the Jesuit Missionaries in*

between the Ming and Qing Dynasties (1949) by Xu Zongze; *Jesuit Missionaries in China* (1965) translated by Thomas Ryan; *Catholics in China* (1976) by Lin Moye; *Christianity in China* (1976) by Lin Chi-ping, *The History of Chinese-Western Communication* (1968) by Fang Hao, *History of Sino-Western Cultural Exchange* (1985) by Shen Fuwei, *A Concise History of the Sino-Western Relationship during the Ming-to-Qing Dynastic Transition* (1987) by Zhang Weihua, Han Qi's "The Discovery of *Principia* and the Spread of Newton's Theory in Pre-nineteenth Century China" issued in *The Chinese Journal for the History of Science and Technology*, no. 2 (1998); Han Qi and Zhan Jialing's "The Dissemination of Western Mathematics in the Palace in the Reign of Kangxi" issued in the *Studies in the History of Natural Sciences*, no. 2 (2003); *Meister Himmlischer Geheimnisse* (Adam Schall the Master of Heavenly Secret, 1989) by Ernst Stürmer, and *Jesuit Missionaries and Science in China* by Fan Hongye (1992).

2. Shangchuan Island is also named Ilha São João (St. John's Island).
3. *Xianhua*, meaning fairy flower, is a common decorative feature in Buddhist painting.
4. Ricci first placed the Meridian in the center, making China in the west of the map. The Chinese were not pleased and refused to study the map. Ricci thus made some changes to the map. See H. Bernard, *History of Catholic Evangelic Missions in Sixteenth Century China*, translated by Xiao Junhua 蕭浚華 (Beijing: The Commercial Press, 1936), 279.
5. Louis Pfister, *Collected Biographies of the Jesuits in China*, translated by Feng Chengjun 馮承鈞. (Taipei: The Commercial Press, 1970), 46.
6. You Dong 尤侗, *Waiguo zhuzhici* 外國竹枝詞 (Collections of Foreign Folk Songs) qtd. in Fang Hao 方豪, *Zhongguo tianzhujiaoshi renwu zhuan* 中國天主教史人物傳 1 (Biographies of Catholics in China 1) (Beijing: Zhonghua Book Company, 1988), 81.
7. Gottfried Wilhelm von Leibniz ed., Mei Qianli 梅謙立 and Yang Baojun 楊葆筠 trans., *Anecdotes in Modern China: To Enlighten the History of Our Times* (Zhengzhou: Daxiang chubanshe, 2005), 38.
8. Wu Boya 吳伯婭, *Kangyongqian sandi yu xixue dongjian* 康熙乾三帝與西學東漸 (Emperor Kangxi, Yongzheng, Qianlong, and the Eastward Dissemination of Western Learning) (Beijing: China Religious Culture Publisher, 2002), 382,
9. Ibid., 383.
10. Qian Cunxun 錢存訓, "Jinshi yishu dui Zhongguo xiandaihua de yingxiang" 近世譯書對中國現代化的影響 (Impact of translation to the Modernization in China), *Wenxian* 文獻 (Documents), No. 2 (1986).
11. The "Astronomical Treatise" of *Huainanzi* 淮南子 suggests that there are nine layers of the heaven.
12. Eight chapters of *On the Revolutions of the Celestial Spheres* were translated, and 17 out of 27 observation records were quoted. Du Shiran 杜石然, *Zhongguo kexue jishu shigao* 中國科學技術史稿 (Drafted History of Science and Technology in China) (Beijing: Science Press, 1982), 214.
13. J. Rbo, "Theory on the Five Planets," qtd. in Fang, *Zhongxi jiaotong shi*, 719.
14. Ruan Yuan 阮元, *Chourenzhuan huibian* 疇人傳彙編 (*Biographies of the Astronomers*) (Yangzhou: Guangling shushe, 2009), 544.
15. Fang, *Zhongxi jiaotong shi*, 721.
16. Wang Chongmin 王重民 ed., *Xu Guangqi ji* 徐光啟集 (Collections of Xu Guangqi) (Beijing: Zhonghua Book Company, 1963), 319.
17. Encroachment of the five stars, also known as the transits of planets in modern astronomical context, means the passing of Mercury, Venus, Mars, Jupiter, and Saturn between the Earth and the other stellar bodies.
18. Hong Weilian 洪煨蓮, "Kao Li Madou de shijie ditu" 考利瑪竇的世界地圖 (A Research on Ricci's World Map), *The Chinese Historical Geography* 禹貢, Vol. 5, No. 3-4.

19. There are altogether 53 maps, including the world map, the Asia map, the India map and its neighboring area, and the Khanate map. Cao Wanru 曹婉如 et al., "Zhongguo yu Ouzhou ditu jiaoliu de kaishi" 中國與歐洲地圖交流的開始 (The Beginning of the Communication between Chinese and European Maps), *Studies in the History of Natural Sciences* 自然科學史研究, No. 4 (1984).
20. Li Zhizao 李之藻, preface to the printed *Zhifang waiji* 職方外紀 (Geography of Foreign Countries to China).
21. Julius Aleni, "Summary of America," chapter 4 of *Geography of Foreign Countries to China*.
22. Ibid., "Summary of Europe."
23. Zhang Yuxiang 張玉祥, *Gudai shijie qida qizhi* 古代世界七大奇蹟 (Seven Wonders in the Ancient World) (Beijing: The Commercial Press, 1982), 1.
24. *Euclid's Elements* (the Arabian translated edition) was first introduced to China in the Yuan Dynasty. It was believed that Kublai Khan presented this book.
25. Li Zhizao李之藻, preface to the *Tongwen suanzhi* 同文算指 (Rules of Arithmetic Common to Cultures).
26. Emperor Kangxi was interested in the study of mathematics. He invited missionaries J. Bouvet and F. G. Joan to explain arithmetic, geometry, trigonometry and logarithm in Manchu language. He mastered the use of various instruments in calculating areas and volumes. Lecture notes of J. Bouvet and F. G. Joan were compiled in the *Elements of Mathematics*.
27. Fang, *Zhongxi jiaotong shi*, 788.
28. Bi Gongchen 畢拱辰, preface to the *Taixi renshen shuogai* 泰西人身說概 (Western Views on Human Body).
29. Cao Xueqin 曹雪芹, *Hongliu meng* 紅樓夢 (Dream of the Red Chamber), translated by H. Bencraft Joly (Hong Kong: Kelly & Walsh, ltd., 1892), chapter 52.
30. Fang, *Zhongxi jiaotong shi*, 908.
31. Lighthouse was translated as "*ruiguangjin* 瑞光鏡" in Chinese, meaning the "mirror of the fortunate light."
32. Cao, *Hongliu meng*, chapter 6.
33. Abstract to the *Tianwen lüe* 天問略 (Questions about Heaven), *Siku quanshu tiyao* 四庫全書提要 (The Catalog of the Four Branches of Literature).
34. Yang Guangxian 楊光先, *Pixie lun* 辟邪論 (An Exposure of Heresy).
35. Ruan, *Chorenzhuan*, 407.
36. Wang's inventions were too numerous for the latter generations to distinguish which were his actual inventions and which were copied from the Western instruments.
37. Fang, *Zhongxi jiaotong shi*, 753.
38. Xu Zongze 徐宗澤, *Mingqing jian Yesuhuishi yizhu tiyao* 明清間耶穌會士譯著提要 (A Summary of the Translated Works of the Jesuits Missionaries in between the Ming and Qing Dynasties) (Beijing: Zhonghua Book Company, 1949).
39. Ruan, *Chorenzhuan*, 407.
40. Mei Wending 梅文鼎, preface to "Arithmetic," *Meishi congshu jiyao* 梅氏叢書輯要 (Essientials of the Collectanea of the Mei).
41. Hang Shijun 杭世駿, "Biography of Mei Wending," *Daogutang ji* 道古堂集 (Collection of the Daogu Hall).
42. Wang ed., *Xu Guangqi ji*, 374.
43. Fang, *Zhongxi jiaotong shi*, 714.

44. Wei Jun 魏浚, "Li shuo huangtang huoshi" 利說荒唐惑世 (Ricci's Teaching Is Ridiculous and Confusing the Public), Xu Changzhi 徐昌治 ed., *Shengchao poxie ji* 聖朝破邪集 (Collected Papers on Overcoming Evil Ideologies).
45. Sima Qian 司馬遷, "Collected Biography of Mencius and Sunzi," chapter 74 of *Shiji* 史記 (Records of the Grand Historian) (Beijing: Zhonghua Book Company, 1959), 2344.
46. Li Weizhen 李維楨, "Compendium of Geography," chapter 15 of the *Dabi shanfang ji* 大泌山房集 (Collections of the Dabi Mountain Studio).
47. Abstract to the *Kunyu tushuo* 坤輿圖說 (Illustrated Explanation of the Entire World), chapter 71 of *Siku quanshu tiyao*.
48. Yang Guangxian 楊光先, "Budeyi" 不得已 (I Cannot Do Otherwise).
49. Yu Zhengxie, "Comments to the Completion of *A Treatise on the Human Body*," *A Variety of Manuscripts Written in 1833*.
50. Mei Wending 梅文鼎, "Addendum to the Diagram of Hemispherical Universe" *Wu'an lisuan shumu* 勿庵曆算書目 (Mathematical Treatises of Wu'an).
51. Quan Zuwang 全祖望, "Memorial Inscription to Huang Lizhou," *Jieqi ting ji* 鮚埼亭集 Collections of the Jieqi Neighbourhood.
52. Zhang Tingyu 張廷玉 et al., "Monographs on Astronomy and the Calendar," chapter 31 of *Mingshi* 明史 (History of the Ming Dynasty) (Beijing: Zhonghua Book Company, 1974), 544.
53. Fang, *Zhongxi jiaotong shi*, 746.
54. Abstract of *Ceyuan haijing* 測圓海鏡 (Sea Mirror of Circle Measurements), chapter 107 of *Siku quanshu tiyao*.
55. Zhang Weihua 張維華, *A Concise History of the Sino-Western Relationship during the Ming-to-Qing Dynastic Transition* (Ji'nan: Qilu Press, 1987), 196.

Chapter 3

1. Based upon the recommendation of a Chinese person residing in London, Yong Sam-tak travelled to London by a ship of the British East India Company in 1804. He studied English in a youth school in a London suburb. Having heard of the presence of Yong, the London Missionary Society ordered Morrison to contact Yong for his mission in China. Yong thus moved to London to live with Morrison, taught Chinese to Morrison, and helped him to transcribe part of the Chinese Bible. Despite several arguments between Yong and Morrison, they established a firm friendship during Morrison's stay in Guangzhou. Su Ching 蘇精, *Malixun yu Zhongwen yinshua chuban* 馬禮遜與中文印刷出版 (Morrison and Chinese Publications), 57-64. Also Elizabeth Morrison, *Malixun huiyilu* 馬禮遜回憶錄 (Memoirs of the Life and Labours of Robert Morrison), translated by Gu Changsheng 顧長聲 (Guilin: Guangxi Normal University Press, 2004), 43.
2. W. Milne (1785–1822) joined the London Missionary Society in 1809. He was recommended to study at the Gosport Missionary Academy, where he befriended Morrison. He contributed mainly to the evangelic missions in Southeast Asia. During his last years, he devoted himself to the operation of the Anglo-Chinese School. He died on June 2, 1822.
3. W. H. Medhurst (1796–1857) was born in April 29, 1796, in London. He departed England for Malacca at the age of 20. He first arrived in China in 1835, with Guangzhou as his first station. He soon travelled along to the coast, and he reached Shanghai in 1843. He settled in Shanghai with his friend William Lockhart, and they established the London Missionary Society Mission Press. He returned to the United Kingdom to report for duty and to visit his relatives in December 1865, but he died after a month and never returned to China. He was one of the most influential figures in the history of the dissemination of Western learning in the late-Qing era. During his lifetime, he published 90 titles written in Chinese, English, and Malay. The

Medhurst College in Shanghai was named after him to memorialize his contributions.

4. William Young belonged to the English Baptist Church. The Malaya-born missonary befriended W. H. Medhurst in Batavia, where he settled in his early times. He was employed as the assistant of Medhurst in 1828 on the missions in Southeast Asia. After the opening of China in 1842, Young started his evangelic missions in Fujian and Amoy. He moved to Australia to start preaching to the overseas Chinese who arrived in Australia due to the Gold Rush.

5. Born in New York, William Dean (1807–1895) belonged to the American Baptist Church. In 1834, he was dispatched for evangelic missions in Thailand. During his travelling from Singapore to Thailand, he nearly died at the hands of pirates. He thus stayed in Singapore to learn Chinese. After Hong Kong became a British colony in 1842, Dean moved to Hong Kong, where he established a church for the Chaochou people. He retired in 1884 and he returned to the United States. He died of sickness on August 13, 1895, in Santiago, California.

6. David Abeel (1804–1846) was a Dutchman born in New Jersey. He demonstrated his interest in medical studies, world history, and geography during his childhood. He contributed most to establishing the network between the churches in the United States and Europe. During his time in China, he befriended Xu Jiyu, who had learned much from Abeel to complete *A Short Account of the Maritime Circuit*. He returned to New York in 1845.

7. K. F. A. Gutzlaff (1803–1851) was a German. He began his education at the Janike Institute in Berlin. He joined the Netherlands Missionary Society in Rotterdam at the age of 20, and was dispatched to China three years later. Gutzlaff was a man with language talents. He was proficient in English, Mandarin, Cantonese, Fujianese, German, Japanese, and Latin, and he had been engaged in the study of several Arabic and Turkish languages. He was employed as one of the translators during the signing of the Treaty of Nanjing in 1842. In the interest of the convenience of preaching, he adopted a Chinese name Ko Shih-lee, and dressed and talked like the Chinese. He published approximately 70 titles in English, German, Japanese, and Chinese during his lifetime. Hong Kong's Gutzlaff Street in Central is named after him.

8. Elijah C. Bridgman (1801–1861) was born in Massachusetts. Bridgman entered a theological seminary after graduating from the university. In October 1829, he was dispatched to China by the American Board of Commissioners for Foreign Missions. He learned Chinese from Morrison. He established the *Chinese Repository* in Guangzhou in 1832, and he was the chief-editor until 1847. He was employed as the translator during the signing of the Treaty of Wanghia in 1844. After resigning from the post of chief-editor of the *Chinese Repository*, he started evangelic missions in the Lower Yangtze area. During his five years of travels, he helped edit the Chinese version of *The Bible*. He was elected as the President of the Royal Asiatic Society of Great Britain and Ireland (Northeast China Branch) for his enormous achievements.

9. Joshua Marshman was born in England, but he spent his life in India. He arrived in Calcutta in 1799, and he started to learn Chinese from an American from Macau in 1805. He had never been to China, but he was regarded as one of the pioneers in the development of Christianity in China due to his translation of several parts of *The Bible*. He had four other works that introduced Chinese classics to the West.

10. David Collie studied in the Gosport Missionary Academy together with Morrison before his missions to Malacca. He joined the Anglo-Chinese College as a Chinese teacher and the library curator.

11. Samuel Kidd (1799–1843) also studied in the Gosport Missionary Academy together with D. Collie and Morrison. He was also a Chinese teacher at the Anglo-Chinese College. He returned to the United Kingdom and he was employed as a Professor of Chinese Language at London University.

12. Samuel Dyer (1804–1843) belonged to the London Missionary Society. After graduating from Cambridge University, he started his evangelic missions in Penang. He moved and settled in Malacca in 1835 to manage the Malacca Press. The most important contribution of Dyer was the invention of copper movable printing.

13. Marshall Broomhall, *Robert Morrison: a Master-Builder* (London: Church Missionary Society, 1924), 84.

14. Zhang Shijuan 張施娟, "Meiguo: dayang bi'an de qiyi guodu" 美國：大洋彼岸的奇異國度 (The United States: a Mysterious State on another side of the great ocean), in Gong Ying'an 龔纓晏, *Xifangren donglai zhihou* 西方人東來之後 (After the Coming of the Westerner to the East) (Hangzhou: Zhejiang University Press, 2006).
15. "Regulation of the Society for the Diffusion of Useful Knowledge," *Chinese Repository*, Dec 1834, 384.
16. Ira Tracy was appointed as a clergyman by the American Board of Commissioners for Foreign Missions in 1832. He was dispatched to Singapore to be the chief manager of the Singaporean Press in 1833. He retired due to sickness in 1841.
17. Su, *Malixun yu Zhongwen yinshua chuban*, 34.
18. These articles were compiled as the *Brief Introduction of World Geography*, which was published in 1822.
19. Su, *Malixun yu Zhongwen yinshua chuban*, 167.
20. "On the Revolution of the Earth around the Sun," *Chinese Monthly Magazine*, 1816, 20.
21. Ibid.
22. *A Monthly Record of Important Selections*, Jul 1823.
23. Huang Shijian 黃時鑒, preface to the *Dongxiyang kao meiyue tongjizhuan yingyinben* 東西洋考每月統記傳影印本 (Eastern Western Monthly Magazine [Copied Edition]) (Beijing: Zhonghua Book Company, 1997). The magazine stopped publication for a year in 1836.
24. Ibid., Jun 1833, 8.
25. Ibid., Nov 1837, 294-296.
26. Ibid., Apr 1838, 354.
27. Ibid., Mar 1838, 339.
28. "Landun shiyong," 蘭敦十咏 (Ten Odes on London), ibid., Dec 1833.
29. Walter H. Medhurst, *Dili biantong lüezhuan* 地理便童略傳 (Brief Introduction of Geography) (Malacca: Anglo-Chinese College, 1819), 9-10.
30. Ibid.
31. Huang comp., *Dongxiyang kao meiyue tongjizhuan yingyinben*, 16.
32. Zou Zhenhuan 鄒振環, *Xifang chuanjiaoshi yu wanqing xishi dongjian* 西方傳教士與晚清西史東漸 (Western Missionaries and the Eastward Dissemination of Western History in Late-Qing China) (Shanghai: Shanghai guji press, 2007), 65.
33. A microfilm of the *Narrative Record of the Countries of the World, Past and Present* is stored in the Library of the Yenching Association of the Harvest University.
34. Zou, *Xifang chuanjiaoshi yu wanqing xishi dongjian*, 97-103.
35. Su, *Malixun yu Zhongwen yinshua chuban*, 113-127.
36. Zhang, "Meiguo: dayang bi'an de qiyi guodu," 207.
37. Elijah C. Bridgman, *Meilige heshengguozhi lüe* 美理哥合省國志略 (A Brief History of the United States of America) (Shanghai: London Missionary Society Mission Press, 1861), chap four.
38. Gutzlaff, K. F. A., *Maoyi tongzhi* 貿易通志 (A General Account of Trade) (Singapore: Jianxia shuyuan, 1840), 5.
39. Ge Gongzhen 戈公振, *Zhongguo baoxue shi* 中國報學史 (History of China's Newspapers) (Taipei: Student Book Co., Ltd., 1982), 92. Cai Wu 蔡武, "Tantan Dongxiyang kao meiyue tongjizhuan" 談談《東西洋考每月統記傳》 (On the *Eastern Western Monthly Magazine*), *National Central Library Bulletin* 國立中央圖書館館刊, No. 2 (4).

40. Zhang Xiumin 張秀民, *Zhongguo yinshua shi* 中國印刷史 (The History of Publication in China) (Shanghai: Shanghai People's Publishing House, 1989), 581.
41. *The Indo-Chinese Gleaner*, Oct 1818.
42. James Humphrey belonged to the London Missionary Society. He was dispatched to succeed W. Milne as the Principal of the Anglo-Chinese College. He returned to the United Kingdom in 1829.
43. Cacob Tomlin belonged to the London Missionary Society. After graduating from Cambridge University, Tomlin was dispatched to Malacca to start evangelic missions in Southeast Asia. Prior to his employment as the Principal of the Anglo-Chinese College, he was a Chinese and English teacher in the school. He left the Anglo-Chinese College to be the dean of a newly established theological college in Malacca in 1834. He travelled to Bangladesh to continue preaching after leaving the theological college in 1836.
44. John Evans belonged to the London Missionary Society. He had been a Professor of Classical Literature, Mathematics, and Hebrew at Cambridge and Oxford before his mission to Malacca in 1834. He succeeded Cacob Tomlin to be the Principal of the Anglo-Chinese College. Following his return to the United Kingdom, he died of cholera.
45. James Legge (1815–1897) belonged to the London Missionary Society. He arrived at Malacca in January 1840 to be the seventh Principal of the Anglo-Chinese College. He was responsible for the relocation of the college to Hong Kong and he continued to preside over the school until 1845, when he returned to England for a vacation. He returned to China to participate in the translation of Chinese classics. The Sinologue was a friend of Wang Tao, a Chinese reformer. He returned to England to be the Professor of Chinese Studies at Oxford University.
46. Tan Shulin 譚樹林, *Malixun yu Zhongxi wenhua jiaoliu* 馬禮遜與中西文化交流 (Robert Morrison and Sino-Western Cultural Exchanges) (Hangzhou: China Academy of Art Press, 2004), 198-216.
47. "Constitution of the Morrison Education Society," *Chinese Repository*, Dec 1836, 375-377.
48. Samuel Robbins Brown (1810–1880) belonged to the American Presbyterian Church. After graduating from Yale University at the age of 22, he continued his study at Columbia Theological Seminary. With a recommendation from Yale, Brown was employed as the Principal of the Morrison Educational Society School in 1839.
49. Lancelot Dent, "The Third Annual Report of the Morrison Education Society," *Chinese Repository*, Oct 1841, 569-70.
50. *Macau Newspaper*, July 11, 1840.
51. Dr. Peter Parker (1804–1889) was born in a peasant family in Massachusetts. After receiving a Bachelor of Arts degree in 1831, he continued to study in both medical science and theology. In 1834, he graduated as a Doctor of Medicine and he was ordained as a Presbyterian clergyman.
52. Thomas R. Colledge et al., "Suggestions for the formation of a Medical Missionary Society," *Chinese Repository*, Dec 1836, 370-373.
53. *Macau Newspaper*, July 11, 1840.

Chapter 4

1. Wei Jingsheng 衛京生, "Fuzhou kaipi wei tongshang kouan zaoqi de qingkuang" 福州開闢為通商口岸早期的情況 (Situation in Fuzhou in Its Early Days of Opening as a Treaty Port), *Fujian wenshi zhiliao* 福建文史資料 (Fujian Humanity and Historical Materials), No. 1 (1962).
2. George Lanning and Samuel Couling, *The History of Shanghai* (Shanghai: Kelly & Walsh, 1921), 295-296.
3. H. B. Morse, *The International Relations of the Chinese Empire* (Taipei: Wen Hsing Book Store, 1963), 391-392.

4. John Lewis Shuck was born in Virginia, the United States. After his ordainment by the American Baptist Church in 1835, Shuck was dispatched to Southeast Asia for evangelic mission. He first arrived at Penang in 1835, and he headed to Singapore, where he learnt Chinese and Malay. His journey to China began in September 9, 1836. Before his settling in Hong Kong, he had been travelling to Macau and Guangzhou. He opened the Wang Ngai College in Hong Kong. He later moved to Shanghai, where he was devoted in the translation of *The Bible*. He returned to the United States in 1881, preaching to the overseas Chinese in California.

5. Dyer Ball was an American missionary graduated from the Yale University with the degree of literature and medical studies. In 1838, seven years after his ordainment, he was dispatched to Singapore to start an evangelic mission. He travelled to Macau and Hong Kong in 1841 and 1843, respectively, providing medical service, publishing books, and preaching. He settled in Guangzhou since 1858. He had more than 10 titles published in Chinese.

6. *Chinese Serial*, No. 1 (1853).

7. Zhao Liewen, an assistant of Zeng Guofan, loaned the whole collection of the *Chinese Serial* to his intellectual friend. *Chinese Serial*, No. 5 (1855).

8. Andrew Patton Happer (1818–1894) started his journey to China after his graduation from the Pennsylvanian University as a Medical Doctor in 1844. He started working as a physician in Macau, and he moved to Guangzhou in 1847. He later shifted to education service after the arrival of John Glasgow Kerr in 1854. He opened the Canton Christian College (former Lingnan University of Guangzhou) in 1887 with the funds he raised in the United States and worked as the Director of the college. He returned to the United States in 1819 due to illness.

9. Benjamin Hobson, "Diqiu yi xingxing lun" 地球亦行星論 (The Earth is also a Planet), *Tianwen lüelun* 天文略論 (A Short Discourse on Astronomy).

10. The academic circle generally agreed that the *Discourse of Astronomy* (published in 1859 in Shanghai) was the earliest reference work of astronomy in Chinese. However, the *Catechism of Astronomy* that was published in 1849 was in fact the earliest astronomy treatise. Therefore, the actual year of the introduction of Western astronomy in China was 1849 instead of 1859.

11. Benjamin Hobson, preface to *Xiyi lüelun* 西醫略論 (First Lines of the Practice of Surgery in the West) (Shanghai: Renji Hospital, 1857).

12. Ji Yun 紀昀, *Yuewei caotang biji* 閱微草堂筆記 (Random Jottings from the Cottage of Close Scrutiny), vol. 9.

13. Zeng Guofan 曾國藩, "Tongzhi yuannian qiyue siri" 同治元年七月四日 (July 4 of the 1st Year of the Reign of Tongzhi), *Zeng Guofan quanji* 曾國藩全集 (The Complete Collection of Zeng Guofan).

14. Stephen John was born in Connecticut, the United States. He studied in Massachusetts and New York in his early days. After graduating from the Auburn Seminary, he was ordained and dispatched to Southeast Asia. He mainly worked in Siam and Singapore. He headed to China in 1846, arriving at Fuzhou on January 2, 1847.

15. For a detailed biography of Jostus Doolittle, refer to the doctor thesis of Lin Liqiang. Lin Liqiang 林立強, "Meiguo chuanjiaoshi Lu Gongming yu wanqing Fujian shehui" 美國傳教士盧公明與晚清福建社會 (An American Missionary Justus Doolittle and the Society in Fujian in the Late Qing Period), Doctor diss., Fujian Normal University, 2004.

16. Fred W Drake, *Xu Jiyu ji qi Yinghuan zhilüe* 徐繼畬及其《瀛寰志略》 (Xu Jiyu and His *A Short Account of the Maritime Circuit*), translated by Ren Fuxing 任復興 (Beijing: Wenjin chubanshe, 1990), 30. Originally published as *China Charts the World: Hsu Chi-Yu and His Geography of 1848*.

17. Xu Jiyu 徐繼畬, preface to *Yinghuan zhilüe* 瀛寰志略 (A Short Account of the Maritime Circuit).

18. D. B. McCartee (1820–1900), a physician-missionary from the American Presbyterian Church, was born in Philadelphia. He arrived in Hong Kong in February 1843, and four months later, he departed for Ningbo, where he had been working for 28 years. He was employed as a Professor of Legal Studies and

Natural History of the Tokyo Imperial University (present-day University of Tokyo) during 1872 to 1875. He was then appointed as the Grand Minister Consultant of China in the Japanese Embassy.

19. John J. Heeren, *On the Shantung Front: a History of the Shantung Mission of the Presbyterian Church in the U. S. A. 1861–1940 in Its Historical, Economic and Political Setting* (New York: Board of Foreign Missions of the Presbyterian Church in the United States, 1940), 227.

20. "*Huahua*" means China and the United States. The first "*hua*" denotes China, and the second "*hua*" represents "the flower flag," symbolizing the fancy flag of the United States. It was renamed as Americano-Chinese Bookstore after its relocation to Shanghai in 1860.

21. W. M. Lowrie (1819–1847) of the American Presbyterian Church was born in Pennsylvania, the United States. After his graduation from the university in 1837, he continued his study in the Princeton Theological Seminary. One year after his ordainment, he was appointed to in China. Before his arrival at Ningbo in 1845, he had been working in Hong Kong and Macau. He died by drowning in August 1847 due to a piracy attack.

22. M. S. Culbertson (1819–1862) of the American Presbyterian Church was born in Pennsylvania, the United States. After graduating from West Point Military Academy in 1840, he continued his study at the Princeton Theological Seminary. He joined the evangelic mission in China in 1844, working in Macau and Hong Kong before heading to Ningbo. He stayed in Ningbo from April 1845 to July 1850, after which he moved to Shanghai.

23. A. W. Loomis of the American Presbyterian Church was dispatched to China together with Culbertson in 1844. He arrived at the Chusan Archipelago on March 30, 1844. He visited Ningbo in August of the same year. Due to unsatisfactory health, he returned to the United States in 1849, and he started preaching to the overseas Chinese in California.

24. M. S. Coulter of the American Presbyterian Church was born in Virginia. After graduating from a university in Indiana in 1848, he started his evangelic mission in China. He arrived at Ningbo in the following year, managing the church's press. He died in Ningbo in 1852.

25. Richard Q. Way (1819–1895) of the American Presbyterian Church was born in Georgia. He was dispatched to China in 1844. He arrived at Macao and Ningbo in July and August, respectively. He helped manage the church's press and The Ningpo Boys' Academy. The boarding school was later combined with the Presbyterian school in Hangzhou as the Hangchow University. He returned to the United States in 1859.

26. Richard Q. Way, *Diqiu shuolüe* 地球說略 (A Brief Discourse on the Earth) (Ningbo: The Chinese and American Holy Classic Book Establishment, 1856). Also Wei Yuan 魏源, *Haiguo tuzhi* 海國圖志 (Illustrated Gazetteer of the Maritime Countries (Pingaing: Jinggudao, 1876)), vol. 100, 2.

27. Wang Xiaoqiu 王曉秋, "Changnei kaihua changwai xiang — wanqing hanyi xishu zai Riben de chuanbo" 牆內開花牆外香——晚清漢譯西書在日本的傳播 (The Dissemination of Chinese Books to Japan in the Late Qing Period), Huang Aiping 黃愛平 and Huang Xingtao 黃興濤 ed., *Xixue yu Qingdai wenhua* 西學與清代文化 (Western Learning and the Culture of the Qing Dynasty) (Beijing: Zhonghua Book Company, 2008), 748.

28. These six natures included incompatibility, the presence of a subject, shape, separateness, non-automaticity, and attraction.

29. Andrew P. Happer, *Tianwen wenda* 天文問答 (Catechism of Astronomy) (Ningbo: The Chinese and American Holy Classic Book Establishment, 1849), 33.

30. Daniel J. MacGowan, *Bowu tongshu* 博物通書 (Philosophical Almanac in Chinese) (Ningbo: The Chinese and American Holy Classic Book Establishment, 1851). The advertisement was written in seal script characters.

31. *Six Talks on Gambling* was a revised version of the 1819 edition published in Malacca.

32. *Six Talks on the Abandon of Opium Smoking* was a revised version of the 1835 edition published in Singapore.

33. Both *Luren risheng* and *Tianlu licheng* were the translated edition of John Bunyan's *The Pilgrim's Progress*.
34. Cai Yutian 蔡育天 et al. ed., *Shanghai daoqi juanyi* 上海道契卷一 (Collections of the Title Deeds of Shanghai, volume one) (Shanghai: Shanghai guji chubanshe, 1998), 35-36.
35. Elijah C. Bridgman, "What I have Seen in Shanghai," *Chinese Repository*, no. 10 (1849), 517. Also Wang Tao, *Manyou suilu* 漫遊隨錄 (Jottings of My Roaming).
36. Su, *Malixun yu Zhongwen yinshua chuban*, 229.
37. Ibid, 231.
38. Wang Tao 王韜, *Yingruan zazhi* 瀛壖雜誌 (Miscellaneous Records of the Shore).
39. W. C. Milne was born during his fathers' journey to Guangzhou. He had been living in Malacca before returning to study in the United Kingdom. He was ordained in 1839 by the London Missionary Press and dispatched to China. He arrived at Macau in 1839 and taught in the Morrison Education Society School. He stated his evangelic missions in Dinghai and Ningbo from 1842 to 1843. He and W. H. Medhurst were selected representatives of the translation of *The Bible* during a meeting in Hong Kong in August 1843. Three years after the meeting, he started the translation of *The Bible* with Medhurst and J. Stronach. He returned to the United Kingdom in 1854, leaving the London Missionary Society two years later. In 1858, he returned to China as a translator in the British Embassy in Fuzhou. He was promoted as the instructor of translation in the British Embassy in Beijing in 1861. He died on May 15, 1863 in Beijing due to illness.
40. Wylie from the London Missionary Society was dispatched to China in 1847 due to his mastery of Chinese. He arrived in Shanghai on August 26, assisting W. H. Medhurst in managing the London Missionary Society Mission Press. Wylie, a man with profound knowledge, was responsible for not only the publication of *The Bible*, but also the compilation and translation of a series of science reference works. He was also the chief editor of *Universal Miscellany*, the first Chinese journal in Shanghai. He also contributed to the translation projects of the Jiangnan Arsenal. He returned to the United Kingdom in 1862, leaving the London Missionary Society in the same year. In November 1863, he returned to China as the Director of The Bible Society of the Great United Kingdom, promoting *The Bible*. He retired in July 1877 due to eye disease.
41. Wylie was well respected by the Chinese scholars. Shen Yugui from Shanghai presented a poem to the missionary in his farewell, recognizing his contributions in the dissemination of Western learning and his good characters. Shen Yugui 沈毓桂, "Weilie xiansheng jianggui Yingguo fuci zengbie" 偉烈先生將歸英國賦此贈別 (A Poem to Mr. Wylie for His Return to the United Kingdom), *Shun Pao* 申報, June 30, 1877.
42. W. Muirhead from the London Missionary Society was dispatched to China in 1847. He arrived at Shanghai in August 26 of the same year. He was active in Shanghai, making friends with local intellectuals such as Wang Tao and Jiang Dunfu. He was the main contributor of *The Church News* since its establishment in 1868. He produced numerous works in both Chinese and English, among which the *Universal Geography* and *A General Gazetteer of the Great Britain* were the most notable. He died in Shanghai in 1900.
43. J. Edkins from the London Missionary Society was dispatched to China in 1848. He arrived in Hong Kong on July 2, and he reached Shanghai in September 2 of the same year. He had been working as the director of the London Missionary Society Mission Press prior to his employment as the translator in the Custom at the request of Robert Hart. He was notable among the British missionaries for his expertise to Chinese affairs. Representative works of Edkins included the *Peking Magazine* and *An Elementary Treatise on Mechanics*.
44. Guo Songtao 郭嵩燾, *Guo Songtao riji* 郭嵩燾日記 (The Diary of Guo Songtao 1) (Changsha: Hunan People's Press, 1981), 33.
45. Alexander Wylie, preface to the *Shuxue qimeng* 數學啟蒙 (Compendium of Arithmetic).

46. Liang Qichao 梁啟超, *Xixue shumu biao* 西學書目表 (Bibliography of Western Knowledge), 1.
47. Wang Tao 王韜, *Wang Tao riji* 王韜日記 (The Diary of Wang Tao) (Beijing: Chung Hwa Press, 1987), 157.
48. Li Shanlan 李善蘭, preface to *The Sequel of Euclid's Elements*, qtd. in Xu Shichang 徐世昌, *Qingru xuean* 清儒學案 (Records of Qing Scholars), vol. 176.
49. Hang Yingbi, also Hang Duiyu (pseudonym Luqing), was born in Songjiang, Jiangsu Province. Han, a holder of the "recommended man" degree, was proficient in Western learning as well. He sponsored the publication of *The Sequel of Euclid's Elements* and participated in the editing of science titles in the London Missionary Society Mission Press. Ruan, *Biographies of Astronomers*, 737. See also Alexander Wylie, *Memorials of Protestant Missionaries to the Chinese*, 173.
50. Zhang Wenhu 張文虎, preface to *The Sequel of Euclid's Elements*, qtd. in Ge Shijun 葛士浚, *Huangchao jingshiwen xinzeng xubian* 皇朝經世文新增續編 (Newly-Collected Essays about Statecraft of the Qing Dynasty), vol. 6, 1897.
51. Wang, *The Diary of Wang Tao*, 69.
52. "Chuanjiaoshi Ai Yuese deng wuren fu Suzhou yejian Ganwang he Zhongwang de jingguo" 傳教士艾約瑟等五人赴蘇州謁見干王和忠王的經過 (The Meeting of Joseph Edkins and four missionaries, King Gan, and King Zhong in Suzhou), The Institute of History of the Shanghai Academy of Social Science ed., *Taipingjun zai Shanghai — Beihua jiebao suanyi* 太平軍在上海——《北華捷報》選譯 (Taiping Army in Shanghai: Selective Translations of the North-China Herald) (Shanghai: Shanghai People's Publishing House, 1983), 62.
53. Alexander Wylie and Wang Tao 王韜, *Zhongxue qianshuo* 重學淺說 (An Elementary Treatise on Mechanics), 19.
54. Xu Weize 徐維則 and Gu Xieguang 顧燮光, *Zengban dongxixue shulu* 增版東西學書錄 (Bibliography of Japanese-Western Knowledge Revised Edition).
55. Li Shanlan 李善蘭, preface to *Zhiwuxue* 植物學 (Elements of Botany).
56. Alexander Wylie, preface to *Tantian* 談天 (Discourse on Astronomy).
57. Ibid.
58. Ruan, preface to *Chourenzhuan*.
59. Wang, *Wang Tao riji*, 109.
60. Liang Qichao 梁啟超, *Du xixue shufa* 讀西學書法 (A Research on Western Learning).
61. William Muirhead, "On United Kingdom," *Universal Geography*.
62. Ibid.
63. Shionoya Tōin, preface to *Universal Geography*, qtd. in Wang, "The Dissemination of Chinese Books to Japan in the Late Qing Period," Huang and Huang ed., *Western Learning and the Culture of the Qing Dynasty*, 747.
64. William Muirhead, *A General Gazetteer of the Great Britain* (Shanghai: London Missionary Society Mission Press, 1856), 1.
65. Wang Zichun 汪子春, "Woguo zhuanbo jindai zhiwuxue zhishi de diyibu yizhu *Zhiwuxue*" 我國傳播近代植物學知識的第一部譯著《植物學》(*Elements of Botany*: the First Translated Reference Work of Modern Botany in China), *Studies in the History of Natural Sciences* 自然科學史研究, No. 3 (1984), vol. 1.
66. Liang, *Du xixue shufa*.
67. Wong Chi-min 王吉民 and Wu Lien-the 伍連德, *History of Chinese Medicine* (Shanghai: National Quarantine Service, 1936), 365.
68. Ibid.

69. Benjamin Hobson, preface to *Practice of Medicine and Materia Medica*.
70. Wang, *Wang Tao riji*, 15-16.
71. Ibid, 55.
72. "Diqianyue shuo" 地牽月說 (The Effect of Gravity on the Moon), *Chinese Almanac* (Shanghai: London Missionary Society Mission Press, 1854), 24.
73. Wang, *Wang Tao riji*, 18-19.
74. For the latest studies of the *Universal Miscellany*, refer to Shen Guowei 沈國威 ed., *Liuhe congtan* 六合叢談 (Universal Miscellany) (Shanghai: Shanghai Lexicographical Publishing House, 2006).
75. Alexander Wylie, "*Liuhe congtan* xiaoyin" 《六合叢談》小引 (Introduction to the *Universal Miscellany*), *Universal Miscellany* 六合叢談, No. 1 (1857).
76. A revised version of the 1835 edition.

Chapter 5

1. Wei, *Haiguo tuzhi*, 4.
2. *The International Law* was first published in French in 1758. It was translated into English in the next year. By 1839, this book had become a masterpiece in the West, with more than 10 and seven editions published in Britain and the United States, respectively.
3. Wang Weijian 王維儉, "Lin Zexu fanyi xifang guojifa zhuzuo kaolüe" 林則徐翻譯西方國際法著作考略 (A Study of the Translation of the International Law by Lin Zexu) *Journal of Sun Yat-sen University* 中山大學學報, No. 1 (1985). Refer to verse 94, chapter 8 of volume 1 of the International Law (English edition), verse 100-102, chapter 8 of volume 2, and verse 1-2, chapter 1 of volume 3 for these terms.
4. Liang Tingnan 梁廷枏, *Yuehai guanzhi* 粵海關志 (Gazetteer of the Guangdong Customs) Shen Yunlong 沈雲龍 ed., *Jindai Zhongguo shiliao congkan xubian dishijiu ji* 近代中國史料叢刊續編第十九輯 (The Sequel of the Collectanea of Historical Sources of Modern China 19) (Taipei: Wen Hai Press Company, 1975), 1651-1652. Actually it is inappropriate to address Italy as a country before its unification in 1871.
5. Ibid., 1663.
6. Ibid., 1671-1672.
7. Liang Tingnan 梁廷枏, *Hesheng guoshuo* 合省國說 (On the United States), in Liu Xiao 劉驍 and Luo Yi 駱驛 ed., *Haiguo sishuo* 海國四說 (Four Essays on Off-shore Countries) (Beijing: Zhonghua Book Company, 1993), 64.
8. Ibid., 57-58.
9. Ibid., 59.
10. Ibid., 63.
11. Ibid., 72.
12. Ibid., 74.
13. Ibid., 77.
14. Ibid., 51.
15. Ibid., 88-89.
16. Liang did not indicate the exact completion year of *An Account of London*, but in the preface of the *Four Essays on Off-shore Countries*, Liang proclaimed the compilation of these four titles, *An Account of London* included, was completed in January, the 26th year of the reign of Daoguang (1846). Therefore, it was believed that *An Account of London* was completed in 1846.
17. Liang Tingnan 梁廷枏, *Lanlun oushuo* 蘭侖偶說 (An Account of London), Liu and Luo ed., *Four Essays on Off-shore Countries*, 114.

18. Ibid., 136.
19. Ibid., 140.
20. Ibid., 159. The description of the English education system was similar to *Geography of Foreign Countries to China*. It was believed that Liang had referred to this work.
21. Ibid., 160.
22. Xu Jiyu 徐繼畬, preface to *Yinghuan kaolüe* 瀛寰考略 (A Short Account of the Maritime Circuit) (Taipei: Wen Hai Press Company, 1974).
23. Ibid.
24. M. A. Ozon and Rev. George Smith, "Notices of Fuhchau fú," *Chinese Repository*, No. 15 (1846), 216.
25. "The *Ying Hwan Chi-lioh* or *General Survey of the Maritime Circuit, a Universal Geography* by His Excellency Su Ki-yu of Wutai in Shansi, the present Lieutenant-governor of Fuhkien," *Chinese Repository*, No. 4 (1851), 169-170.
26. Ozon and Smith, "Notices of Fuhchau fú," 216. The Maynooth Grant was a controversial issue in 1845. The British government, seeking to improve its relationship with Dublin, suggested increasing the annual subsidy to the Maynooth College in Ireland. Smith cited such example to demonstrate Xu's familiarity with the internal affairs of the United Kingdom.
27. Xu, *Yinghuan zhilüe*, vol. 7.
28. Ibid.
29. Chen Sheng and Wu Guang were the leaders of the anti-Qin uprising. Cao Cao and Liu Bei were the kings of the Kingdom of Wei and Shu, respectively, during the period of the Three Kingdoms. These men were notable for their military achievements. "America in China," *The New York Times*, March 29, 1868. Originally published in Xu, *A Short Account of the Maritime Circuit*, vol. 2, 209.
30. Wang Tao 王韜, "Yinghuan zhilüe ba" 《瀛寰志略》跋 (Postscript to *A Short Account of the Maritime Circuit*) *Taoyuan wenlu waibian* 弢園文錄外編 (Addendum to the Collected Essays of the Tao Garden), vol.9.
31. Kang Youwei 康有為, "Kang Nanhai zibian nianpu" 康南海自編年譜 (The Annals of Kang Nanhai) Association of Chinese Historians 中國史學會, ed., *Wuxu bianfa* 戊戌變法 (On the Hundred Days' Reform) (Shanghai: Shanghai People's Publishing House, 1957), vol. 4, 116.
32. Liang Qichao 梁啟超, "Sanshi zishu" 三十自述 (A Self-narration at the Age of 30), Liang Qichao, *Yinbingshi wenji* 飲冰室文集 (Complete Works of the Master of the Ice-Drinker's Studio) (Beijing: Zhonghua Book Company, 1989).
33. Liang Qichao 梁啟超, *Zhongguo jinsanbainian xueshu shi* 中國近三百年學術史 (Chinese Academic History in the Recent 300 Years).
34. Zhang Yilin 張一麐, "Tang Jiwu wei Liang Boqiang Zunrenzhensan xiansheng mubei wengao tici" 湯濟武為梁伯強尊人震三先生墓碑文稿題詞 (Memorial Poetry from Tang Jiwu to Liang Boqiang), Zhang Yilin, *Xintaipingshi ji* 心太平室集 (Collections of the Xintaiping Study) (Taipei: Wenhai chubanshe, 1966), vol. 2.
35. Fang Wen 方聞, *Qing Xu Songkan xiansheng Jiyu nianpu* 清徐松龕先生繼畬年譜 (The Annals of Xu Jiyu) (Taipei: The Commercial Press, 1982), 323.
36. Guo brought along a copy of *A Short Account of the Maritime Circuit* with him, taking out the book and comparing the description with the real situation whenever he visited one place. Guo Songtao 郭嵩燾, *Guo Songtao riji* 郭嵩燾日記 (The Diary of Guo Songtao) (Changsha: Hunan People's Publishing House, 1981), vol. 3, 74, 82, 86.
37. "*A Compendious Description of the World* (lit. the Oceanic Circle) by Seu Sung Lung in 6 Vols," *The North China Herald*, September 28, 1850. The Press editor misunderstood the character *kan* 龕 as *long* 龍, and thus spelling Xu's name as Sung Lung instead of Songkan.

38. One can find the inscription at the Washington Monument nowadays.
39. Pan Zhenping 潘振平, "Xu Jiyu he Yinghuan zhilüe" 徐繼畬和《瀛寰志略》(Xu Jiyu and *A Short Account of the Maritime Circuit*) *Journal of East China Normal University* 華東師範大學學報, No. 6 (1981).
40. Fang, *Qing Xu Songkan xiansheng Jiyu nianpu*, 328-329.
41. "America in China," *The New York Times*, March 29, 1868.
42. Only titles published in the Ming and Qing Dynasties were listed as the remaining titles were too outdated or general to list.
43. José Martinho Marques (1810–1867) was a Macanese who studied in the Seminário de São José (Seminary of San Jose). He was qualified as a translator in 1833, after when he began his business as a translator in Leal Senado (The Loyal Senate). During 1848 to 1861, he served as a translator for the French, American, and Prussian diplomats to China. His publications included *Official Language and the Cantonese Conversation* (*Guanhua yu yueyu huihua* 官話與粵語會話) and other religious titles. Wu Zhen 吳震 and Zhao Lifeng 趙利峰, "Aomen tusheng Puren Hanxuejia Majishi yu Xinshi dili beikao" 澳門土生葡人漢學家瑪吉士與《新釋地理備考》(A Macanese Sinologue José Martinho Marques and *A Study of Geography*), *Ji'nan Journal (Philosophy and Social Science)*, No. 2, 2006.
44. Wu and Zhao, "A Macanese Sinologue José Martinho Marques and *A Study of Geography*."
45. Wei, *Haiguo tushuo*, vol. 1.
46. Ibid., vol. 60.
47. Ibid., vol. 58.
48. Xiao Zhizhi 蕭致治, "Ping Weiyuan de Haiguo tuzhi" 評魏源的《海國圖志》(An Evaluation of the *Illustrated Gazetteer of the Maritime Countries*), Ning Jing 寧靖 ed., *Yanpian zhanzhengshi lunwen zhuanji xubian* (The Sequel of the Collected Essays of the Opium War) 鴉片戰爭史論文專集續編 (Beijing: People Publishing House, 1984).
49. Liang Qichao 梁啟超, *Lun Zhongguo xueshu sixiang bianqian zhi dashi* 論中國學術思想變遷之大勢 (On the Basic Trends of Chinese Intellectual Change).
50. Inoue Kiyoshi 井上清, *Riben jindaishi* 日本近代史 (The History of Modern Japan), translated by Lu Ming 呂明 (Beijing: Shenghuo dushu xinzhi sanlian shudian, 1956), vol. 1, 214.
51. John Fryer, "Jiangnan zhizao zongju fanyi xishu shilüe" 江南制造總局翻譯西書事略 (An Outline of Translation of Books), *Chinese Scientific Magazine* 3格致匯編, no. 5 (1880).
52. Qian Baozong 錢寶琮, *Zhongguo shuxue shi* 中國數學史 (The History of Mathematics in China) (Beijing: Science Press, 1981), 317-329.
53. Wang, *Wang Tao riji*, 57.
54. Wang was given the nickname of "the Long Hair *Zhuangxuan*" by the Jiangnan commoners for his profound knowledge and also his support to the Taiping Uprising.
55. A. Wylie and Wang Tao 王韜, *Xiguo tianxue yuanliu* 西國天學源流 (A History of Astronomy of the Western Countries) (Shanghai: Songyinglu, 1889), 28.
56. Ibid.
57. Wang Tao 王韜, "*Zhongxi tongshu* xu" 《中西通書》序 (Preface to the *Chinese Almanac*), Wang, *Wang Tao riji*, 19.
58. Wylie and Wang, *Xiguo tianxue yuanliu*, 29.
59. Wang, *Wang Tao riji*, 107.
60. Ibid., 92.
61. Wang Tao 王韜, *Yingru zazhi* 瀛壖雜誌 (Miscellaneous Records of the Shore) (Shanghai: Shanghai guji chubanshe, 1989), vol. 5, 93.

62. Ibid., 77.

63. Science titles amounted to only a quarter of the publication. The remaining titles were religious materials.

64. Wang Zhongyang 汪仲洋, "Gengzi liuyue wen zhousan jing" 庚子六月聞舟山警 (Hearing the Alarm from the Chusan Archipelago in June 1840), Aying 阿英 ed., *Yapian zhanzheng wenxue ji* 鴉片戰爭文學集 (Collected Literature on the Opium War) (Beijing: Zhonghua Book Company, 1957), 257.

65. Ye Zhongjin 葉鍾進, *Jiweishanfang zaji* 寄味山房雜記 (Miscellaneous Records of the Jiwei Mountain Studio).

66. Editorial Department, Zhonghua Book Company, *Chouban yiwu shimo Daoguang chao* 籌辦夷務始末道光朝 (The Management of Barbarian Affairs in Its Entirety, the Reign of Daoguang) (Beijing: Zhonghua Book Company, 1964), vol. 19 and 41.

67. Ibid., vol. 18.

68. Ibid., vol. 2.

Glossary

A Brief Explanation of the World Map	《地球圖說略》
A Brief Record of England	《英吉利小記》
A Complete List of the Translated Works of Lin Shu	《林紓翻譯作品全目》
A Complete Map of the Globe	《地球全圖》
A Comprehensive Study of Human Body	《全體通考》
A Desultory Account of the Malayan Archipelago	《海島逸志》
A Dictionary of the Hok-Keën Dialect of the Chinese Language	《福建土話字典》
A Guide to Chinese Grammar	《中文語法指南》
A Primer in Verse	《幼學詩釋句》
A Sketch of Chinese History	《中國史綱》
A Variety of Manuscripts Written in 1833	《癸巳類稿》
A View of China: for Philological Purposes	《中國：國家與風景》
Additional Law on Business	《生意人事廣益法》
Administrator	總辦
An Exposure of Heresy	《辟邪論》
Anglo-Cantonese Dictionary	《英粵字典》
Anglo-Chinese College	英華書院
Anglo-Chinese College (Heling)	鶴齡英華書院
Anqing Arsenal	安慶內軍械所
Aozhou College	鼇洲書院
Assistant Provincial Surveillance Commissioner of Lingxi	嶺西按察司副使
Books for Beginners of Chinese and Western Learning	《中西學門徑書七種》
Brigade vice Commander	都司
Brilliant Opinion on Gambling	《賭博明論》
Catalog of Books Published before 1911 Revolution	《辛亥革命書征》
celestial globe of various stars	列宿紀象大儀
celestial sphere	渾天星球
celestial template	平懸渾儀
Censorate	都察院
Chamberlain for Ceremonials	太常卿
Chief Minister of the Court of Judicial Review	大理寺卿
China Christian Education Association	中國基督教教育會
China Opened	《開放的中國》
China: Dialogues Between A Father and His Two Children Concerning the History and Present State of That Country	《父子對話: 中國的歷史和現狀》
Christian College in China	廣州格致書院
Circuit Intendant	道台
Collected Essays of the Qianyan Hall	《潛研堂文集》
Collection of Historical Souces on Sino-Western Communication	《中西交通史料匯編》

Glossary

Collections of the Jieqi Neighbourhood	《鮚埼亭集》
Commentaries and Sub-Commentaries on the Thirteen Classics	《十三經注疏》
Commissioner-in-chief	都督
Compendium of Geography	《方輿勝略》
Court of Colonial Affairs	理藩院
Court of Imperial Armaments	武備院
Court of Imperial Ceremonial	鴻臚寺
Court of the Imperial Clan	宗人府
Datong Calendar	大統曆
Denoted Dictionary of the Amoy Dialect	《廈門話標誌》
Dialogues and Detached Sentences in the Chinese Language	《中文會話與斷句》
Director	郎中
Discourse on Ma-tsoo-po	《媽祖婆論》
Discovery of Astronomy	《天文揭要》
Disquisition on Filial Piety	《辨孝論》
Disquisition on Human Nature	《辨性論》
Disquisition on Slander	《辨毀謗》
Educational Association of China	中國學塾會
Education Commissioner	學政
Elements of Chinese Grammar	《中國言法》
equator globe	赤道經緯儀
Erudite of the Water Clock	漏刻博士
Essential Notes for Cantonese Learners	《初學粵語切要》
Ewo Hong	豐泰行
Foochow College	福州格致書院
Fucheng Gate	阜城門
Further Study of Christianity	《景教續考》
Governor-general	總督
Grammar of the Chinese Language	《中國語法》
Grand Master for Splendid Happiness	光祿一品大夫
Grand Master for Thorough Counsel	通議大夫
Grand Minister Consultant	參贊
Guyue Library	古越藏書樓
Heian tenkōdō	平安天香堂
History of Catholic Evangelic Missions in Sixteenth Century China	《天主教十六世紀在華傳教志》
Hōshūdō	寶集堂
Household Administration of the Heir Apparent	詹事府
Idioms in the Four Books	《四書俚語啟蒙》
Illustrations of the Symbols, Philosophy, Antiquities, Customs, Superstition's, Laws, Government, Education, and Literature of the Chinese	《中國: 特徵、哲學、法律、教育和文學諸方面的素描》
Imperial Foreign Language Institute	同文館
Imperial Household Department	內務府

Imperial Parks Administration	奉宸院卿
Imvestigating Censor	監察御史
Jesuit Novitiate	耶穌會初學院
Jesuits Missionaries in China	《耶穌會士在中國》
Journey across the Small Sea	《裨海紀遊》
Junior Compiler in the Hanlin Academy	翰林院編修
Kansendō	甘泉堂
Kum-le-fow Hospital	惠愛醫館
La Chine à Tire-d'aile	《中國一瞥》
Mathematical Treatises of Wu'an	《勿庵曆算書目》
Medhurst College	上海梅溪書院
Medical Missionary Society of China	中華醫藥傳道會
Minister of Justice	刑部尚書
Minister of Revenue	戶部尚書
Minister of Rites	禮部尚書
Ministry of Civil Office	吏部
Ministry of Foreign Affairs	總理各國事務衙門
Ministry of Revenue	戶部
Monographs on Astronomy and the Calendar	《律曆志》
Morrison Education Society School	馬禮遜學堂
National Central Library Bulletin	《國立中央圖書館館刊》
Neighbourhood	亭
Notes about Migration to the United States	《往金山要訣》
Notices Concerning China and the Port of Canton	《關於中國與廣州》
Office of Imperial Stables	太僕寺
Office of Transmission	通政使司
On the Earth and Astronomy	《地球天文合論》
On the Eastern and Western Oceans	《東西洋考》
On the Hanshi and Ching Ming Festival	《寒食清明論》
On the Watchmaker Analogy	《鐘表匠論》
Palace Study	上駟院
Phonetic Notation of the Canton Dialect	《廣州土話注音》
Prefect	知府
Primer for Enlightenment	《蒙養啟明》
Primer for Kids	《蒙童訓》
Provincial Administration Commissioner	布政使
quadrant of the seven stars	七政象限大儀
Questions and Answers to Book Catalogs	《書目答問》
Record of August Military Achievements of the Qing Court	《聖武記》
Record of Things Seen and Heard in the Western Regions	《西域聞見錄》
Records of Macao	《澳門紀略》
Records of Waterways in the Western Region	《西域水道記》
Renji Hospital	倫敦會仁濟醫院
Rōka Fukudaie	浪華福田家

Glossary

Sanitary Board	潔淨局
Sea Mirror of Circle Measurements	《測圓海鏡》
Secretary	主事
Secretary in the Grand Secretariat	內閣中書
Seven Talks on the Abandonment of Opium Smoking	《鴉片速改七戒文》
Shanghai Institute for Dialects	上海廣方言館
Shanghai Journal of Mathematics Office	上海算學報館
Shanghai Nanyang College	上海南洋公學
Shixian Calendar	時憲曆
Singapore Chronicle	《新加坡年鑒》
Sino-Western Calendric Treatise	《華洋和合通書》
Shoushi Calendar	授時曆
Sōkairō	爽快樓
Sub-prefectural Magistrate	同知
Sun Tau Lan Street	新豆欄街
Superintendent of Training	提學使
Surveillance Commissioner of Zhejiang Province	浙江按察使
Surveillance Governor	巡警道
Taipan	大班
telescope for the wax and waning of the seven stars	測候七政交食遠鏡
The American Presbyterian Mission Press	美華書館
The Analects	《論語》
The Causes of Poverty of the Chinese	《華人貧窶之故》
The China Mail	《德臣西報》
The Chinese Mail	《華字日報》
The Court of Sacrificial Worship	太常寺
The Encyclopedia of China and the West	《西洋中華通書》
The Encyclopedia of China and the United Kingdom	《英華通書》
The Ningpo Boys' Academic	崇信義塾
The Ningpo Girls' Academic	寧波女塾
The Overall Survey of the Ocean's Shores	《瀛涯勝覽》
the policy of single-port trading	一口通商
The Sacred Edicts	《上諭》
The Territory of England with Illustrations	《英吉利地圖說》
Three Thousands Common Words in Chinese	《中文最常用三千字》
Tianjin Armaments College	天津武備學堂
Tōjuen	桃樹園
Translation College of the Jiangnan Arsenal	江南機器制造局翻譯館
Translation of a Comparative Vocabulary of the Chinese, Corean and Japanese Languages	《中朝日語對照》
Treatise on the Composition of the Universe	《空際格致》
Universal Geography	《萬國地理全集》
Vice Director	員外郎
Vice Minister	少卿

Vice Minister of the Ministry of Military	兵部侍郎
Vocabulary of the Canton Dialect	《廣東省土話字彙》
Vocabulary of the Fukien Dialect	《福建土話字彙》
Wang Ngai College	宏藝書塾
Warehouseman	司庫
Wen Shan Girls' School	文山女塾
Yuying Middle School	毓英女校
zodiac globe	黃道經緯儀
Zhuxue Study	鑄學齋

References

Personal Works

Allen, Young J. and Cai Erkang 蔡爾康. *Zhongdong zhanji benmo* 中東戰紀本末 (Tales of the Sino-Japanese War). Shanghai: SDK, 1896, 1897, 1990.

Allen, Young J. and Kreyer, Carl T. ed. *Xiguo jinshi huipian* 西國近事匯編 (Collection of Recent Events in the West). Shanghai: Translation College of the Jiangnan Arsenal, 1873.

Allen, Young J. *Yindu liying shier yishuo* 印度隸英十二益說 (Twelve Benefits of the Indian Subordination to the United Kingdom). Shanghai: SDK, 1898.

An Kejia 晏可佳. *Zhongguo Tianzhujiao jianshi* 中國天主教簡史 (A Brief History of Catholics in China). Beijing: China Religious Culture Publisher, 2001.

Association of Chinese Historians ed. *Wuxu bianfa* 戊戌變法 (On the Hundred Days' Reform). Shanghai: Shanghai People's Publishing House, 1957.

—— ed. *Xinhai gemin* 辛亥革命 (1911 Revolution). Shanghai: Shanghai People's Publishing House, 1957.

—— ed. *Yangwu yundong* 洋務運動 (Self-Strengthening Movement). Shanghai: Shanghai People's Publishing House, 1961.

—— ed. *Yapian zhanzheng* 鴉片戰爭 (The Opium War). Shanghai: Shanghai xinzhishi chubanshe, 1955.

Aying 阿英 ed. *Wanqing wenyi baokan shulüe* 晚清文藝報刊述略 (A Brief Account of the Literary Journal in Late Qing Dynasty). Shanghai: Shanghai gudian wenxue chubanshe, 1958.

——. *Yapian zhanzheng wenxue ji* 鴉片戰爭文學集 (Collected Literature on the Opium War). Beijing: Zhonghua Book Company, 1957.

Bai Limin 白莉民. *Xixue dongjian yu Mingqing zhiji jiaoyu sichao* 西學東漸與明清之際教育思潮 (The Eastward Dissemination of Western Learning and the Educational Thoughts in the Ming-to-Qing Transitional Period). Beijing: Educational Science Publishing House, 1989.

Barnett, Suzanne Wilson. "Practical Evangelism: Protestant Missions and the Introduction of Western Civilization into China (1820–1850)." PhD diss., Harvard University, 1973.

Bellamy, Edward, Lin Tiandou 林天斗 and Zhang Zimou 張自謀 trans. *Huigu* 回顧 (Looking Backward 2000–1887). Beijing: The Commercial Press, 1984.

——. *Bainian yijiao* 百年一覺 (Centennial Awakening). Shanghai: SDK, 1894. Originally published as Looking backward, 2000–1887.

Bennett, Adrian Arthur. *John Fryer: The Introduction of Western Science and Technology into Nineteenth-century China.* Cambridge: Harvard University Press, 1967.

——. *Missionary Journalist in China: Young J. Allen and His Magazines* (1860–1883). Athens: University of Georgia Press, 1983.

——. *Research Guide to the Chiao-hui-hsin-pao (The Church News) 1868–1874*. San Francisco: Chinese Materials Center, 1975.

——. *Research Guide to the Wan-kuo-kung-pao (The Globe Magazine)* 1874–1883. San Francisco: Chinese Materials Center, 1975.

References

Bernard, Henry. *Tianzhujiao shiliu shiji zaihua chuanjiaozhi* 天主教十六世紀在華傳教志 (History of Catholic Evangelic Missions in Sixteenth Century China) Translated by Xiao Junhua 蕭浚華. Beijing: The Commercial Press, 1936.

Biggerstaff, Knight. *The Earliest Modern Government Schools in China*. Ithaca: Cornell University Press, 1961.

Blair, John. *Siyi biannian biao* 四裔編年表 (The Annals of the Four Barbarians). Translated by Allen, Young J., and Yan Liangxun 嚴良勛. Shanghai: Translation College of the Jiangnan Arsenal, 1874.

Bloxam, Charles L. *Huanxue jianyuan bupian* 化學鑒原補編 (Additional Principle and Applications of Chemistry). Translated by John Fryer and Xu Shou 徐壽. Shanghai: Translation College of the Jiangnan Arsenal, 1879.

——. *Huanxue jianyuan Xupian* 化學鑒原續編 (The Sequel of the Principle and Applications of Chemistry). Translated by John Fryer and Xu Shou 徐壽. Shanghai: Translation College of the Jiangnan Arsenal, 1875.

Bluntschli, Johann Kaspar. *Gongfa huitong* 公法會通 (An Interpretation of Public Law). Translated by Lian Fang 聯芳, W. A. P. Martin, and Qing Chang 慶常. Beijing: Imperial Foreign Language Institute, 1880.

Bowman, John E. *Huaxue fenyuan* 化學分原 (Chemical Analysis). Translated by John Fryer and Xu Jianyan 徐建寅. Shanghai: Translation College of the Jiangnan Arsenal, 1871.

Bridgman, E. C. *Meilige heshengguozhi lüe* 美理哥合省國志略 (A Brief History of the United States of America). Singapore: Jianxia shuyuan, 1838.

Britton, Roswell S. *The Chinese Periodical Press*, 1800–1912. Shanghai: Kelly and Walsh, 1934.

Broomhall, Marshall. *Robert Morrison: a Master-Builder*. London: Church Missionary Society, 1924.

Burton, Margaret E. *The Education of Women in China*. New York: Fleming H. Revell Co.

Cai Shangsi 蔡尚思 and Fang Xing 方行 ed. *Tan Sitong quanji* 譚嗣同全集 (A Complete Collection of Tan Sitong). Beijing: Zhonghua Book Company, 1981.

Cai Wu 蔡武. "Tantan Dongxiyang kao meiyue tongjizhuan" 談談 東西洋考每月統記傳 (On the Eastern Western Monthly Magazine), *National Central Library Bulletin* 國立中央圖書館館刊, No. 2 (4).

Cai Yutian 蔡育天 et al. ed. *Shanghai daoqi juanyi* 上海道契卷一 (Collections of the Title Deeds of Shanghai, volume one. Shanghai: Shanghai guji chubanshe, 1998.

Cao Lizhen 曹履貞 and Zhang Zhiben 張知本 trans. *Fazheng congpian* 法政叢編 (Collectanea on Law and Administration). Tokyo: Sh   ransha, 1905.

Cao Wanru 曹婉如 et al. "Zhongguo yu Ouzhou ditu jiaoliu de kaishi" 中國與歐洲地圖交流的開始 (The Beginning of the Communication between Chinese and European Maps), *Studies in the History of Natural Sciences* 自然科學史研究, No. 4 (1984).

Cao Zengyou 曹增友. *Chuanjiaoshi yu Zhongguo kexue* 傳教士與中國科學 (Missionaries and Chinese Science). Beijing: China Religious Culture Publisher, 1999.

Chen Pingyuan 陳平原 and Milena Doleželová-Velingerová ed. *Jindai Zhongguo de baike quanshu* 近代中國的百科全書 (Encyclopedia of Modern China). Beijing: Peking University Press, 2007.

Chen Shoupeng 陳壽彭 trans. *Wanguo shilüe* 萬國史略 (A Short History of Myraid Countries) Jinling: Jiangchu bianyiju, 1906.

Chen Song 陳崧 and Ding Weizhi 丁偉志. *Zhongxitiyong zhi jian — wanqing Zhongxi wenhuaguan shulun* 中西體用之間—晚清中西文化觀述論 (Between the Chinese Fundamental Learning and the Western Technical Practice: a Study on the Cultural Perspective of Sino-Western Culture in the Late Qing Dynasty). Beijing: China Social Sciences Press, 1997.

Chen Xulu 陳旭麓. *Jindai Zhongguo shehui de xinchen daixie* 近代中國社會的新陳代謝 (Metabolism of Modern Chinese Society). Shanghai: Shanghai People's Publishing House, 1992.

——. *Jindaishi sibianlu* 近代史思辯錄 (Record of Moral Reasoning in Modern History). Guangzhou: Guangdong People's Publishing House, 1984.

Chen Yuan 陳垣. "Jidujiao ruhua shilüe" 基督教入華史略 (A Brief History of the Coming of Christianity to China). *Truth Monthly*, No. 18 (1924).

Chen Zhengqing 陳正青. *Guangfangyanguan quanan* 廣方言館全案 (The Complete Information of the Institute for Dialects). Shanghai: Shanghai guji chubanshe, 1989.

Chen Zhongyi 陳忠倚 ed. *Huangchao jingshiwen sanbian* 皇朝經世文三編 (Collected Essays about Statecraft of the Qing Dynasty 3). Shanghai: Baowen shuju, 1898.

Chen Zhu 陳洙 ed. *Jiangnan zhizaoju yishu tiyao* 江南制造局譯書提要 (Summary of the Translated Works of the Jiangnan Arsenal). Shanghai: Jiangnan Arsenal, 1909.

Chu Guishan 儲桂山 ed. *Huangchao jingshiwen xinbian xuji* 皇朝經世文新編續集 (The Sequel of the Newly-Collected Essays about Statecraft of the Qing Dynasty).Yiji shuju, 1902.

Clyde, Paul H, and Burton F. Beers. *The Far East: a History of the Western Impacts and the Eastern Reponses, 1830–1975*. Englewood Cliffs, N.J.: Prentice-Hall, 1975.

Cohen, Paul A. *China and Christianity: the Missionary Movement and the Growth of Chinese Antiforeignism, 1860–1870*. Cambridge: Harvard University Press, 1967.

Cohen, Paul A., and John E. Schrecker. *Reform in Nineteenth-century China*. Cambridge: Harvard University Press, 1976.

Collingwood, R. G. He Zhaowu 何兆武 et al., trans. *Lishi de guannian* 歷史的觀念 (The Idea of History). Beijing: China Social Sciences Press, 1986.

Couling, Samuel, and George Lanning. *The History of Shanghai. Shanghai*: Kelly & Walsh, 1921.

Crawford, Martha. *Zao Yangfan shu* 造洋飯書 (Foreign Cookery). Shanghai: American Presbyterian Mission Press, 1866.

Cuncui xueshe 存萃學社 ed. *Li Madou yanjiu lunwenji* 利瑪竇研究論集 (Collected Research Reports on Matteo Ricci). Hong Kong: Chongwen shudian, 1971.

Dai Hongci 戴鴻慈 and Duan Fang 端方 et al. ed. *Lieguo zhengyao* 列國政要 (Essentials of Government of Various Countries). Shanghai: The Commercial Press, 1907.

Dai Nihon Shin Hōten Kōshūkai 大日本新法典講習會 ed. *Hanyi xinfalu cidian* 漢譯新法律詞典 (Chinese Translation of the Dictionary of the New Law). Translated by Xu Yongxi 徐用錫. Beijing: Jingshi yixueguan, 1905.

Dana, James Dwight. *Jinshi shibie* 金石識別 (Discrimination of Mineral). Translated by Daniel Jerome MacGowan and Hua Hengfang 華蘅芳. Shanghai: Translation College of the Jiangnan Arsenal, 1872. Originally published as *The System of Mineralogy of James Dwight Dana, 1837-1868, Descriptive Mineralogy*.

Department of History, Sun Yat-sen University ed. *Lin Zexu Ji* 林則徐集 (Collections of Lin Zexu). Beiing: Zhonghua Book Company, 1985.

References

Drake, Fred W. *Xu Jiyu ji qi Yinghuan zhilüe* 徐繼畬及其《瀛寰志略》(Xu Jiyu and His *A Short Account of the Maritime Circuit*) Translated by Ren Fuxing 任復興. Beijing: Wenjin chubanshe, 1990. Originally published as *China Charts the World: Hsu Chi-Yu and His Geography of 1848*.

Du Shiran 杜石然. *Zhongguo kexue jishu shigao* 中國科學技術史稿 (Drafted History of Science and Technology in China). Beijing: Science Press, 1982.

Editorial Department, Zhonghua Book Company ed. *Chouban yiwu shimo Daoguang Chao* 籌辦夷務始末 道光朝 (The Management of Barbarian Affairs in Its Entirety, Reign of Daoguang). Beijing: Zhonghua Book Company, 1964.

—— ed. *Chouban yiwu shimo Xianfeng Chao* 籌辦夷務始末 咸豐朝 (The Management of Barbarian Affairs in Its Entirety, Reign of Xianfeng). Beijing: Zhonghua Book Company, 1979.

—— ed. *Chouban yiwu shimo Tongzhi Chao* 籌辦夷務始末 同治朝 (The Management of Barbarian Affairs in Its Entirety, Reign of Tongzhi). Beijing: Zhonghua Book Company, 2008.

Edkins, Joseph et al. *Zhongxi tongshu* 中西通書 (Chinese Almanac). Shanghai: London Missionary Society Mission Press, 1853–1855.

Edkins, Joseph. *Xixue qimeng* 西學啟蒙 (Primers for Western Learning). Shanghai: Superintendence of Trade, 1886.

Etiemble, Rene and Jacques Gernet. *Mingqing ruhua Yesuhuishi he Zhongxi wenhua jiaoliu* 明清入華耶穌會士和中西文化交流 (Jesuits Missionaries in the Ming-to-Qing Transitional Period and the Sino-Western Cultural Communication). Translated by Geng Sheng 耿昇. Chengdu: Sichuan bashu shushe, 1993.

Evans, Charles W. DeLacy. *Yannian yishou lun* 延年益壽論 (On the Prolongation of Life). Translated by John Fryer. Shanghai: School and Textbook Series Committee, 1892. Originally published as Can *We Prolong Life?: An Inquiry into the Cause of Old Age and Natural Death, Showing the Diet and Agents Best Adapted for a Lengthened Prolongation of Existence* (London: Baillière, 1879).

Faber, Ernst. *Zixi cudong* 自西徂東 (Civilization, China and Christian). Hong Kong: Zhonghua yinwu zongju, 1884.

Fairbank, John K. ed. The *Cambridge History of China* (Vol. 10: Late Ch'ing, 1800–1911). Cambridge: Cambridge University Press, 2008.

——. *The Missionary Enterprise in China and America*. Cambridge: Harvard University Press, 1974.

——. *Trade and Diplomacy on the China Coast: the Opening of the Treaty Ports, 1842–1854*. Stanford, California: Stanford University Press, 1969.

Fan Hongye 樊洪業. *Yesuhuishi yu Zhongguo kexue* 耶穌會士與中國科學 (Jesuit Missionaries and Science in China). Beijing: China Renmin University Press, 1992.

Fan Junzhi 范均之, Liu Jianting 廖淦亭, and Ma Youyu 馬幼漁 trans. *Shijie tongshi* 世界通史 (General History of the World). Shanghai: Shanghai tongshe, 1903.

Fang Hao 方豪. *Zhongguo Tianzhujiao chuanjiaoshi gailun* 中國天主教史人物傳 (Biographies of the Chinese Catholics). Beijing: Zhonghua Book Company, 1988.

——. *Zhongxi jiaotongshi* 中西交通史 (The History of Sino-Western Communication). Changsha: Yuelu Publishing House, 1987.

Fang Wen 方聞 ed. *Qing Xu Songkan xiansheng Jiyu nianpu* 清徐松龕先生繼畬年譜 (The Annals of Xu Jiyu). Taipei: The Commercial Press, 1982.

Fang Xing 方行 and Tang Zhijun 湯志鈞. *Wang Tao Riji* 王韜日記 (The Diary of Wang Tao). Beijing: Zhonghua Book Company, 1987.

Fawcett, Henry. *Fuguoce* 富國策 (Strategies to Enrich the State). Translated by Wang Fengzao 汪鳳藻 and edited by W. A. P. Martin. Beijing: Imperial Foreign Language Institute, 1881.

Ferdinand Dagenais. *Calendar of the Correspondence, Publications, and Miscellaneous Papers of John Fryer (1839–1928), with Selected Excerpts*. Berkeley: University of California, 1997.

Fresenius, Karl Remigius. *Huaxue kaozhi* 化學考質 (Manual of Quanlitative Chemical Analysis). Translated by John Fryer and Xu Shou 徐壽. Shanghai: Translation College of the Jiangnan Arsenal, 1883.

——. *Huaxue qiushu* 化學求數 (Quantitative Chemical Analysis). Shanghai: Translation College of the Jiangnan Arsenal, 1883.

Fryer, John and Ying Zuxi 應祖錫 trans. *Zuozhi cuyan* 佐治芻言 (Chambers's Educational Course: Political Economy for Use in Schools and for Private Instruction). Shanghai: Translation College of the Jiangnan Arsenal, 1885.

Fryer, John ed. *Lixue xuzhi* 理學須知. Shanghai: Chinese Scientific Book Depot, 1888.

Fryer, John trans. "Diary of Voyage to China, from March 10, 1861 to August 6, 1861." In *John Fryer Papers*, Online Archive of the University of California.

——. "Jiangnan zhizao zongju fanyi xishu shilüe" 江南制造總局翻譯西書事略 (An Outline of Translation of Books in the Jiangnan Arsenal). *Chinese Scientific Magazine* 3 格致匯編, No. 5, (1880).

——. *An Account of the Department for the Translation of Foreign Books at the Kiangnan Arsenal, Shanghai: with Various Lists of Publications in the Chinese Language*. Shanghai: American Presbyterian Mission Press, 1880.

——. *Haitong weisheng bian* 孩童衛生編 (Hygine of Children). Shanghai: Chinese Scientific Book Depot, 1894.

——. *The Educational Directory for China: an Account of the Various Schools and Colleges Connected with Protestant Missions as well as of Government and Private Schools under Foreign Instruction*. Shanghai: Educational Association of China, 1895.

——. *Youtong weisheng pian* 幼童衛生編 (The Hygiene of Young Children). Shanghai: Chinese Scientific Book Depot, 1893.

Fu Weikang 傅維康 ed. *Zhongguo yixueshi* 中國醫學史 (The History of Medical Studies in China). Shanghai yixueyuan chubanshe, 1990.

Fujii, Kenjirō 藤井健次郎. *Zhexue fanlun* 哲學泛論 (General Discourse on Philosophy). Translated by Fan Diji 范迪吉. Shanghai: Huiwen xueshe, 1903.

Fukui, Junzō 福井準造. *Jinshi shehui zhuyi* 近世社會主義 (Socialism of the Modern World). Translated by Zhao Bizhen 趙必振. Shanghai: Guangzhi shuju, 1903. Originally published as *Kinsei shakai shugi* 近世社會主義 (Tokyo: Yūhikaku Shobō, 1899).

Gao Mingkai 高名凱 and Liu Zhengtan 劉正埮 ed. *Hanyu wailaici cidian* 漢語外來詞詞典 (Dictionary for the Foreign-imported Terms in the Chinese Language). Shanghai: Shanghai Lexicographical Publishing House, 1984.

Ge Gongzhen 戈公振. *Zhongguo baoxue shi* 中國報學史 (History of China's Newspapers). Taipei: Student Book Co., Ltd., 1982.

References

Ge Shijun 葛士浚 ed. *Huangchao jingshiwen xinzeng xubian* 皇朝經世文新增續編 (Newly-Collected Essays about Statecraft of the Qing Dynasty). Shanghai: Saoye shanfang, 1897.

——. *Huangchao jingshiwen xubian* 皇朝經世文續編 (The Sequel of the Collected Essays about Statecraft of the Qing Dynasty). Shanghai: Tushu jicheng ju, 1888.

Geffcken, F. Heinrich and Martens, Karl von. *Xingyao zhizhang* 星軺指掌 (Guide to Diplomatic Prctice). Translated by Lian Fang 聯芳 and Qing Chang 慶常, edited by W. A. P. Martin. Beijing: Imperial Foreign Language Institute, 1876.

General Conference of the Protestant Missionaries of China and Matthew Tyson Yates, ed. *Records of the General Conference of the Protestant Missionaries of China Held at Shanghai, 1877*. Shanghai: American Presbyterian Mission Press, 1878.

——. *Records of the General Conference of the Protestant Missionaries of China Held at Shanghai, 1890*. Shanghai: American Presbyterian Mission Press, 1890.

Gong Ying'an 龔纓晏 et al. *Xifangren donglai zhihou* 西方人東來之後 (After the Eastward Travelling of the Westerners). Hangzhou: Zhejiang University Press, 2006.

Gu Changsheng 顧長聲. *Chuanjiaoshi yu jindai Zhongguo* 傳教士與近代中國 (Missionaries and Modern China). Shanghai: Shanghai People's Publishing House, 1981.

——. *Cong Malixun dao Shituleideng* 從馬禮遜到司徒雷登 (From Robert Morrison to John Stuart Leighton). Shanghai: Shanghai People's Publishing House, 1985.

Gu Weimin 顧衛民. *Jidujiao yu jindai Zhongguo shehui* 基督教與近代中國社會 (Christianity and Modern Chinese Society). Shanghai: Shanghai People's Publishing House, 1996.

——. *Zhongguo Tianzhujiao biannianshi* 中國天主教編年史 (The Annals of Catholic in China). Shanghai: Shanghai Bookstore, 2003.

Gu Xieguang 顧燮光. *Yishu jingyanlu* 譯書經眼錄 (Records of Translation). Hangzhou: Jingjiashi haolou, 1935.

Guo Songtao 郭嵩燾. *Guo Songtao Riji* 郭嵩燾日記 (The Diary of Guo Songtao). Changsha: Hunan People's Publishing House, 1981.

Guo Weidong 郭衛東 ed. *Jindai waiguo zaihua wenhua jigou zonglu* 近代外國在華文化機構綜錄 (A Record of the Foreign Cultural Agents in Modern China). Shanghai: Shanghai People's Publishing House, 1993.

Gutzlaff, K. F. A. *Daying guotong zhi* 大英國統志 (A General Gazetteer of the Great Britain). Singapore: Jianxia shuyuan, 1834.

——. *Gujin wanguo gangjian* 古今萬國綱鑒 (Narrative Record of the Countries of the World, Past and Present). Singapore: Jianxia shuyuan, 1838.

——. *Maoyi tongzhi* 貿易通志 (A General Account of Trade). Singapore: Jianxia shuyuan, 1840.

Guy, William A., David Ferrier ed. *Falu yixue* 法律醫學 (Forensic Medical Studies). Translated by John Fryer, Xu Shou 徐壽, and Zhao Yuanyi 趙元益. Shanghai: Translation College of the Jiangnan Arsenal, 1899. Originally published as *Principles of Forensic Medicine* (London: H. Renshaw, 1895).

Han Guang 寒光. *Lin Qinnan* 林琴南 (Lin Qinnan). Beijing: Zhonghua Book Company, 1935.

Han Qi 韓琦. "Shuli gezhi de faxian — jianlun shijiu shiji yiqian Niudun xueshuo zai Zhongguo de chuanbo"《數理格致》的發現—兼論十九世紀以前牛頓學說在中國的傳播 (The Discovery of *Principia* and the Spread of Newton's Theory in Pre-nineteenth Century China).

The Chinese Journal for the History of Science and Technology 中國科技史科, No. 2 (1998).

Han Qi 韓琦 and Zhan Jialing 詹嘉玲. "Kangxi shidai xifang shuxue zai gongting de chuanbo — yi Anduohe suanshu zuanyao zonggang de bianzuan weili" 康熙時代西方數學在宮廷的傳播—以安多和《算法纂要總綱》的編纂為例 (The Dissemination of Western Mathematics in the Palace in the Reign of Kangxi) *History of Natural Sciences* 自然科學史研究, No. 2 (2003).

Hang Shijun 杭世駿. *Daogutang ji* 道古堂集 (Collection of the Daogu Hall).

Happer, Andrew Patton, *Tianwen wenda* 天文問答 (Catechism of Astronomy). Ningbo: The Chinese and American Holy Classic Book Establishment, 1849.

Harrison, Brian. *Waiting for China: the Anglo-Chinese College at Malacca, 1818–1843, and Early Nineteenth-century Missions*. Hong Kong: Hong Kong University Press, 1979.

Haswell, Chas H. *Suanshi jiyao* 算式集要 (Collected Mathematical Questions). Translated by Jiang Heng 江衡 and John Fryer. Shanghai: Translation College of the Jiangnan Arsenal, 1877.

Haven, Joseph. *Xinlingxue* 心靈學 (Mind Spirit Study). Translated by Yan Yongjing 顏永京. Shanghai: School and Textbook Series Committee, 1889.

He Dajin 何大進, Lei Yutian 雷雨田 and Zhao Chunchen 趙春晨. Jidujiao yu jindai lingnan wenhua 基督教與近代嶺南文化 (Christianity and Modern Lingnan Culture). Shanghai: Shanghai People's Publishing House, 2002.

He Dajin 何大進. *Wanqing Zhongmei guanxi yu shehui biange: wanqing Meiguo chuanjiaoshi zaihua huodong de lishi kaocha* 晚清中美關係與社會變革 晚清美國傳教士在華活動的歷史考察 (Sino-American Relationship and Social Transformation in the Late Qing China: a Historical Study of the Activities of American Missionaries in Late Qing China). Nanchang: Jiangxi People's Publishing House, 1998.

He Liangdong 何良棟 ed. *Huangchao jingshiwen sibian* 皇朝經世文四編 (Collected Essays about Statecraft of the Qing Dynasty 4). Shanghai: Baohong shuju, 1902.

Headland, Frederick W. and Royle, J. Forbes. *Xiyao dacheng* 西藥大成 (Materia Medica and Therapeutics). Shanghai: Translation College of the Jiangnan Arsenal, 1879. Originally published as *A Manual of Materia Medica and Therapeutics: Including the Preparations of the British Pharmacopoeia, and Many Other Approved Medicines*.

Headland, Frederick W. *Rumen yixue* 儒門醫學 (A Medical Handbook). Translated by John Fryer and Zhao Yuanyi 趙元益. Shanghai: Translation College of the Jiangnan Arsenal, 1876.

Heeren, John J. *On the Shantung Front: a History of the Shantung Mission of the Presbyterian Church in the U. S. A. 1861–1940 in Its Historical, Economic and Political Setting*. New York: Board of Foreign Missions of the Presbyterian Church in the United States, 1940.

Hobson, Benjamin. *Bowu xinpian* 博物新編 (Natural Philosophy and Natural History). Guangzhou: Canton Hospital, Pok Tsai, 1855.

——. Guan Sifu 管嗣復 ed. *Fuying xinshuo* 婦嬰新說 (Treatise on Midwifery and Diseases of Children). Shanghai: London Missionary Society Mission Press, 1858.

——. *Neike xinshuo* 內科新說 (Practice of Medicine and Materia Medica). Shanghai: London Missionary Society Mission Press, 1858.

——. *Quanti xinlun* 全體新論. Guangzhou: Kum-le-fow Hospital, 1851

——. *Tianwen lüelun* 天文略論 (A Short Discourse on Astronomy).

——. *Xiyi lüelun* 西醫略論 (First Lines Of the Practice of Surgery in the West). Shanghai: Renji Hospital, 1857.

Hobson, Benjamin and Komuro Seiichi 小室誠一. *Gōtō hakubutsu shinpen* 鼇頭博物新編 (Natural Philosophy and Natural History, the First Volume).

Høffding, Harald and Mary E. Lowndes. *Xinlixue gailun* 心理學概論 (An Outline of Psychology). Translated by Wang Guowei 王國維. Shanghai: The Commercial Press, 1915.

Hong Weilian 洪煨蓮. "Kao Li Madou de shijie ditu" 考利瑪竇的世界地圖 (A Research on Ricci's World Map). *The Chinese Historical Geography* 禹貢, Vol. 5, No. 3-4.

Houston, Edwin J., and Kennelly, Arthur E. *Suanshi jiefa* 算式解法 (Solutions to Mathematical Questions). Translated by Hua Hengfang 華蘅芳 and John Fryer. Shanghai: Translation College of the Jiangnan Arsenal, 1899. Originally published as *The Interpretation of Mathematical Formulae* (New York: American Technical Book Co., 1898).

Hu Fengxiang 胡逢祥 and Zhang Wenjian 張文建. *Zhongguo jindai shixue sichao yu liupai* 中國近代史學思潮與流派 (Ideas and Schools of Historiography of Modern China). Shanghai: East China Normal University Press, 1991.

Hu Weiqing 胡衛清. *Pupian zhuyi de tiaozhan: Jindai Zhongguo Jidujiao jiaoyu yanjiu 1877–1927* 普遍主義的挑戰 近代中國基督教教育研究 1877–1927 (A Challenge to Universalism: a Study of Christian Education in Modern China 1877–1927. Shanghai: Shanghai People's Publishing House, 2000.

Hu Zhusheng 胡珠生 ed. *Chen Qiu ji* 陳虬集 (Collections of Chen Qiu). Hangzhou: Zhejiang People's Publishing House, 1992.

Hua Hengfang 華蘅芳 and Carl T. Kreyer trans. *Cehou congtan* 測候叢談 (Climatic Miscellany). Shanghai: Translation College of the Jiangnan Arsenal, 1877.

Huang Aiping 黃愛平 and Huang Xingtao 黃興濤. ed. *Xixue yu Qingdai wenhua* 西學與清代文化 (Western Learning and the Culture of the Qing Dynasty). Beijing: Zhonghua Book Company, 2008.

Huang Naichang 黃乃裳. *Da Meiguo shilüe* 大美國史略 (A Short History of the United States). Fuzhou: American Presbyterian Mission Press, 1899.

Huang Qingcheng 黃慶澄 ed. *Zhongxi putong shumu biao* 中西普通書目表 (Common Titles of Chinese and Western Books). Woodblock-printed edition, 1898.

Huang Shijian 黃時鑒. *Dongxi wenhua jiaoliu shi lungao* 東西文化交流史論稿 (Drafted History of the Eastern Western Cultural Communication). Shanghai: shanghai guji chubanshe, 1998.

—— ed. *Dongxiyang kao meiyue tongjizhuan yingyinben* 東西洋考每月統記傳影印本 (Eastern Western Monthly Magazine [Copied Edition]). Beijing: Zhonghua Book Company, 1997.

Huang Yanpei 黃炎培. *Bashinianlai* 八十年來 (In the Past 80 Years). Beijing: Zhongguo wenshi chubanshe, 1982.

Hymers, John. *Sanjiao shuli* 三角數理 (Explanation to Trigonometry). Translated by John Fryer. Shanghai: Translation College of the Jiangnan Arsenal, 1878.

Ienaga, Toyokichi 家永豐吉 and Motora Yujiro 元良勇次郎, Shao Xiyong 邵希雍 trans. Bankoku *shiko* 萬國史綱 (An Outline of the History of Myriad Countries). Zhina fanyi huishe, 1903.

Inoue, Enryō 井上圓了. *Yaoguaixue jiangyilu* 妖怪學講義錄 (Notes on the Ghosts). Translated by Cai Yuanpei 蔡元培. Shanghai: The Commercial Press, 1906.

——. *Zhexue yaoling* 哲學要領 (Guideline to Philosophy). Shanghai: Guangzhi shuju, 1902. Originally published as *Tetsugakuyōryō* 哲學要領 (Tokyo: Tetsugaku shoin, 1886).

Inoue, Kiyoshi 井上清. *Riben jindaishi* 日本近代史 (The History of Modern Japan). Translated by Lu Ming 呂明. Beijing: Shenghuo dushu xinzhi sanlian shudian, 1956.

Institute of History of the Shanghai Academy of Social Sciences ed. *Shanghai Xiaodaohui qiyi shiliao huibian* 上海小刀會起義史料匯編 (Collection of the Historical Sources of the Uprising of the Society of Little Swords in Shanghai). Shanghai: Shanghai People's Publishing House, 1980.

——. *Taipingjun zai Shanghai — Beihua jiebao suanyi* 太平軍在上海 — 北華捷報 選譯 (Taiping Army in Shanghai: Selective Translations of the *North-China Herald*). Shanghai: Shanghai People's Publishing House, 1983.

Jacques Gernet, Geng Sheng 耿昇 trans. Zhongguo yu Jidujiao 中國與基督教 (China and Christianity). Shanghai: Shanghai guji chubanshe, 2003.

Jevons, W. S. *Bianxue* 辨學 (A Study on Logic). Translated by Wang Guowei 王國維. Beijing: Yishen yinshua ju, 1908.

Ji Yun 紀昀. *Yuewei caotang biji* 閱微草堂筆記 (Random Jottings from the Cottage of Close Scrutiny).

Jiang Wenhan 江文漢. *Mingqing jian zaihua de Tianzhujiao Yesuhuishi* 明清間在華的天主教耶穌會士 (Jesuits Missionaries in the Ming-to-Qing Transitional Period). Beijing: Zhishi chubanshe, 1987.

Johnston, Jas. F. W. John Fryer and Luan Xueqian 欒學謙 trans. *Huaxue weisheng lun* 化學衛生論 (On Chemical Hygiene). Shanghai: Chinese Scientific Book Depot, 1890.

Kang Zhijie 康志杰. *Xixue dongjian de xianhengzhe: Tang Ruowang* 西學東漸的先行者 湯若望 (Adam Schall: a Pioneer in the Eastward Dissemination of Western Learning). Nanjing: Jiangsu guji chubanshe, 1993.

Keishū, Sanetō 實藤惠秀, Lam Kai-yin 林啟彥 and Tam Yue-him 譚汝謙 trans. *Zhongguoren liuxue Riben shi* 中國人留學日本史 (The History of the Chinese Overseas Studies to Japan). Beijing: SDX Joint Publishing Company, 1983.

Kerr, John Glasgow and He Liaoran 何了然 trans. *Kexue chujie* 化學初階 (First Step in Chemistry). Guangzhou: Canton Hospital, Pok Tsai, 1871.

Kerr, John Glasgow and Kong Qinggao 孔慶高 trans. *Xiyi neike quanshu* 西醫內科全書 (Complete Works of Western Internal Medicine). Guangzhou: Canton Hospital, Pok Tsai, 1882.

Kerr, John Glasgow and Lin Xiangdong 林湘東 trans. *Neike chanwei quanshu* 內科闡微全書 (The Complete Works of Internal Medicine). Guangzhou: Canton Hospital, Pok Tsai, 1873.

——. *Xiyao lüeshi* 西藥略釋 (A Brief Explanation of Western Medicine). Guangzhou: Canton Hospital, Pok Tsai, 1875.

Kishimoto, Nobuta 岸本能武太. *Shehuixue* 社會學 (An Outline of Sociology). Translated by Zhang Taiyan 章太炎. Shanghai: Guangzhi shuju, 1902. Originally published as *Shakaigaku* (Tokyo: Dainihon tosho, 1900).

Koeber, Raphael Gustav von. *Zhexue yaoling* 哲學要領 (Guideline to Philosophy). Shanghai: The Commercial Press, 1903. Translated by Shimoda Jirō 下田次郎 and Cai Yuanpei 蔡元培.

Kōtoku, Shūsui 幸德秋水. *Ershi shiji zhi guaiwu diguo zhuyi* 二十世紀之怪物帝國(Imperialism: The Specter of the Twentieth Century). Translated by Zhao Bizhen. Hong Kong: Guangzhi shuju, 1902. Originally published as *Nijūseiki kaibutsu teikoku shugi* 二十世紀怪物帝国主義.

Kubota, Sadanori 久保田貞則 ed. *Xinli jiaoyuxue* 心理教育學. (Psychological Education). Shanghai: Guangzhi shuju, 1902.

Kuwahara, Jitsuzō 桑原藏. *Tongyang shiyao* 東洋史要 (The Summarized History of Asia). Translated by Fan Bingqing 樊炳清. Shanghai: Dongwen xueshe, 1899. Originally published as Tōyō shiyō 東洋史要.

Leibniz, Gottfried Wilhelm von ed. *Zhongguo jinshi — weiliao zhaoliang wo men zhege shidai de lishi* 中國近事—為了照亮我們這個時代的歷史 (Anecdotes in Modern China: To Enlighten the History of Our Times) Translated by Mei Qianli 梅謙立 and Yang Baojun 楊葆筠. Zhengzhou: Daxiang chubanshe, 2005.

Lei Yutian 雷雨田 ed. *Jindai laiyue chuanjiaoshi pingzhuan* 近代來粵傳教士評傳 (Comments and Biographies of the Missionaries in Canton in Modern Period). Shanghai: Baijia chubanshe, 2004.

Leung Yuen-sang 梁元生. *Lin Lezhi zaihua shiye yu Wanguo gongbao* 林樂知在華事業與 萬國公報 (The Business of Young J. Allen in China and the Globe Magazine). Hong Kong: The Chinese University of Hong Kong Press, 1978.

Li Chucai 李楚材 ed. *Tiguo zhuyi qinhua jiaoyushi zhiliao: jiaohui jiaoyu* 帝國主義侵華教育史資料 教會教育 (Documents of the History of Foreign Education in China: the Church Education). Beijing: Educational Science Publishing House, 1987.

Li Hongzhang 李鴻章. *Li Wenzhong gong quanji* 李文忠公全集 (A Complete Collected Works of Li Hongzhang). Taipei: Wen Hai Press Company, 1980.

Li Qingsong 李清悚 et al. ed. *Diguo zhuyi zai Shanghai de jiaoyu qinlüe huodong zhiliao jianpian* 帝國主義在上海的教育侵略活動資料簡編 (A Brief Compilation of the Documents of Foreign Education in Shanghai). Shanghai: Shanghai Educational Publishing House, 1982.

Li Shanlan 李善蘭 and Alexander Wylie trans. *Daishuxue* 代數學 (Elements of Algebra). Shanghai: London Missionary Society Mission Press, 1859.

Li Shuqing 李樹青. *Tuibian zhong de Zhongguo shehui* 蛻變中的中國社會 (The Transforming Chinese Society). Taipei: Sanrenheng chubanshe, 1974.

Li Tai 李杕 trans. *Lingxingxue* 靈性學 (On Spiritualogy). Shanghai: Tou Se We Press, 1907.

——. *Xixue guanjian* 西學關鍵 (Key to Western Learning). Shanghai: Tou Se We Press, 1903.

——. *Zhexue tigang: minglixue* 哲學提綱 : 名理學 (An Outline of Philosophy: the Study of Logic). Shanghai: Tou Se We Press, 1908.

Li Xiaoqian 李孝遷. *Xifang shixue zai Zhongguo de chuanbo* 西方史學在中國的傳播 (Dissemination of Western Historiography in China). Shanghai: East China Normal University Press, 2007.

Li Zehou 李澤厚. *Zhongguo jindai sixiang shilun* 中國近代思想史論. Beijing: People's Publishing House, 1979.

Li Zhigang 李志剛. *Jidujiao zaoqi zaihua chuanjiaoshi* 基督教早期在華傳教史 (History of Early Proselytization of Christianity in China). Taipei: The Commercial Press, 1995.

Liang Qichao 梁啟超 ed. *Lun Zhongguo xueshu sixiang bianqian zhi dashi* 論中國學術思想變遷之大勢 (On the Basic Trends of Chinese Intellectual Change).

——. *Xizheng congshu* 西政叢書 (Collectanea of the Western Administration). Shanghai: Shenji shuzhuang, 1897.

——. *Xixue shumu biao* 西學書目表 (Bibliography of Western Knowledge). Stone lithography edition, 1896.

——. *Yinbingshi wenji* 飲冰室文集 (Complete Works of the Master of the Ice-Drinker's Studio). Beijing: Zhonghua Book Company, 1989.

——. *Zhongguo jinsanbainian xueshu shi* 中國近三百年學術史 (Chinese Academic History in the Recent 300 Years).

Liang Tingnan 梁廷枏. *Hesheng guoshuo* 合省國說 (On the United States). In Liu Xiao 劉驍 and Luo Yi 駱驛 ed. *Haiguo sishuo* 海國四說 (Four Essays on Off-shore Countries). Beijing: Zhonghua Book Company, 1993.

——. *Yuehai guanzhi* 粵海關志 (Gazetteer of the Guangdong Customs) In Shen Yunlong 沈雲龍 ed. *Jindai Zhongguo shiliao congkan xubian dishijiu ji* 近代中國史料叢刊續編第十九輯 (The Sequel of the Collectanea of Historical Sources of Modern China 19). Taipei: Wen Hai Press Company, 1975.

Lin Chi-Ping 林治平 ed. *Jidujiao ruhua baiqishinian jinianji* 基督教入華百七十年紀念集 (Memorial Collections on the 170 Years Introduction of Christianity in China). Taipei: Cosmic Light Press, 1984.

——. *Jidujiao yu Zhongguo* 基督教與中國 (Christianity and China). Taipei: Cosmic Light Press, 1975.

——. *Zhongguo Jidujiao daxue lunwen ji* 中國基督教大學論文集 (Collected Essays of the Christian Universities in China). Taipei: Cosmic Light Press, 1992.

Lin Liqiang 林立強. "Meiguo chuanjiaoshi Lu Gongming yu wanqing Fujian shehui" 美國傳教士盧公明與晚清福建社會 (An American Missionary Justus Doolittle and the Society in Fujian in the Late Qing Period). Doctor diss., Fujian Normal University, 2004.

Lin Moye 林漠野. *Tianzhujiao zai Zhongguo* 天主教在中國 (Catholics in China). Hong Kong: Zhongguo xueren chubanshe, 1976.

Lindley, John. *Zhiwuxue* 植物學 (Elements of Botany). Translated by A. Williamson, Joseph Edkins, and Li Shanlan 李善蘭. Shanghai: London Missionary Society Mission Press, 1859. Originally published as *An Introduction to Botany* (London: Longman, 1832).

Liu Shixun 劉式訓 trans. *Taixi lisu xinbian* 泰西禮俗新編 (New Treatise on the Custom of Europe).

Liu Tianlu 劉天路 and Tao Feiya 陶飛亞. *Jidujiao yu jindai Shandong shehui* 基督教與近代山東社會 (Christianity and Modern Shandong Society). Ji'nan: Shandon University Press, 1995.

Liu Zexi 劉澤熙 and Yang Du 楊度 trans. *Fazheng cuibian* 法政粹編 (Essentials of Law and Administration). Tokyo: Tokyo Namiki Kappanjo, 1905.

Liu, Kwang-ching. *American Missionaries in China*. Cambridge: Harvard University East Asian Center, 1966.

Lo Hsiang-lin 羅香林. *Xianggang yu Zhongxi wenhua jiaoliu* 香港與中西文化交流 (Hong Kong and the Sino-Western Cultural Communication). Hong Kong: Hong Kong University Press, 1961.

Lund, Thomas. *Daishu lanti* 代數難題 (Difficult Questions on Algebra). Translated by John Fryer and Hua Hengfang 華蘅芳. Shanghai: Translation College of the Jiangnan Arsenal, 1879. Originally published as *A Short and Easy Course of Algebra*.

Luo Bingxiang 羅秉祥 and Zhao Dunhua 趙敦華 ed. *Jidujiao yu jindai Zhongxi wenhua* 基督教與近代中西文化 (Christianity and Modern Sino-Western Culture). Beijing: Peking University Press, 2000.

Lutz, Jessie G. *China and the Christian Colleges, 1850–1950*. Ithaca: Cornell University Press, 1971.

——. *Zhongguo jiaohui daxueshi* (1850–1950) 中國教會大學史 (1850–1950) (The History of Christian Universities in China) (1850–1950). Translated by Zeng Jusheng 曾鉅生. Hangzhou: Zhejiang Education Publishing House, 1987. Originally published as *China and the Christian Colleges, 1850–1950*.

Lyell, Charles. *Dixue qianshi* 地學淺釋 (Elements of Geology). Translated by Hua Hengfang 華蘅芳 and Daniel Jerome MacGowan. Shanghai: Translation College of the Jiangnan Arsenal, 1873. Originally published as *Principles of Geology, or, The Modern Changes of the Earth and Its Inhabitants Considered as Illustrative of Geology* (New York: D. Appleton and Co., 1872).

Ma Min 馬敏 and Zhang Kaiyuan 章開沅 ed. *Jidujiao yu Zhongguo wenhua songkan* 基督教與中國文化叢刊 (Collectanea of Christianity and Chinese Culture). Wuhan: Hubei Education Press, 1984.

Ma Zuyi 馬祖毅. *Zhongguo fanyi jianshi* 中國翻譯簡史 (A Short History of Translation in China). Beijing: China Translation and Publishing Corporation, 1984.

MacGowan, Daniel Jerome. *Bowu tongshu* 博物通書 (Philosophical Almanac in Chinese). Ningbo: Zhenshentang, 1851.

——. *Hanghai jinzhen* 航海金針 (The Navigators' Golden Needle). Ningbo: The Chinese and American Holy Classic Book Establishment, 1853.

Mackenzie, Robert. *Taixi xinshi lanyao* 泰西新史攬要 (A New History of Europe). Translated by Cai Erkang 蔡爾康 and Richard Timothy. Shanghai: SDK, 1895.

Madam Morrison ed., Gu Changsheng 顧長聲 trans. *Malixun huiyilu* 馬禮遜回憶錄 (Memoir of Robert Morrison). Guilin: Guangxi Normal University Press, 2004.

Mai Zhonghua 麥仲華 ed. *Huangchao jingshiwen xinbian* 皇朝經世文新編 (Newly-Collected Essays about Statecraft of the Qing Dynasty). Shanghai: Datong yishuju, 1898.

Martin, Frederick. *Lieguo suiji zhengyao* 列國歲計政要 (Annual Balance and Political Events of Various Countries). Translated by Young J. Allen and Zheng Changyan. Shanghai: Translation College of the Jiangnan Arsenal, 1878.

Martin, W. A. P., Shen Hong 沈弘 et al. trans. *Huajia yiji: yiwei Meiguo chuanjiaoshi yanzhong de Wanqing diguo* 花甲憶記 一位美國傳教士眼中的晚清帝國 (A Cycle of Cathay: or China, South and North; with Personal Reminiscences). Guilin: Guangxi Normal University Press, 2004.

Matsudaira, Yasukuni 松平康國. *Shijie jinshishi* 世界近世史 (History of the Modern World). Shanghai: Guangzhi shuju, 1903. Translated by Zuoxinsha 作新社. Originally published as *Sekai kinseishi* 世界近世史 (Tokyo : Tokyo senmon gakkō shuppanbu, 1901).

McCartee, D. B. ed. *Ping'an tongshu* 平安通書 (An Encyclopedia for Safety Adventure). Ningbo: The Chinese and American Holy Classic Book Establishment, 1850.

Medhurst, Walter Henry. *Dili biantong lüezhuan* 地理便童略傳 (Brief Introduction of Geography). Malacca: Anglo-Chinese College, 1819.

Mei Wending 梅文鼎. *Meishi congshu jiyao* 梅氏叢書輯要 (Essientials of the Collectanea of the Mei).

——. *Wu'an lisuan shumu* 勿庵曆算書目 (Mathematical Treatises of Wu'an).

Merton, Robert K. "Science, Technology and Society in Seventeenth-century England." Osiris 4 (1938): 360-632.

Milner, *Thomas. Daying guozhi* 大英國志 (An Account of the Great Britain). Translated by William Muirhead. Shanghai: London Missionary Society Mission Press, 1856.

Minegishi, Yoneō 峯岸米造 and Mitsukuri, Genpachi 箕作元八. *Ouluoba tongshi* 歐羅巴通史 (General History of Europe). Translated by Hu Jingyi 胡景伊, Tang Renjie 唐人傑, and Xu Youcheng 徐有成. Dongya yishuhui, 1900. Originally published as Seiyō shi kō (Tokyo: Rokumeikan, 1899).

Morgan, Augustus De. *Shuxueli* 數學理 (Explanation to Mathematics). Translated by John Fryer and Zhao Yuanyi 趙元益. Shanghai: Translation College of the Jiangnan Arsenal, 1879.

Mori, Arinori 森有禮. *Wenxue xingguo ce* 文學興國策 (Education in Japan). Translated by Ren Tingxu 任廷旭 and Young J. Allen. Shanghai: SDK, 1896. Originally published as *Education in Japan*.

Morse, Hosea Ballou. *The International Relations of the Chinese Empire*. Taipei: Wen Hsing Book Store, 1963.

Morton, William J. *Tongwu dianguang* 通物電光 (All-piercing Electric Light). Translated by John Fryer and Wang Jilie 王季烈. Shanghai: Translation College of the Jiangnan Arsenal, 1899.

Muirhead, William. *Dili quanzhi* 地理全志 (Universal Geography). Shanghai: London Missionary Society Mission Press, 1854.

Myers. P. V. N. *Maier tongshi* 邁爾通史 (A General History for Colleges and High Schools). Translated by Huang Zuoting 黃佐廷 and Zhang Zaixin 張在新. Taiyuan: Shanxi daxuetang yishuyuan, 1905. Originally published as *A General History for Colleges and High Schools*.

Nakae, Chōmin 中江兆民. *Lixue gouxuan* 理學鈎玄 (Exploration to Logic). Trasnalted by Chen Peng 陳鵬. Shanghai: Guangzhi shuju, 1902. Originally published as *Rigaku kōgen* 理學鈎玄 (Tokyo: Sh seisha, 1886).

Nakamura, Shingo 中村進午. *Xiyi guoji gongfa* 新譯國際公法 (New Translated International Law). Translated by Yuan Xilian 袁希濂. Shanghai: Zhongguo tushu gongsi, 1907.

Needham, Joseph 李約瑟. *Zhongguo kexue jishu shi* 中國科學技術史 (Science and Civilization in China). Beijing: Science Press, 1990.

Ning Jing 寧靖 ed. *Yanpian zhanzhengshi lunwen zhuanji xubian* 鴉片戰爭史論文專集續編 (The Sequel of the Collected Essays of the Opium War). Beijing: People Publishing House, 1984.

Noad, Henry M. *Dianxue* 電學 (On Electrical Science). Translatd by John Fryer and Xu Jianyan 徐建寅. Shanghai: Translation College of the Jiangnan Arsenal, 1879. Originally published as *A Manual of Electricity*.

Ogawa, Ginjirō 小川銀次郎. *Xiyang shiyao* 西洋史要 (Essentials of the History of the West). Translated by Fan Bingqing 樊炳清 and Sha Duan 薩端. Shanghai: Jinsuzhai yishushe, 1901. Originally published as *Seiyō shiryaku* 西洋史略 (Tokyo: Kinkō dō, 1900).

Okamoto, Kansuke 岡本監輔. *Bankoku shiki* 萬國史記 (The Historical Records of the Myriad Countries). Shanghai: Shanghai Shun Pao Office, 1880.

Ōnishi, Hajime 大西祝. Lun lixue 論理學 (Discourse on Logic). Translated by Hu Maoru. Hebei: Hebei yishushe, 1906. Originally published as *Ronrigaku* 論理學 (Tōkyō : Keiseisha Shoten, 1903).

Osgood, Dauphin William ed. *Quanti chanwei* 全體闡微 (Analysis on Human Body). Fuzhou: Shengjiao yiguan, 1881.

Pan Zhenping 潘振平. "Xu Jiyu he Yinghuan zhilüe" 徐繼畬和《瀛寰志略》(Xu Jiyu and *A Short Account of the Maritime Circuit*). Journal of East China Normal University 華東師範大學學報, No. 6 (1981).

Pfister, Louis 費賴之. *Mingqingjian zaihua Yesuhuishi liezhuan 1552–1773* 明清間在華耶穌會士列傳 1552–1773 (Collected Biographies of the Jesuits in China) Translated by Mei Chengjun 梅乘駿. Shanghai: Catholic Shanghai Diocese Guangqi Society, 1997).

——. *Rihua Yesuhuishi liezhuan* 入華耶穌會士列傳 (Collected Biographies of the Jesuits in China). Taipei: Commercial Press, 1970. Translated by Feng Chengjun 馮承鈞.

Phillimore, Robert J. *Geguo jiaoshe bianfa lun* 各國交涉便法論 (Commentaries on International Private Law). Translated by John Fryer. Shanghai: Translation College of the Jiangnan Arsenal, 1894.

——. *Geguo jiaoshe gongfa lun* 各國交涉公法論 (Commentaries on International Law). Translated by John Fryer and Yu Shijue 嚴世爵. Shanghai: Translation College of the Jiangnan Arsenal, 1894. Originally published as *Commentaries upon International Law*.

Qi Rushan 齊如山. *Qi Rushan huiyilu* 齊如山回憶錄 (Memoir of Qi Rushan) Beijing: Theatre Book, 1989.

Qi Yinping 戚印平. *Riben zaoqi Yesuhui shi yanjiu* 日本早期耶穌會史研究 (A Study of the Early History of the Society of Jesus). Beijing: The Commercial Press, 2003.

Qian Baozong 錢寶琮. *Zhongguo shuxueshi* 中國數學史 (History of Mathematics in China). Beijing: Science Press, 1981.

Qian Cunxun 錢存訓. "Jinshi yishu dui Zhongguo xiandaihua de yingxiang" 近世譯書對中國現代化的影響 (Impacts of Translation to the Modernization of China). *Wenxian* 文獻, No. 2 (1986).

Qian Zhongshu 錢鍾書 et al. *Lin Shu de fanyi* 林紓的翻譯 (The Translation Works of Lin Shu). Beijing: The Commercial Press, 1934.

Qiushizhai 求是齋 ed. *Huangchao jingshiwen wubian* 皇朝經世文五編 (Collected Essays about Statecraft of the Qing Dynasty 5). Shanghai: Yijinshi, 1902.

Qiuziqiangzhai zhuren 求自強齋主人 ed. *Huangchao jingshi wenbian* 皇朝經世文編 (Collected Essays about Statecraft of the Qing Dynasty). Shanghai: Shenji shuzhuang, 1901.

Quan Zuwang 全祖望. *Jieqi ting ji* 鮚埼亭集 Collections of the Jieqi Neighbourhood.

Richard, Timothy 李提摩太. *Baxing zhiyi zonglun* 八星之一總論 (A Summary of the Earth). Shanghai: SDK, 1898.

——. *Daguo cidi kao* 大國次第考 (A Study of the Ranking of the Great Powers). Shanghai: SDK, 1898.

——. *Forty-five Years in China*, Reminiscences. London: T. Fisher Urwin Ltd., 1916.

——. *Lieguo biantong xingsheng ji* 列國變通興盛記 (Reform and Rise of Various Countries). Shanghai: SDK, 1898.

——. *Ouzhou bada diwang zhuan* 歐洲八大帝王傳 (The Biographies of the Eight Great Kings of Europe). Shanghai: SDK, 1899.

——. *Qiguo xinxue beiyao* 七國新學備要 (Essentials of new knowledge from seven countries). Shanghai: SDK, 1898.

——. *Shengli fenli zhi bielun* 生利分利之別論 (Another Discourse on Production and Consumption). Shanghai: SDK, 1898.

——. *Tianxia wuzhou gedaguo zhiyao* 天下五洲各大國志要 (A Brief Record of the Great Powers in the Five Continents). Shanghai: SDK, 1897.

——. *Xin zhengce* 新政策 (New Policies). Shanghai: SDK, 1898.

Robertson, Edmund, John Fryer and Wang Zhensheng 汪振聲 trans. *Gongfa zonglun* 公法總論 (A General Discourse on the International Law). Shanghai: Translation College of the Jiangnan Arsenal, 1894.

Rousseau, Jean-Jacques. *Minyue tongyi* 民約通義 (The Social Contract). Translated by Nakae Chōmin 中江兆民. Shanghai: Tongwen shuju, 1898.

Ruan Yuan 阮元 et al. ed. *Chourenzhuan huibian* 疇人傳彙編 (Biographies of the Astronomers). Yangzhou: Guangling shushe, 2009.

Ryan, Thomas F. *Yesuhuishi zai Zhongguo* 耶穌會士在中國 (Jesuits Missionaries in China). Translated by Tao Yiwei 陶翼為. Hong Kong: Catholic Truth Society, 1965.

Sakamoto, Kajima 坂本嘉治馬. *Bankoku shinreikishi* 萬國新歷史 (The New History of the Myriad Countries). Translated by Xue Guang'e 薛光鍔. Shanghai: Yizhi xueshe, 1903.

Scheliha, Viktor Ernst Karl Rudolk von. *Fanghai xinlun* 防海新論 (A New Treatise on Coastal Defense). Translated by Hua Hengfang 華蘅芳 and John Fryer. Shanghai: Translation College of the Jiangnan Arsenal, 1874. Originally published as *A Treatise on Coast-defence: Based on the Experience Gained by Officers of the Corps of Engineers of the Army of the Confederate States*.

Shao Zhitang 邵之棠 ed. *Huangchao jingshiwen tongbian* 皇朝經世文統編 (Combined Collected Essays about Statecraft of the Qing Dynasty). Shanghai: Baoshanzhai, 1901.

Sheffield, Devello Zelotos ed. *General Knowledge about the World* 萬國通鑑 (Wango tongjian). Shanghai: American Presbyterian Mission Press, 1882.

Shen Fuwei 沈福偉. Zhongxi wenhua jiaoliushi 中西文化交流史 (The History of Sino-Western Cultural Communication). Shanghai: Shanghai People's Publishing House, 1985.

Shen Guowei 沈國威 *Liuhe congtan* 六合叢談 (Universal Miscellany). Shanghai: Shanghai Lexicographical Publishing House, 2006.

Shen Weibin 沈渭濱 ed. *Jindai Zhongguo kexuejia* 近代中國科學家 (Scientists of Modern China). Shanghai: shanghai People's Publishing House, 1988.

Shen Zhaoyi 沈兆禕. *Xinxue shumu tiyao* 新學書目提要 (Summary of Western Reference Works). Shanghai: Shanghai Tongya shuju, 1904.

Shi He 史和 et al. *Zhongguo jindai baokan minglu* 中國近代報刊名錄 (Lists of Journals in Modern China). Fuzhou: Fujian People's Publishing House, 1991.

Shi Jinghuan 史靜寰 and Wang Lixin 王立新. *Jidujiao jiaoyu yu Zhongguo zhishi fenzi* 基督教教育與中國知識分子 (Christian Education and Chinese Intellectuals). Fuzhou: Fujian Education Press, 1998.

Shu Xincheng 舒新城 ed. *Zhongguo jindai jiaoyushi zhiliao* 中國近代教育史資料 (Documents of the History of Education in Modern China). Beijing: People's Education Press, 1961.

Sima Qian 司馬遷. *Shiji* 史記 (Records of the Grand Historian). Beijing: Zhonghua Book Company, 1959.

Soothill, W. E. *Timothy Richard of China*. London: Seeley, Service & Co.Ltd., 1924.

Spence, Jonathan D. *Gaibian Zhongguo* 改變中國 (To Change China: Western Advisers in China). Translated by Cao Dejun 曹德駿 et al. Beijing: SDX Joint Publishing Company, 1990.

Spencer, Herbert. *Yiye yaolan* 肄業要覽 (On Education). Translated by Yan Yongjing 顏永京. Shanghai: American Presbyterian Mission Press, 1882

Steele, Joel Dorman. *Gewu zhixue* 格物質學 (Popular Physics). Translated by Pan Shenwen 潘慎文 and Xie Honglai 謝洪賚. Shanghai: American Presbyterian Mission Press, 1898.

Stürmer, Ernst. *Tongxuan jiaoshi Tang Ruowang* 通玄教師湯若望 (Meister Himmlischer Geheimnisse). Translated by Zhang Xiaohu 張曉虎. Beijing: China Renmin University Press, 1989.

Su Ching 蘇精. *Malixun yu Zhongwen yinshua chuban* 馬禮遜與中文印刷出版. Taipei: Student Book Co., Ltd., 2000.

——. *Qingji Tongwenguan ji qi shisheng* 清季同文館及其師生 (The Imperial Foreign Language Institute of the Qing Dynasty, Its Teachers and Students). Taipei: Shanghai yinshuachang, 1985.

Sun Baoxuan 孫寶瑄. *Wangshanlu riji* 忘山廬日記 (The Diary of the Wangshan House). Shanghai: Shanghai guji chubanshe, 1983.

Swinton, William. *Wanguo shiyao* 萬國史要 (Essentials of the History of Myriad Countries). Translated by Zhang Xiang 張相. Hangzhou: Shixuezhai, 1903.

Tam Yue-him 譚汝謙. *Zhongguo yi Riben shumu zonghe mulu* 中國譯日本書目綜合目錄. Hong Kong: The Chinese University of Hong Kong Press, 1980.

Tan Shuangquan 譚雙泉. *Jiaohui daxue zai jinxiandai Zhongguo* 教會大學在近現代中國 (Church School in Modern China). Changsha: Hunan Educational Publishing House, 1995.

Tan Shulin 譚樹林. *Malixun yu Zhongxi wenhua jiaoliu* 馬禮遜與中西文化交流 (Robert Morrison and the Sino-Western Cultural Communication). Hangzhou: China Academy of Art Press, 2004.

Tang Christopher Ching 湯清. *Zhongguo jidujiao bainianshi* 中國基督教百年史 (The Centennial History of Christianity in China). Hong Kong: Hong Kong Taosheng Publishing House, 1987.

Tang Zhenchang 唐振常 and Shen Hengchun 沈恒春 ed. *Shanghai shi yanjiu* 上海史研究 (A Study of the History of Shanghai). Beijing: Academia Press, 1989.

Tang Zhenchang 唐振常 ed. *Shanghai shi* 上海史 (The History of Shanghai). Shanghai: Shanghai People's Publishing House, 1989.

The Commercial Press ed. *Shangwu yinshuguan jiushinian* 商務印書館九十年 (Ninety Years of the Commercial Press). Beijing: The Commercial Press, 1987.

——. *Shangwu yinshuguan jiushiwunian* 商務印書館九十五年 (Ninety-five Years of the Commercial Press). Beijing: The Commercial Press, 1992.

Tyndall, John. *Guangxue* 光學 (On Optics). Translated by Carl T. Kreyer and Zhao Yuanyi 趙元益. Shanghai: Translation College of the Jiangnan Arsenal, 1876. Originally published as *Notes of a Course of Nine Lectures on Light*.

Ukita, Kazutami 浮田和民. *Shixue tonglun* 史學通論 (General Explanation to Historiography). Translated by Li Haosheng 李浩生. Hangzhou: Hecong yishuju, 1903. Originally published as Shigaku tsūron 史學通論 (Tokyo: Tokyo senmon gakkō).

Wallace, William. *Daishushu* 代數術 (Algebra). Translated by Hua Hengfang 華蘅芳 and John Fryer. Shanghai: Translation College of the Jiangnan Arsenal, 1873.

Wang Bing 王冰. *Zhongwai wuli jiaoliushi* 中外物理交流史 (The History of the Sino-Western Exchanged Learning on Physics). Changsha: Hunan Educational Publishing House, 2001.

Wang Chongmin 王重民 ed. *Xu Guangqi ji* 徐光啟集 (Collections of Xu Guangqi). Beijing: Zhonghua Book Company, 1963.

Wang Erh-min 王爾敏. *Shanghai Gezhi shuyuan zhilüe* 上海格致書院志略 (A Brief History of the Shanghai Polytechnic Institute) Hong Kong: Chinese University of Hong Kong Press, 1980.

Wang Jiajian 王家儉. *Wei Yuan dui xifang de renshi ji qi haifang sixiang* 魏源對西方的認識及其海防思想 (Wei Yuan's Understanding to the West and His Thoughts on Coastal Defense). Taipei: Jinghua yinshuguan, 1964.

Wang Lan 王瀾 and Zhou Liu 周流 ed. *Taixi xuean* 泰西學案 (The Study of European Academia). Shanghai: Mingquanshe, 1903.

Wang Li 王力. *Hanyu cihui shi* 漢語詞匯史 (History of Vocabularies in the Chinese Language). Ji'nan: Shandong Education Press, 1980.

Wang Rongbao 汪榮寶 and Ye Lan 葉瀾 ed. *Xin erya* 新爾雅 (The New Approcahing Elegance: a Dictionary). Shanghai: Mingquanshe, 1903.

Wang Shi 王栻 ed. *Yan Fu ji* 嚴復集 (Collected Essays of Yan Fu). Beijing: Zhonghua Book Company, 1986.

Wang Tao 王韜 and Alexander Wylie trans. *Xiguo tianxue yuanliu* 西國天學源流 (A History of Astronomy of the Western Countries). Shanghai: Wang Tao, 1889.

Wang Tao 王韜 ed. *Gezhi shuyuan keyi* 格致書院課藝 (Textbook of the Shanghai Polytechnic Institute). Shanghai: Tao Yuan, 1887–1894.

——. *Manyou suilu* 漫遊隨錄 (Jottings of My Roaming).

——. *Xixue yuanshi kao* 西學原始考 (An Inquiry into the Beginnings of Western Learning). Shanghai: Wang Tao, 1890.

——. *Yingru zazhi* 瀛壖雜誌 (Miscellaneous Records of the Shore). Shanghai: Shanghai guji chubanshe, 1989.

Wang Xiaoqiu 王曉秋. *Jindai Zhongri wenhua jiaoliu shi* 近代中日文化交流史 (The History of Cultural Communication in Modern Period). Beijing: Zhonghua Book Company, 1992.

Wang Weijian 王維儉. "Lin Zexu fanyi xifang guojifa zhuzuo kaolüe" 林則徐翻譯西方國際法著作考略 (A Study of the Translation of the International Law by Lin Zexu). *Journal of Sun Yat-sen University* 中山大學學報, No. 1 (1985).

Wang Yanwei 王彥威 et al. ed. *Qingji waijiao shiliao* 清季外交史料 (Historical Documents of the Diplomacy of the Qing Dynasty). Beijing: Bibliography and Document Publishing House, 1987.

Wang Yusheng 王渝生 ed. *Xixue dongchuan renwu congshu* 西學東傳人物叢書 (Collectanea of the Historical Figures in the Eastward Dissemination of Western Learning). Beijing: Science Press, 2000.

Wang Zhixin 王治心. *Zhongguo Jidujiao shigang* 中國基督教史綱 (An Outline of the History of Christianity in China). Shanghai: Shanghai guji chubanshe, 2004.

Wang Zichun 汪子春. "Woguo zhuanbo jindai zhiwuxue zhishi de diyibu yizhu Zhiwuxue" 我國傳播近代植物學知識的第一部譯著《植物學》(Elements of Botany: the First Translated Reference Work of Modern Botany in China). *Studies in the History of Natural Sciences* 自然科學史研究, No. 3 (1984), vol. 1.

Washington, Irving. *Huashengdun quanzhuan* 華盛頓全傳 (A Complete Biography of George

Washington). Translated by Cai Guozhao 蔡國昭 and Li Ruqian 黎汝謙. Woodblock edition, 1886. Originally published as *Life of George Washington*.

Watson McMillen Hayes and Zhou Wenyuan 周文源 trans. *Tianwen jieyao* 天文揭要 (Discovery of Astronomy). Shanghai: School and Textbook Series Committee, 1898.

Way, Richard Quarterman. *Diqiu shuolüe* 地球說略 (A Brief Discourse on the Earth). Ningbo: The Chinese and American Holy Classic Book Establishment, 1856.

Wong Chi-min 王吉民 and Wu Lien-the 伍連德. *History of Chinese Medicine* Shanghai: National Quarantine Service, 1936.

Wei Jingsheng 衛京生. "Fuzhou kaipi wei tongshang kouan zaoqi de qingkuang" 福州開闢為通商口岸早期的情況 (Situation in Fuzhou in Its Early Days of Opening as a Treaty Port). *Fujian wenshi zhiliao* 福建文史資料 (Fujian Humanity and Historical Materials), No. 1 (1962).

Wei Yuan 魏源. *Haiguo tuzhi* 海國圖志 (Illustrated Gazetteer of the Maritime Countries). Pingqing: Jinggudao shu, 1876.

Wells, David Ames. *Huaxue jianyuan* 化學鑒原 (Principle and Applications of Chemistry). Translated by John Fryer and Xu Shou 徐壽. Shanghai: Translation College of the Jiangnan Arsenal, 1871.

Wells, S. Williams. Gu Jun 顧鈞 and Jiang Li 江莉 trans. *Wei Sanwei shengping ji shuxin: yiwei Meiguo laihua chuanjiaoshi de xinlu licheng* 衛三畏生平及書信 一位美國來華傳教士的心路歷程 (The Biography and Letters of S. Williams Wells: the Experience of an American Missionary in China) Guilin: Guangxi Normal University Press, 2004.

Weng Tonghe 翁同龢. *Weng Tonghe riji* 翁同龢日記 (The Diary of Weng Tonghe). Beijing: Zhonghua Book Company, 1989.

Wheaton, Henry. *The Law of Nations*. Translated by W. A. P. Martin. Beijing: Chongshiguan, 1864.

Whewell, William. *Zhongxue* 重學 (An Elementary Treatise on Mechanics). Translated by Joseph Edkins and Li Shanlan 李善蘭. Shanghai: London Missionary Society Mission Press, 1859. Originally published as *Demonstration that All Matter is Heavy* (Cambridge: 1841).

Wood, Henry. *Zhixin mianbing fa* 治心免病法 (Ideal Suggestion Through Mental Photography). Translated by John Fryer. Shanghai: School and Textbook Series Committee, 1896. Originally published as Ideal Suggestion Through Mental Photography (Boston: Lee & Shepard, 1893).

Woolsey, Theodore Swight, Feng Yi 鳳儀 and Wang Fengzao 汪鳳藻 trans., W. A. P. Martin ed. *Gongfa bianlan* 公法便覽 (Introduction to International Law). Beijing: Imperial Foreign Language Institute, 1877.

Wu Boya 吳伯婭. *Kangyongqian sandi yu xixue dongjian* 康熙乾三帝與西學東漸 (Emperor Kangxi, Yongzheng, Qianlong, and the Eastward Dissemination of Western Learning). Beijing: China Religious Culture Publisher, 2002.

Wu Guoyi 胡國義 ed. *Shixue tonglun sizhong hekan* 史學通論四種合刊 (Four Titles of General Discourse of Historiography). Shanghai: East China Normal University Press, 2007.

Wu Xiaoxin 吳小新 and Zou Ailign 鄒愛蓮 ed. *Qing zhongqianqi xiyang Tianzhujiao zaihua huodong dang'an shiliao* 清中前期西洋天主教在華活動檔案史料 (Historical Sources of the Western Catholics in China in mid-Qing Period). Beijing: Zhonghua Book Company, 2003.

Wu Yixiong 吳義雄. *Zai Zongjiao yu shixu zhijian*: Jidujiao Xinjiao chaunjiaoshi zai huanan yuanhai de zaoqi huodong yanjiu 在宗教與世俗之間 基督教新教傳教士在華南沿海的早期活動研究 (In Between Religion and Secularity: a Study on the Early Activities of the Protestant

Missionaries in the South China Coast). Guangzhou: Guangdong Education Publishing House, 2000.

Wu Zhen 吳震 and Zhao Lifeng 趙利峰. "Aomen tusheng Puren Hanxuejia Majishi yu Xinshi dili beikao" 澳門土生葡人漢學家瑪吉士與 新釋地理備考 (A Macanese Sinologue José Martinho Marques and *A Study of Geography*). *Jinan Journal (Philosophy and Social Science)*, No. 2, 2006.

Wu Ziming 吳梓明. *Jiduzongjiao yu Zhongguo daxue jiaoyu* 基督宗教與中國大學教育 (Christianity and Chinese University Education). Beijing: China Social Sciences Press, 2003.

Wylie, Alexander. *Memorials of Protestant Missionaries to the Chinese: Giving a List of Their Publications, and Obituary Notices of the Deceased*. Shanghai: American Presbyterian Mission Press, 1867.

Xiang Da 向達. *Zhongxi jiaotongshi* 中西交通史 (The History of Sino-Western Communication). Beijing: Zhonghua Book Company, 1934.

Xiong Yuezhi 熊月之 ed. *Wanqing xinxue shumu tiyao* 晚清新學書目提要 (Summary of the Titles of New Learning Published in the Late Qing Period). Shanghai: shanghai guji chubanshe, 2007.

——. *Zhongguo jindai minzhu sixiangshi* 中國近代民主思想史 (A History of China's Modern Democratic Thought). Shanghai: Shanghai People's Publishing House, 1986.

Xu Changzhi 徐昌治 ed. *Shengchao poxie ji* 聖朝破邪集 (Collected Papers on Overcoming Evil Ideologies).

Xu Jiyu 徐繼畬. *Yinghuan kaolüe* 瀛寰考略 (A Short Account on the Maritime Circuit). Taipei: Wen Hai Press Company, 1974.

Xu Mushi 許牧世. *Guangxuehui de lishi ji qi gongxian* 廣學會的歷史及其貢獻 (The History and Contributions of the Society for the Diffusion of Christian and General Knowledge Among the Chinese). Hong Kong: Chinese Christian Literature Council, 1977.

Xu Shichang 徐世昌. *Qingru xuean* 清儒學案 (Records of Qing Scholars).

Xu Weize 徐維則. *Dongxixue shulu* 東西學書錄 (Bibliography of Japanese-Western Knowledge). Stone lithography edition, 1899.

——. *Zengban dongxixue shulu* 增版東西學書錄 (Bibliography of Japanese-Western Knowledge [enlarged edition]). Edited by Gu Xieguang 顧燮光. 1902.

Xu Zongxe 徐宗澤 ed. *Mingqingjian Yesuhuishi yizhu tiyao* 明清間耶穌會士譯著提要 (A Summary of the Translated Works of the Jesuits Missionaries in between the Ming and Qing Dynasties). Beijing: Zhonghua Book Company, 1949.

——. *Zhongguo Tianzhujiao chuanjiaoshi gailun* 中國天主教傳教史概論 (Summary of Catholics in China). Shanghai: Shanghai Tou Se We Press, 1938.

Yan Fu 嚴復 trans. *Yanyi mingzhu congkan* 嚴譯名著叢刊 (Translation Works of Yan Fu) Beijing: The Commercial Press, 1981.

Yang Mo 楊模 ed. *Xijin sizhe shishi huicun* 錫金四哲事實彙存 (Four Philosophers of Xijin). Yangzhou: Guangling shushe, 2007.

Yang Tianhong 楊天宏. *Jidujiao yu jindai Zhongguo* 基督教與近代中國 (Christianity and Modern China). Chengdu: Sichuan People's Publishing House, 1994.

Yang Yinhang 楊蔭杭 trans. *Mingxue jiaokeshu* 名學教學書 (Textbook On Logic). Shanghai: Wenming shuju, 1903.

Ye Zhongjin 葉鍾進. *Jiweishanfang zaji* 寄味山房雜記 (Miscellaneous Records of the Jiwei Mountain Studio).

Yao Minquan 姚民權. *Shanghai Jidujiao shi (1843–1949)* 上海基督教史 (1843–1949) (The History of Christianity in Shanghai: from 1843 to 1949). Shanghai: National Committee of Three-Self Patriotic Movement of the Protestant Churches, 1980).

Yao Songling 姚崧齡. *Yingxiang woguo weixin de jige waiguoren* 影響我國維新的幾個外國人 (A Few Foreigners Who Affected the Modernization of China). Taipei: Biographical Literature Press, 1971.

Yu Sanle 余三樂. *Zaoqi xifang chuanjiaoshi yu Beijing* 早期西方傳教士與北京 (Early Western Missionaries and Beijing) Beijing: Beijing Publishing Group, 2001.

Zhang Jinglu 張靜廬 ed. *Zhongguo jindai chuban shiliao* 中國近代出版史料 (Historical Sources of Publication of Modern China). Beijing: Zhonghua Book Company, 1957.

Zhang Kaiyuan 章開沅 ed. *Wenhua chuanbo yu jiaohui daxue* 文化傳播與教會大學 (Cultural Dissemination and the Church Universities). Wuhan: Hubei Education Press, 1996.

Zhang Tingyu 張廷玉 et al. *Mingshi* 明史 (History of the Ming Dynasty). Beijing: Zhonghua Book Company, 1974.

Zhang Weihua 張維華. *Mingqing zhiji Zhongxi guanxi jianshi* 明清之際中西關係簡史 (A Brief History of the Sino-Western Relationship in the Ming-to-Qing transitional Peirod). Ji'nan: Qilu Press, 1987.

Zhang Xingliang 張星烺. *Ouhua dongjianshi* 歐化東漸史 (The History of European Cultural Dissemination into China). Beijing: The Commercial Press, 1934.

——. *Zhongxi jiaotong shiliao huibian* 中西交通史料匯編 (Compilation of the Historical Sources of the Sino-Western Communication). Beijing: Zhonghua Book Company, 1977.

Zhang Xiumin 張秀民. *Zhongguo yinshua shi* 中國印刷史 (The History of Publication in China). Shanghai: Shanghai People's Publishing House, 1989.

Zhang Yilin 張一麐. *Xintaipingshi ji* 心太平室集 (Collections of the Xintaiping Study). Taipei: Wenhai chubanshe, 1966.

Zhang Yuxiang 張玉祥, *Gudai shijie qida qizhi* 古代世界七大奇蹟 (Seven Wonders in the Ancient World). Beijing: The Commercial Press, 1982.

Zhao Hongjun 趙洪鈞. *Jindai Zhongxiyi lunzhengshi* 近代中西醫論爭史 (A Conflict between Chinese and Western Medicine in Modern Period). Hefei: Anhui Science & Technology Publishing House, 1989.

Zeng Guofan 曾國藩. *Zeng Guofan quanji* 曾國藩全集 (The Complete Collection of Zeng Guofan).

Zheng Dedi 鄭德弟 et al. trans. *Yesuhuishi Zhongguo shujian ji: Zhongguo huiyilu* 耶穌會士中國書簡集 中國回憶錄 (A Memoir of China: Collections of Letters of the Jesuits Missionaries in China). Zhengzhou: Daxiang chubanshe, 2001.

Zhong Shaohua 鍾少華. *Renlei zhishi de xingongju — Zhongri jindai baike quanshu yanjiu* 人類知識的新工具—中國近代百科全書研究 (New Tool for Human Knowledge: a Study of the modern Chinese and Japanese Encyclopedia). Beijing: Beijing Library, 1996.

Zhou Changshou 周昌壽. *Yikan kexue shuji kaolüe* 譯刊科學書籍考略 (A Study on the Translated Science Works). Hong Kong: Mengshi tushu gongsi, 1972.

Zou Zhenhuan 鄒振環. *Wanqing xifang dilixue zai Zhongguo* 晚清西方地理學在中國 (Western Geography in the Late Qing China). Shanghai: Shanghai gudian wenxue chubanshe, 2000.

——. *Xifang chuanjiaoshi yu wanqing xishi dongjian* 西方傳教士與晚清西史東漸 (Western Missionaries and the Eastward Dissemination of Western history in Late-Qing China). Shanghai: Shanghai guji chubanshe, 2007.

——. *Yingxiang Zhongguo jindai shehui de yibaizhong yizuo* 影響中國近代社會的一百種譯作 (100 Translated Works That Affected the Modern Chinese Society). Beijing: China Translation and Publishing Corporation, 1996.

Zuoxinshe 作新社 ed. *Wanguo lishi* 萬國歷史 (The History of Myriad Countries). Shanghai: Zuoxinshe yishuju, 1902.

Journals and Newspaper

A Review of the Times 萬國公報.

Chinese and Foreign Weekly 中外新聞七日錄.

Chinese Monthly Magazine 察世俗每月統紀傳.

Chinese Scientific Magazine 格致匯編.

Chuban shiliao 出版史料 (Publication of Historical Materials).

Eastern Western Monthly Magazine 東西洋考每月統記傳.

Historical Research 歷史研究.

Journal of Dialectics of Nature 自然辨證法通訊.

Kexueshi yicong 科學史譯叢 (Collectanea of the Translation Works in the History of Science).

Modern Chinese History Studies 近代史研究.

Shun Pao 申報.

Studies in the History of Natural Sciences 自然科學史研究.

The Chinese Journal for the History of Science and Technology 中國科技史料.

The Chinese Progress 時務報.

The Chinese Shipping List & Advertiser 上海新報.

The Church News 教會新報.

The Globe Magazine 萬國公報.

The New York Times.

Universal Miscellany 六合叢談.

Xinwen bao 新聞報 (News Daily).

Yishu gonghui bao 譯書公會報 (Translation Society Weekly Edition).

Index

CPSIA information can be obtained at www.ICGtesting.com
Printed in the USA
LVOW03*0857170815
450396LV00004B/7/P

9 789814 332248